Be Not Afraid

BE NOT AFRAID
Collected Writing

Cardinal George Pell

Edited by Tess Livingstone

Duffy & Snellgrove
Sydney

Published by Duffy & Snellgrove in 2004
PO Box 177 Potts Point NSW 1335 Australia
info@duffyandsnellgrove.com.au

Distributed by Pan Macmillan

© Cardinal George Pell 2004
© foreword Cardinal Francis Arinze

Cover design by Alex Snellgrove
Cover photographs by WinkiPoP Media
Typeset by Cooper Graphics
Printed by Griffin Press

ISBN 1 876631 97 X

visit our website: www.duffyandsnellgrove.com.au

*To the memory of my parents,
George Arthur Pell and
Margaret Lillian Pell (Burke),
and my first bishop, Sir James Patrick O'Collins,
Bishop of Ballarat 1941–1971.*

Readers are invited to send comments to:
benotafraidcomment@hotmail.com

Contents

Foreword by Cardinal Francis Arinze — xi
A Word of Thanks — xiii

1 My Lord and My God

Love and the Cosmos	1
Corpus Christi	6
'Who Do You Say I Am?' Sacrament of Confirmation	10
Neither Male nor Female	14
Christ the King	18
The Sacred Heart	21
The Loaves and Fishes	26
Christ's Wisdom and Justice	30

2 The Great Feasts of the Liturgical Year

The Narrow Doorway to Salvation	35
A Simple, Beautiful Story	38
Turning Point of All History	42
The Transfiguration	44
Healing the Eyes of our Heart	48
Jubilee Year 2000 Chrism Mass	51
Good Friday	54
Easter	59
The Third Eye	63
Pentecost	67

3 Mary, Mother and Role Model

Our Lady Help of Christians	71
The Immaculate Conception	75
The Assumption of our Blessed Lady	80
The Rosary	84

4 Heroes through the Centuries

25th Anniversary of Election of Pope John Paul II	89
Saints Peter and Paul	95
Mother Mary of the Cross	98
Edith Stein	104
The Forty English Martyrs	109
St Patrick's Day Mass	112
Isidore the Priest	117
Frederic Ozanam (Founder of the Society of St Vincent de Paul)	119
Mother Teresa of Calcutta	124
The Faith and Devotion of St Therese	130
St Thomas Becket	133
Our Lady of Lavang and the Vietnamese Martyrs	138

5 The Faithful of Tomorrow

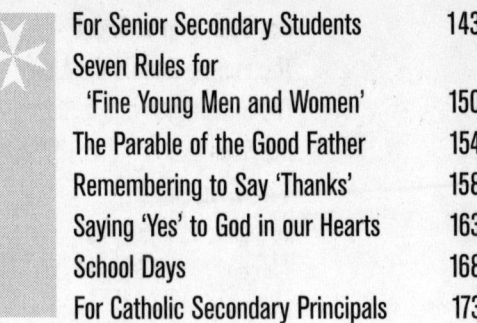

For Senior Secondary Students	143
Seven Rules for 'Fine Young Men and Women'	150
The Parable of the Good Father	154
Remembering to Say 'Thanks'	158
Saying 'Yes' to God in our Hearts	163
School Days	168
For Catholic Secondary Principals	173

6 Love and Life

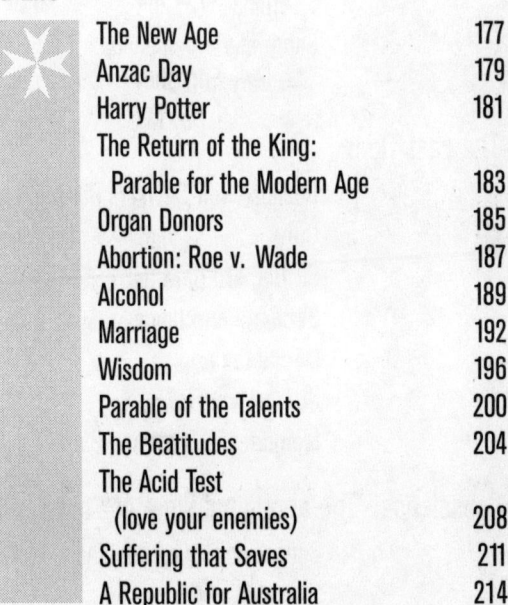

The New Age	177
Anzac Day	179
Harry Potter	181
The Return of the King: Parable for the Modern Age	183
Organ Donors	185
Abortion: Roe v. Wade	187
Alcohol	189
Marriage	192
Wisdom	196
Parable of the Talents	200
The Beatitudes	204
The Acid Test (love your enemies)	208
Suffering that Saves	211
A Republic for Australia	214

7 The Church, Yesterday, Today and Tomorrow

Matthew, the Fine Poet	219
The Picture Behind the Altar	222
The Priesthood	225
Religious Life in the Third Millennium	230
A New Parish	234
Installation Sermon as Archbishop of Sydney	237
The Church and the World	243
From Roman Student to Cardinal … Light	245
Santa Maria Domenica Mazzarello (2004)	248

8 The Last Things

Because Non-Smokers Die Too	251
Duty	254
Sir Bernard Callinan	257
Elizabeth Anscombe	262
BA Santamaria	265
Sr Clare Forbes	271
Memories of Mum and Dad	277

9 Conscience: 'The aboriginal Vicar of Christ'

Conscience: 'the aboriginal Vicar of Christ'	283

Four Catholic Foundations	301
Picture Acknowledgments	303
Gospel Index	305

Foreword

IN these three hundred pages of *Be Not Afraid*, George Cardinal Pell speaks to us as a fellow believer in Jesus Christ and His Church, as a pastor, as a scholar and as a witness to the love of God revealed in the Incarnated Word.

The attention to Holy Scripture, the fidelity to the Catholic Faith, a warm Marian devotion, and the clarity and directness of these sermons make this book particularly precious.

It is a joy to read this volume and to share something of Cardinal Pell's great spirit. The Church and the world need more of such witnesses.

I warmly recommend *Be Not Afraid* to clerics, consecrated people and lay faithful.

Francis Cardinal Arinze
Feast of the Transfiguration of the Lord
6 August 2004
Vatican City

A Word of Thanks

As a priest at Ballarat East I was very friendly with a wonderful Italian family and their two grown-up children. We shared a common faith, a love of Italy and music, especially Puccini and Verdi.

The elderly mother regularly proclaimed 'Father Pell preach a beautiful sermon'. 'Mamma,' her daughter would complain, 'but you don't understand English.' 'I know', my old friend would reply, 'but Father Pell preach a lovely sermon.'

Not all my listeners have been as sympathetic and enthusiastic, but after some years of experience you can tell whether many are listening, whether you are losing the crowd, whether some are becoming hostile. Therefore my first debt of thanks is to the thousands of people who have listened to me (as for every priest) and have helped me with their feedback, commendation or criticism.

Special thanks is due to the editor, Ms Tess Livingstone, who encouraged this project, trawled through hundreds of sermons, made the basic selection and helped with her input and editing. Father Charles Portelli, PP, my Master of Ceremonies in Melbourne, must also be thanked for his input and his constant good advice, some of which I followed, as must Fr Peter Joseph for his meticulous proofreading.

For a priest it is an honour and a duty to try to break open the Word of God for His people. I hope that this selection from nearly forty years of speaking and writing will in fact carry a breath of the Spirit so that the love of God, found especially in the life and teaching of Jesus His Son, will burn more brightly in the hearts of many readers.

+ George Cardinal Pell
Archbishop of Sydney
Feast of Our Lady of Mt Carmel
16 July 2004

1

My Lord and My God

Love and the Cosmos

Readings: *Acts 10:25-26, 34-35, 44-48; 1 John 4:7-10 (In this letter, St John explains that God revealed His love for us by sending His Son into the world so that we might have life through Him.)*
Gospel: *John 15:9-17 (St John relates how Jesus told His followers that He loves us just as the Father loves Him. He urges us to remain in His love by keeping the Commandments, and reveals that He has told us everything He has heard from His Father. He says He chose us, not the other way around and urges us to love one another.)*

Sixth Sunday of Easter – Year B

ONCE upon a time, in the olden days as the primary school children say to me, I was giving religious education classes regularly to a number of teenagers from the local state high schools. I remember this particular occasion because there were a few of them who were explaining to me the theory of evolution that they were being taught then at school. They were also completely happy with the Genesis narrative of creation from the first book of the Old Testament – not just the basic thrust, but the details, they had no problem about that – and without telling them directly, I could not even provoke or chide or entice them into realizing that there might have been a tension between the scientific account of how the world came to be and the religious story in the first book of the Old Testament.

Today we have two beautiful readings on the centrality of love, which most of us would have very little difficulty in accepting. In Christian tradition we must love one another, in deeds not just in words, and the second element present in both those readings is that love comes from God, that our God loves us. That Supreme Intelligence is interested in each one of us. As the scriptures relate, sending His Son among us is the prime evidence of that love. The love shows itself in many ways – through the service of others, through genuine gratitude. Gratitude unlocks joy. Gratitude releases us from our self-absorption. Love shows itself through good planning. There are many examples of this – parents with their children, what school will they send them to, keeping an eye on their friends, making sure the teenagers are not accessing pornography through the Internet, not reading too many of the wrong sorts of magazines.

But how can we reconcile the importance of love with the big picture, the total picture; you might say the scientific picture? Most of us have been in aeroplanes and looked down at the tiny humans and cars that are travelling on earth; a different perspective. How can we reconcile the importance of love with the immensity of the Universe, where our planet is comparable to a grain of sand on an immense beach?

I want to take a few thoughts from an article that appeared earlier this month in an English Catholic magazine, *The Tablet*, from the other side of the world. The article was written by Russell Stannard, a retired professor of philosophy at the Open University in England. He was talking about the place of God and love in the cosmos, in the history of evolution. One of the remarkable things today is that so many of the new pagans (unlike the pagans in the days of the Roman Empire, who did not know or could not acknowledge the one true God) are saying quite explicitly that the whole of creation is a giant fluke. There is no purpose to it. It came from nowhere, came by chance and is going nowhere. This is quite remarkable and remarkably bleak.

I mentioned the size of the Universe being beyond our comprehension. Most places in the Universe are hostile to life; they are either too hot or too cold. For most of the history of the Universe there has been no intelligent life, certainly at least no human intelligent life. There seems to be no doubt that the Universe is expanding after the Big Bang and that eventually it will slow down and drift back to a Big Crunch. There will be a heat dearth as everything cools down. There is no need for us to be personally too much worried because that is billions and billions of years into the future. But each star has only a limited amount of fuel for nuclear fission and while new stars are coming into being there is no doubt that there are limits to that energy.

How do we look on all this? Stannard suggests that God is a good planner and he produces some very interesting evidence for that. He speaks of the Universe as the womb in which human life developed. We believe that our one true God had the responsibility and the capacity for designing the Universe. How violent was He to make the Big Bang? If the forces in that initial and mysterious explosion had been less, the whole of the Universe would have come together in a Big Crunch in a time shorter than the 12,000 million years that were needed for evolution here on earth. If the forces in the Big Bang had been much greater, the velocity of the gases coming out of the Big Bang would have been so fast that they would not have had time to collect together. In the production of life there is a very small window of opportunity for the creation of intelligent creatures.

The same with the force of gravity. If gravity was a lesser force there was a great risk there would have been no stars in the Universe. If in fact the force of gravity was greater, the stars would have been massive as some stars are and would have burned themselves out very quickly. And then there is a question of the materials that constitute living bodies. Apparently the two gases that first came from the Big Bang were hydrogen and helium and it was through nuclear fusion that these two basic elements were changed, especially into the carbon that is necessary for life. The odds that are needed to go from carbon to human life are astronomical, almost beyond our imagining.

I spoke about this once before and a maths lecturer came up to me and said: 'Do you realize just how immense those odds are?' And I said, being mathematically pretty illiterate, 'I don't really.' But they are many, many, many times beyond winning a great lottery not once, but every time since it began.

The scientists call this the anthropic principle. The Universe has bent over backwards to accommodate us and to enable human life to commence and to exist and to thrive. As one scientist said, the Universe knew we were coming.

So we thank God for the gift of faith, but we also

thank God for the genius of men and women of learning who have been able to puzzle out so much of the mystery of the Universe and through modern technology have been able to enhance our lives so wonderfully. And we thank God for the world of communication. How different our world would be without the mass media. Just personally I'd find it very difficult to imagine breakfast without all the morning papers. More seriously, what a diminished society ours would be without a free press.

As always, we often realize these things when we go away. I was travelling through China soon after the Tiananmen Square massacre with people who knew Chinese, but the Chinese press was useless for finding out what was happening. We relied on the BBC. I think it is not by chance that in that country they have massive problems of pollution, as they did everywhere in the Communist world, because there is no press to speak about these things. And there is no doubt too that a free press has helped us in the Church to face up to evils and difficulties within the Church and to purify ourselves, as was necessary.

Gratitude is a wonderful thing, it is a marvellous expression of love, and I want to conclude with a quotation from this morning's *Sunday Herald-Sun*, from Bryan Patterson's 'Faithworks'. I always read it before I preach here on a Sunday because like a magpie I am always going around trying to find something that will prevent me from repeating myself too much. He quoted from the last public statement of Cardinal John O'Connor, the Archbishop of New York, who has just died, and who was here a couple of years ago to consecrate this Cathedral. It is a beautiful expression of love and in the particular form of gratitude. O'Connor wrote this: 'Nothing quite focuses us as does a hospital room ... One reflects on one's failures, one's imperfections, one's hope of what one might have done and perhaps failed to do or should not have done and perhaps did. But washing through it all, refreshing, purifying, is the unyielding sense of the great mercy, and even more the great gentleness of God. I find myself in unutterable peace, a peace born of the grace of God and of the goodness of God's people. Life is such a gift, and after almost eighty years of living it, I have no sentiment so strong as gratitude.'

Sunday, 28 May 2000,
St Patrick's Cathedral, Melbourne

Corpus Christi

Readings: *Ex 24:3-8; Heb 9:11-15.*
Gospel: *Mark 14:12-16, 22-26 (Mark tells of Jesus' last supper with His apostles.)*

Feast of Corpus Christi – Year B

THE Feast of Corpus Christi celebrates one of the strangest and most beautiful truths taught by the Catholic Church community. Mark's gospel gives us one account of the institution of this ritual. Just before He was crucified, Jesus celebrated the Passover with His apostles, His giving them His flesh to eat and His blood to drink under the forms of bread and wine. The bread was broken to prefigure His suffering and death and His blood was described as the blood of the covenant to be poured out for many. This doctrine is controversial even among good Christians today and it has been controversial since Jesus first announced His intentions. John's gospel recounts Jesus telling His followers that if they do not eat the flesh of the Son of Man or drink His blood, they do not have any religious life in them. Those who do so eat and drink will have eternal life and be raised up body and soul on the last day (6:48-66).

Some of His listeners found this type of talk intolerable, left Him and no longer walked with Him.

We are used to the idea of receiving Holy Communion with faith in the dignity and ritual of the Eucharistic celebration. But we should spare a thought for those Jews who were unable to accept this teaching, because there is something shocking and surprising in the thought that we all actually consume the Body and Blood of the Son of God. (Corpus Christi is Latin for Body of Christ.) We can all become victims to routine, so that the stupendous miracle which occurs at the consecration, without the slightest external change, slips by us.

And it is interesting that many Bible Christians, the people who were first called 'fundamentalists', regularly jib at understanding Our Lord's Eucharistic words literally. We should pray for them that they come to a better and fuller understanding of the redeeming mystery of the Eucharist as we continue to work with them and all other Christians to preach and explain the teaching of Christ and the apostles.

The Eucharist is a true banquet. St Ephrem from Syria in the fourth century speaks of those who take communion eating 'Fire and Spirit', the source of eternal life. Another Middle Eastern saint and martyr, Bishop Ignatius of Antioch, who died in 107 AD, spoke of the Eucharistic bread as a 'medicine of immortality, an antidote to death'. We could even say that in taking Communion we consume and digest the secret of the resurrection, our personal resurrection made possible by the resurrection of Christ Our Lord.

Our celebration of Mass expresses and reinforces our communion with the Saints in heaven, with the Church in heaven. The Consecration, when the bread and wine become the Body and Blood of Christ, is the most sacred moment at Mass. This belief only makes sense as a consequence of our belief in the death and resurrection of Christ. A great mystery, it cannot be explained, but its elements are not contradictory. By commemorating the unique saving sacrifice of Jesus, the Lamb of God, we join ourselves to the heavenly liturgy and become part of that great multitude from all the ages who cry out in heaven 'Salvation belongs to Our God who sits upon the throne and to the Lamb' (Rev 7:10).

While the feast reflects the importance of the Eucharist, for many centuries it has been associated with one particular aspect – devotion to the Real Presence of Christ.

The thirteenth century was probably the most remarkable in the history of the Church, beginning with St Francis of Assisi, including St Thomas Aquinas and closing with the great painter Giotto and the writer Dante. During this century, Blessed Juliana of Mont Cornillon near Liege in Belgium, a very holy nun, popularised the feast of Corpus Christi and devotion to the Blessed Sacrament. Pope Urban IV, who had been an Archdeacon at Liege, later made the feast universal throughout the Western Church. However, it was only in the next century that the popularity of the feast deepened and widened. Tradition has it that St Thomas Aquinas wrote many of the Latin prayers and hymns used in the Mass of the feast, speaking of our senses of sight, touch and taste being deceived by this miracle: '*visus, tactus, gustus fallitur.*'

The Protestant Reformation presupposed that one could have apostolic faith through apostolic doctrine.

The Catholic view is that the community preserves the faith – one needs not just doctrine, but a Church in which doctrine takes shape.

There was a famous exchange between a Lutheran scholar and St Robert Bellarmine, the Jesuit, in the years after the Reformation. The Lutheran argued against Eucharistic adoration on the grounds that Christ meant for the Sacrament to be used, not reserved. It was a legitimate theological point. Bellarmine's response was that the Church had adored the Eucharist for a long time, and there was no good reason to abandon the practice. In fact, once the Lutherans jettisoned adoration, they developed a different Eucharistic doctrine that moved away from the enduring 'Real Presence' of Christ. It's a case in which the tradition of the community had protected the faith.

One can analyse this argument in different ways, but it is a reminder of how fundamental a value the idea of community is for Catholics. In an era in which forces such as nationalism, tribalism, and ideological polarization are eating away at the Church's sense of communion, it's an important testimony. Adoration and prayer before the Blessed Sacrament are a source of grace and vocations, and a useful antidote to prevent any weakening of belief in the real presence of Christ in the Eucharistic species.

I wonder sometimes whether the sense of mystery, the common conviction, especially among children, that Christ is present under the appearance of bread and wine, is being somewhat obscured. Recognition that the sanctuary lamp is a sign of Christ's presence in the tabernacle is important. So is a decent genuflection. Youngsters' knees are not gone with praying or football, so a nod or a bob is not good enough! There is a danger of routine, too, especially for the priest.

The community symbolism of Mass, especially the

symbolism of a sacrificial meal, is very beautiful, but it should never be allowed to obscure the great mystery of the Presence of Christ Himself in the elements of bread and wine.

However, this is not the greater mystery. It is even more mysterious that Christ wanted to nourish us with Himself, because in the Old Testament, eating someone else's body was a sign of deadly enmity. We are not physically nourished by the hosts; they are a symbol of spiritual nourishment. But this symbol of spiritual nourishment is neither an easy nor a natural symbol. St Augustine said: 'He gave us His Body to make us into His Body.' The Real Presence of Christ builds up unity among us. Both elements of this mystery are vitally important.

Adapted from a sermon at St Mary's Cathedral, Sydney, 22 June 2003, and an editorial in the Ballarat diocesan newspaper Light, *June 1984*

'Who Do You Say I Am?'

Sacrament of Confirmation

Readings: Is 22:19-23; Rom 11:33-36.
Gospel: Matthew 16:13-20 (Jesus promises to found the Church at Caesarea Philippi, appointing Peter as the first Pope, the rock upon whom 'I'll build my Church'. Giving Peter the 'keys to the Kingdom of heaven' Christ promises that 'whatever you bind on earth shall be bound in heaven; and whatever you loose on earth shall be loosed in heaven'.)

FOR those of us who are believers a number of basic questions can be put, whether we are Christians, or we are Catholics. The most basic question is — is it all true? And then, what difference does it make if we accept all this? We can get a little bit more particular — does God exist? Is there life after death? And more centrally, because in some ways it is the key to so many of these answers — who do you think Christ is? In the Gospel Our Lord used probably his favourite explanation to call Himself the Son of Man; a term taken from the Old Testament and especially from the Book of Daniel, but a mysterious term.

Now 'who do we say Christ is?' is a difficult question because all sorts of practical consequences follow from it. Christ's call was not simply a polite invitation. He didn't say, 'Well if you are a little bit interested in things religious, like some people are interested in stamp collecting, you might come along and hear what I have to say.' Jesus said, 'Come, follow me.' It was insistent.

So His claims are extreme, some of His teachings are difficult; they work, but they are difficult. He had a most unusual life; born in a stable, died as a young man, executed at the age of thirty-three. I am very interested in Aussie Rules football. I also enjoy watching good soccer, rugby union and I'm very interested in test cricket. None of those things really conflict one with the other too much and that was the way in Roman times many people looked on religion. You could have a whole raft of religions, be a bit interested in them all, and choose a bit from this or that or something else. But Jesus called us to base our core values, as we now say, on Him and to believe in His special role as the Son of God.

What is this special role of Jesus? There is no doubt it is enormous. It is now more than 2000 years since He was born. There are one billion Catholics throughout the world and hundreds of millions of other Christians. Is He simply another religious genius like the Buddha or Mohammed, with a special insight into things religious the way Einstein was a genius in science and Beethoven or Mozart were geniuses in music? Is He simply the greatest philosopher, especially for ordinary people, who ever lived?

Or is Jesus a great mistake? Somebody who has led people in the wrong direction, advocating humility rather than empowerment. Advocating forgiveness, turning the other cheek, rather than revenge. Advocating the worship of an unseen God, rather than human autonomy. Promising life after death when there is no such thing.

If Jesus is more right than wrong, or if we think He is basically right in all his fundamental teachings, in what sense is He divine or the Son of God? Is He simply, as we touched on before, the most perfect human who ever lived? So Catholic teaching recognizes Christ as the Son of Mary, that is the human nature, but also as the eternal Son of God, the pre-existent Word, one of the Trinity. That mystery of boundless love from all eternity who took on human nature and came down among us to live and teach us and redeem us.

If and when we accept that Jesus is the Son of God it means that we accept His teachings are true. I can see that some of them are difficult; that His teachings have a unique authority. As we used to say in the olden days, *they give us the good oil* on what life is about. Opinions are divided now as they were divided at the time of the Gospel, when Jesus said to His apostles, 'Who do they reckon I am?' Peter replied, 'Well, some say you are Elijah, some say you are John the Baptist, some say you are one of the prophets.'

So with Confirmation, people are declaring once again that they accept Christ as the Son of God and membership in His Church as something that is beautiful and important. All the Sacraments have a human purpose: Baptism starts us off in the Church; Anointing of the sick often comes towards the end of life. Sunday Mass gives us the strength to believe and to do good. Confirmation completes the Sacraments of Baptism and Eucharist, it is a Sacrament of Initiation, it seals the membership of a person in the Church. After Confirmation they become full members of the Church. It is a Sacrament that can never be repeated and it is a Sacrament whose effects can never be rubbed out or washed out. After Baptism and Confirmation a person is sealed, marked irredeemably.

Now Christ is not a family name, like Portelli or Smith or Nguyen. Christ means *the anointed one*, a Christian, somebody who has been chrismed in the Sacrament of Baptism and Confirmation, and a Christian of course is a follower of Christ.

As an aid to those in the Church, the Gospel also speaks about the special position of Peter, *the rock man*. As I regularly explain to the grade six Confirmation youngsters, Peter's name was Simon. Jesus gave him the name Peter. And I tell the youngsters that Jesus renamed Simon and He called him Rocky because Peter means the rock man, the foundation stone on which the Church will be built.

The Pope in Rome, the Bishop of Rome, is the successor of St Peter, and the city of Rome and the Bishops of Rome have a special role in safeguarding the tradition because both Peter and Paul, the two greatest of the apostles, preached there and both were martyred there.

So it is the Popes and the Bishops who are the guarantors that what is being taught is really and truly the teaching of Christ. The power of the keys was given to Peter, the power to bind and to loose. That is not only a moral power in certain areas, but it is also a power of teaching, of saying what we believe and, more regularly, by isolating and nominating just what is not correct teaching.

To use the Old Testament imagery, as used in the Gospel of Matthew in Jesus' language, we believe that Peter is like a tent peg in firm ground. He is also like a strong old gum tree; a certain point of reference, a guarantee of authenticity and truth and that is a great help in the living of our ordinary lives.

Sunday, 22 August 1999,
St Patrick's Cathedral, Melbourne

Neither Male nor Female

Gospel: *John 6:41-51 (Jesus tells the Jews that He is the bread of life that came down from heaven, and whoever eats this bread shall live forever. The bread that He shall give is His flesh for the life of the world. Jesus reminds them that nobody has seen the Father except 'the one who is from God' – that is, Himself.)*

Nineteenth Sunday in Ordinary Time – Year B

IT is surprising how many people, especially the very young or religiously uninstructed, are surprised to hear that God is not a man, nor a woman. I have sometimes recounted how I made the claim that God was spiritual, not material at all, on talk-back radio and was asked by my host whether this was my personal view or the teaching of the Church. It is of course traditional Christian teaching, common to all the Christian denominations.

Jesus' preferred term for God was father; indeed 'abba' which is the affectionate term young and old would use in the Aramaic language for speaking to their father. This has misled people, as have the paintings or stained glass windows of God the Father as a well built, benign old gentleman with a big beard; the patriarch *par excellence*.

We Christians inherited this view of the one true God as pure Spirit from the Jews. So frightened were they of idolatry, the worship of false gods, that they forbade any image of God to be made or venerated. To this day this is their practice, as it is of the other large group of monotheists, the Moslems, also children of Abraham. In the Holy of Holies, the most sacred spot of the Jewish Temple in Jerusalem, there was originally the Ark of the Covenant, which contained the tablets of the Law given to Moses and an empty throne. This disappeared at the Babylonian captivity and after that the Holy of Holies was empty of any physical object, to signify the transcendent spiritual presence of God – something which (legend tells us) baffled the Roman soldiers who captured and destroyed Jerusalem and the Temple in 70 AD.

One important basis for this belief in the spiritual nature of God is God's revealing His name to Moses as Yahweh: 'I am who I am' (Exodus 20:3-5); a title which says a lot, although it might not seem very helpful at first glance. There is only one God, who is spiritual and is neither part of material creation, nor the sum total of all creation. We are not pantheists, not worshippers of nature, which is often cruel and relentless. Australian conditions often remind us of this.

Our Lord is building on this revelation to His people the Jews, when He explains in today's gospel that nobody has seen the Father, except the one who comes from God; that is Jesus Himself.

I believe our religious situation is much easier than that of the Jews, because Jesus Christ as true God (i.e. Son of God) and true man is a bridge between the omnipotent God, pure Goodness and Beauty, Light and Love and our poor selves, where our spark of divinity is concealed in human weakness and wickedness. There is an infinite gap between God and man, which Christ bridges for us by taking up our sins and achieving their forgiveness when we seek it. This is called redemption. Jesus also is the bridge between this world of ours, with all its beauty, seductiveness and occasional cruelty and the next world, heaven, where our reconstituted bodies and souls will be happy forever, in the permanent NOW which is God.

We need faith to accept this. Jesus is no bridge if He is not divine, not God's Son. Otherwise He is just one of us, a great saint, prophet and mystic. So we must have some sympathy for Jesus' contemporaries, who objected to the claim that He was the bread from heaven. 'We know this man', ran their rebuttal. 'He is the son of Mary and Joseph. What is this nonsense that He came down from heaven?'

So too today people are able to object to the special claims of the Catholic Church, citing our sins and crimes over the centuries and today and our plain ordinariness. They are following precedents going back nearly 2000 years and used by Jesus' own opponents!

It was Catherine of Siena, a remarkable saint and mystic of the fourteenth century, who developed the image of Christ as the bridge, connecting earth and heaven. We have to use the wood of Christ's cross to climb to this bridge, which has stone walls of true solid virtue, a roof of mercy, while the Church is like a hotel, or guest house, or restaurant where the bread of life is served to all those drawn by love to use the bridge to come to God.

Scholars have explained that the bread of life spoken about in today's chapter six from John's gospel refers both to our Lord's teachings and also to the Eucharist, the bread and wine which become the Body and Blood of Jesus.

The Jews escaping from Egypt under Moses ate the manna which fell from heaven, but they still died. The same could almost be said of the great Elijah, who saved the Jews from lapsing into paganism in the ninth century BC and who was sustained on his pilgrimage to the mountain of the Lord by the miraculous scones and jar of water, before he went to heaven in his chariot.

However those who eat Christ's bread of life, offered by the Church, will live forever, possess eternal life. The death which all of us shall suffer is a gateway to reward and happiness for the good.

Jesus, true God and man, is the bridge who has made this possible. He came from heaven to share out inadequacies, tinea, dandruff, the common cold, changing moods, so that we would listen to Him while He taught us and believe that He is our Redeemer, the Bread of Life.

10 August 2003, St Mary's Cathedral, Sydney

Christ the King

Readings: *Ezk 34:11-12, 15-17; 1 Cor 15:20-26, 28.*
Gospel: *Matthew 25:31-46 (Jesus warns His disciples of a final judgment, where some will be welcomed into Heaven and others cast out. He tells them that 'whatever you did for one of the least of my brothers, you did for me.' He was talking about those who were poor, hungry, thirsty, lonely or in prison.)*

Feast of Christ the King – Year A

IF you were asked to write a half page or a page of your views about Jesus Christ, what would you write? Would you be like the young American who got a shock when he realized that he knew more about Abraham Lincoln than he did about Christ Our Lord; although he was happy to acknowledge he was a Christian and never thought of calling himself a Lincolnian!

What would we say to the question 'Who is Christ?' Is Jesus human or divine or a mixture of both? What do we admire in Jesus? What disturbs us in His life or teaching? Is there anything with which we disagree?

We could approach this request from another angle. Would we be able to square what we have written with the evidence we find in the New Testament and in the solemn teachings of the Church, announced by the great church councils in the fourth and fifth centuries? Please God we would not be like the Juror who said that he did not need to study the evidence, because he was going to follow his conscience!

Each one of us is tempted to shape our vision of Christ according to our preferences, perhaps even according to our semi-conscious needs. Sometimes in the press there are appeals made to versions of Christ, which are impossible to reconcile with the full Gospel evidence. We can be told that Christ was all-tolerant, all forgiving and never had a cross word for anyone!

The Christ of the gospels is much more complicated than any one-dimensional image of political correctness. Christ did speak of the primary importance of love, but He listed love of God as the first Commandment with love of our neighbour second. At one stage He drove the money changers from the temple, explained that God's forgiveness only has consequences when we are repentant and ask for forgiveness, and at different times He severely criticized King Herod 'that fox' and some of the Pharisees.

Why do we celebrate Christ as King on the last Sunday before Advent? It is not an ancient feast, being introduced only in 1925 by Pope Pius XI to celebrate the all-embracing authority of Christ, which will lead all people to seek His peace in His Kingdom.

During His lifetime, Jesus did not live like royalty and He was not born into any royal family. He emphasized service, taking the last place for those who wanted to be first in His Kingdom, which is not of this world.

We might pick up a couple of reasons from today's readings to justify the Church's use of the title 'Christ the King'. Paul explains in his first letter to the Christians of Corinth that the resurrection of the dead came about through Christ's redemptive life. In other words, death is not the last word; the inevitable conclusion to every life is not the end-point of existence. Heaven or Hell will follow. Paul explains that through Christ there will be a final time when evil and suffering will be eliminated and

God's Kingdom all-powerful. All people will be brought to life in Christ. In other words Christ is King because He has conquered death.

Jesus is also King because Matthew's gospel shows that on the last day all of mankind will be judged, divided into sheep or goats, those destined for reward and those destined for punishment. It is an unusual fact that today when so many people genuinely yearn for justice, and when most would concede that justice is not achieved for some, perhaps many, in this life that there is a widespread objection to the idea of a final judgment at the end of life, and/or the end of time, when the scales of justice will balance out through reward for the good and punishment for evil doers.

The criteria for judgment as outlined in Matthew's gospel are also interesting, reduced to the presence or absence of an active kindness. This is not the whole story, because all the Commandments still remain in place. Probably those who consistently break the commandments are also those who are consistently selfish, who regularly refuse to help others.

According to Christ the King, our Judge Who is to come, we have obligations to the hungry and thirsty, to strangers and those without clothes or sufficient means, to the sick and the imprisoned. If we refuse to help them, that is equal to refusing to help Christ Himself. If we are kind to those in need this is equivalent to being kind to Christ Himself.

It goes far beyond common sense that our simple acts of kindness should gain such supernatural dividends. But because Christ is the Son of God He is entitled to be called King. Because He is divine, He is able to forgive our sins, to promise us life after death, to reward the good and punish the selfish evildoers. He is indeed our King!

24 November 2002, St Mary's Cathedral, Sydney

The Sacred Heart

JOHN Donne, the Dean of St Paul's Cathedral, London, was the most passionate and eloquent of the Elizabethan poets. His memorable phrases have become part of our language. In his series of homilies he wrote these oft-quoted words:

> No man is an island, entire of itself.
> Every man is a piece of the continent,
> a part of the main.
> Any man's death diminishes me
> because I am involved in mankind;
> And therefore never send to know for whom the
>   bell tolls;
> It tolls for thee.

John Donne's memorial still stands in St Paul's. It was the only piece of sculpture to survive the Great Fire of 1666 that destroyed much of London, including old St Paul's. It was based on a drawing Donne had made of himself in which he insisted on being wrapped in a shroud, tied head and foot, with closed eyes. Donne kept this picture by his sickbed, and his biographer, Izaac Walton, tells how Donne wished that the finished statue should face East, as it was from this point of the compass that he expected the Second Coming of his Saviour.

It was during his last illness that John Donne wrote his poignant 'Hymn to God, my God, in my sickness'. In that poem Donne appeals to God's mercy, revealed most fully in the Crucified Christ. In his illness Donne realized something of the great truth which is contained in the gospel for this feast:

> We think that Paradise and Calvary,
> Christ's Cross and Adam's tree, stood in one place:
> Look, Lord, and find both Adams met in me;
> As the first Adam's sweat surrounds my face,
> May the Last Adam's blood my soul embrace.

The Gospels place us on Calvary, at the most decisive moment in human history. Jesus, the Incarnate Son of God and Son of Mary, who took on our frail human nature, has bowed His head and surrendered His spirit so that we might live no longer as slaves to sin and death, but live forever for God. The Fathers of the Church used to describe the Cross as a ladder which joined heaven to earth, Paradise to Calvary.

There is still one final sorrow that Christ must undergo for our redemption to be complete. The soldier pierces Christ's heart with a lance, and there flows out, as John the evangelist and disciple tells us, blood and water. It is the final act of human aggression against the mercy of God, a battle which began in Eden. It is this last blow which releases the waters of grace for the whole of creation. The water and blood flowing from the heart of Christ are symbols of the new life we share with God because of the sacrifice of His only Beloved Son.

The Sacred Heart of Jesus is the continuing proof that all that is human, good and evil, success and failure, has been taken up into the heart of Christ, and refined there, as gold is tested in a furnace. St Paul tells us that the mystery of life and love, hidden for all the ages, has only now been revealed. Christ's heart is the infinite treasure in which all wisdom is found. There is, because of Christ and through Christ, nothing about human existence that God does not understand. The Sacred Heart of Jesus, in that hour of its human tragedy, began to draw all hearts towards itself. Because Christ loves us with all His heart and soul and body and mind, there is now no limit to our own capacity to love.

It is this ability to love passionately but disinterestedly which must be at the core of what we are about as the Church of Christ. Jesus has given us an example which we, who work in the name of the Church, must follow if our work is to be an authentic expression of the great command given by Christ: Go and make disciples of all nations. The work of those directly involved in the mission of the Church is not solely an act of service. Service is not a virtue, but it springs from virtue, especially that of charity. Service is a manifestation of *agape*, or of a love 'which does not consider its own interests' (1 Cor 1:3) but those of others. It is, as the prayer of St Ignatius puts it, a desire to serve and not to be served, to give without receiving. Service is, all told, a participation in and imitation of God's way of acting.

The one true God is Good, all good and the Supreme Good, who cannot but love and help us disinterestedly. This is why evangelical service is not so much recommended to those who are inferior, to the needy, or the poor, but to those who have much. From the one who has been given much, much will be expected. That is why Jesus says that in His Church, the leader must be the one who serves, and whoever is first must be the slave of all (Mark 10:44). To wash another's feet is to participate in the Sacrament of Christian authority.

Besides being freely given, our service of those in need expresses another aspect of *agape*: humility. Jesus said, 'Learn from me for I am humble and gentle of heart' (Matthew 11:29). Jesus' whole life is a parable of humility: the Eternal Word, through whom all things were made, adopted our frail nature. His death is the final seal of this lesson: the One who sustains all things opened His arms and was nailed to a cross by the indifference and malice of those who would not listen to His teaching. If our work for the service of the Church lacks this humility it will ultimately lead us nowhere. We might become very successful in the volume of our work and its obvious benefits. But our service will become just another way of proving our own righteousness. The blessings promised to the poor in spirit will elude us, and we will have done little to ensure our own place in the Kingdom.

The truth about our work of service is expressed most perfectly in the Eucharist we celebrate. Jesus Christ, whose Body and Blood are present in this Sacrament, sends us out at the end of Mass to love and to serve. The Eucharist is a Sacrament of mission. We love and serve the Lord who identified Himself with the hungry, the sick, the naked: 'Whatsoever you do to the least of these, you do it to me' (Matthew 25). Christ's presence in those in need is a true presence, different from that in the Eucharist, but not imaginary or fictitious. St John Chrysostom once thundered: 'Do you wish to honour the Body of Christ? Then do not allow it to be scorned in its members, in the poor and the naked. Do not honour Him with silk in church, and leave Him cold and naked outside.'

This option for the poor must be first and foremost in any work of service that we undertake in the name of the Church, and therefore of Christ. We must compare our priorities with those of the Gospel and in imitation of those who have gone before us. The Church in Australia is blessed by the selfless witness of service and faith of those who place Christ first and made sure that it was He who was served.

The world can rightly criticize us at times for appearing to shirk from the hard tasks and the difficult decisions. The world condemned Christ because He promised the Kingdom to those who were like little children. We should not expect a milder judgment. At times we may feel that everything depends on us. What the feast of the Sacred Heart reminds us is that everything we do really depends on Christ and on His love for us, a love which can never be measured. God's wisdom, as St Paul told us, is comprehensive.

Our task is to accept the challenges that faith in Christ and in His Church presents and to face them with the gentle, humble love of Him who loved us more than His own life.

We are, as John Donne said, not islands, entire of ourselves. We are part of the great movement of humanity back to the Source of all that is good and true and holy. Your work for the sake of the Gospel is highly valued. My ambition is that all of you will work together to give those who do not or cannot believe in God a reason to search their own hearts more deeply, and hear there the voice of Jesus, the Good Shepherd, calling them to their true home.

Your service is the best book about God that most people will ever read. My prayer for you is that you will grow closer to Christ through your work, and that Christ, in His turn, will strengthen you by proofs of His love, and give your hearts the certainty of knowing that what you do for the least of His brothers and sisters, you do for Him.

6 June 1997, Mass for Catholic Agencies at St Patrick's Cathedral, Melbourne

The Loaves and Fishes

Readings: *Is 55:1-3; Rom 8:35, 37-39.*
Gospel: *Matthew 14:13-21 (A vast crowd followed Jesus into the countryside where He spoke to them and cured the sick. In the evening the crowd was hungry and Jesus changed fives loaves and two fish into enough food for more than 5000 people, with twelve full wicker baskets left over.)*

Eighteenth Sunday in Ordinary Time – Year A

YEARS ago I was looking after a small parish outside Ballarat. It had three churches in different parts of the parish and two or three of the couples who attended one church invited me to join them for lunch at a small country pub after the last Mass. I came in and sat down at the table and the chef sent out a plate to me. On it were a few of slices of bread and a couple of small fish. For a moment I didn't know what was going on, then I realized that he was reminding me of the miracle of the loaves and the fishes. I sent back a message to say that I had knocked off for the day and for that reason I wasn't able to do anything to multiply the loaves and the fishes to help him in his job.

It is an unusual, true little story; an example of how the teachings of the Gospel of Our Lord seep into our subconscious, our unconscious and into our set of values. This miracle is evidence of the fact that the One True God loves us and is interested in us.

Quite a number of people today, an increasing minority, are interested in spirituality. An old English writer, dead for quite some time now, who was a bit of a cynic, but a brilliant journalist and writer, Malcolm Muggeridge, said: 'You can explain a part of the interest in religion by the fact that the sicker you become, the more interested you are in your health.' And there is a little bit of truth in that in the search today. But a fundamental issue in any search for spirituality is whether we believe in the One True God, whether we believe that God is good and whether we believe that God is interested in us. I suppose in the future, increasingly this will come under attack by people who will describe themselves as spiritual and interested in religion.

The feeding of the five thousand is a symbol of our obligation to help one another and especially to help the poor and those who have missed out. It is quite clear from this story and from the whole body of Catholic teaching that Our Lord is not against material things. Our Lord very much values them. It is one reason why we can use the bread and the wine as symbols which become the Body and Blood of Christ. At different stages in Christian history there have been small groups of Christians who denied that Christ was really flesh and blood like us; He was just appearance, He was really a spirit, because somehow matter is inferior or even wicked. The Catholic answer, the traditional Christian answer, has always been 'that is not true'. Material things are good. We pray for our daily bread. But we also know that too much of these material things, or lusting after them too much, can dry our heart up, so that we become unable to feel the needs of others and compassion is finished or very, very limited.

This is the only miracle from Jesus' public life, which is found in all four of the Gospels. Indeed Matthew and Mark have two such accounts. We are not quite sure whether the geographical settings are quite different, whether there were two such incidents or there was just one. And it is clear that right from the start the people there saw it as something more than an expression of Our Lord's compassion for the people, although it was certainly that. We are told in Mark that the people didn't understand what was going on.

Undoubtedly, for many people and for the writers of the Gospels, the miracle was a sign that Jesus was the Messiah, the one for whom the Jews were waiting. An important part of the Old Testament imagery was the understanding that the Messiah would help to feed his people. In his Gospel, John sees it as a pre-figuration of the Eucharist, a pre-figuration of the Messianic feast in heaven, the marriage feast, which is one of the images which is used to describe life after death.

Our Lord had gone to the mountains to pray. The people followed Him there and we are told that they were stuck there without food. Now some people say that this miracle was set soon after Herod had executed John the Baptist and there is no doubt that many of the Jews were wanting to make Jesus a political leader, a political king. One very plausible possibility is that Our Lord went away not only to pray, but so that there would be no political demonstration, no trouble which would give Herod some chance to act against Him. His time had not come.

There is no doubt that quite a number of the people who were there saw the miracle as a foretaste of the political power that they believed Jesus was likely to bring. We are used to the separation of Church and State, something that is comparatively new even in the West. We know that bishops are not premiers, thanks be to God, or prime ministers or governors or anything like that, but with the Jews it was different. Jews were ruled by foreigners, then by the Romans. Their understanding was that often the political leader would be the religious leader. So time and time again Our Lord had to say to them, look I am not interested in a political revolution, I have not come here to free you from the Romans. I suspect that this could be one of the reasons why Judas betrayed Jesus.

We know that he was a thief, he was, as we used to say in the old days, 'tickling the till', he was pinching money from the group, but as well as that he could have been hoping that Jesus would have founded a powerful political movement to restore Israel. When the penny dropped that Jesus was not going to do that, then he felt it was much easier to betray Him.

We also are always tempted to be like the Jews, although we put it in other ways. We are tempted to believe we have (almost) a right to an easier passage through life. Jesus does not promise us that, nor does He promise that because we follow Him our life will be harder, although one or two of the saints were tempted to think like that. It is alleged that after a mishap, St Teresa of Avila said to the good Lord that if this was the way He treated his special friends it wasn't surprising He had so few.

Leaving that aside, there is always an element of the Cross, there is always an element of sacrifice, but just as certainly the burden is light and even the earthly consolations for individuals and for the community that come from following Christ and supporting one another are quite immense.

So let us pray that as individuals and families and as a community we too will follow Christ's lead and that we will help to cure one another and support and feed one another in all sorts of physical and spiritual ways.

Sunday, 1 August 1999,
St Patrick's Cathedral, Melbourne

Christ's Wisdom and Justice

> **Gospel:** Matthew 5:17-19 *(Jesus tells His disciples to uphold and teach the Commandments and warns they will not enter Heaven unless they are more righteous than the scribes and Pharisees.)*
>
> Sixth Sunday of the Year – Year A

THOSE of us who are middle-aged or a little beyond that will remember Pope John XXIII, who died in 1963. His diary was published under the English title *Journal of a Soul* and on one of the very front pages he had a little motto and it said (in Latin) that the high point of philosophy is to be simple and prudent. It was a saying he had taken over from St John Chrysostom. I suppose that is the end point of our Christian living. It is a given that we are working towards that goal as we meditate and think about this challenging and provocative gospel.

As we grow older we often find that life is not as simple as it seemed to be when we were younger. Another writer actually said that one of the points of life is getting to what he called a 'second naivety' where we factored most of the important factors while still retaining our belief in some beautiful and life-giving truths. Some people have said that when we come to understand more we never condemn. I would not agree with that. But, certainly, when we understand more we usually condemn less, although perhaps once in a while we might condemn more severely. This process of Christian growth involves the dismantling of half truths, the destruction of deceptive simplicities, so that we can build more adequate foundations to know what God is like, how we live our life, how we pray, and one of the most difficult things of all, to know ourselves more deeply.

We do not want to lose ourselves in a maze of double-talk or complicated theory. Hang on to the basic truths, challenging or confronting as they might be. There are tensions in the New Testament between the different teachers and teachings. There are tensions in Catholic life between people with different casts of mind on what is the best way to live the Christian truths. A vital factor in all that is our attitude to the Commandments, the Law. One essential element in the whole mix that we have to consider is today's gospel. Matthew seemed to like the law more than some of the other gospel writers, but to me this passage today smacks of truth. Not of Matthew putting these things together, but of Christ Himself talking, not to a great crowd of interested people and enemies and people who had nothing else to do, but to his disciples, people who had already gone some distance on the way with Him.

Basically, what He was saying is that the commandments are necessary, but we can all keep them for the wrong reasons. Our heart has to be in it, just as it is not a question of not committing adultery but of striving to make our hearts pure. It is not just that we avoid murdering somebody but we get hate out of our hearts and we eliminate the insults. It says that there is no great point in going on with a load of prayers, once again if there is hate in our hearts. We need to repent.

So isn't it enough to just follow the Commandments? Obviously it is not. Are members of God's Kingdom simply rule keepers? Obviously that is not enough. Will following the Commandments get us to heaven? I do not think so. Behind all this of course is the concept we have of God.

Do we look at God as a remote, capricious, hard, unforgiving figure or do we look on God as being more loving and understanding and forgiving and compassionate than the wisest and most loving human being that we can possibly imagine?

We know that the Reformation was fought over the issue of just what is necessary for salvation. The Reformers took up that teaching of St Paul, 'Man is saved by faith and not by the law which is powerless to save us'. It is alleged that Luther said 'Sin bravely, but believe more bravely yet'. The Catholic writers appealed more easily to St James who said 'Faith without works is a dead faith'. All the scripture writers are correct, that is why they are in the list of the New Testament books, inspired in a special way by the Holy Spirit.

But to find the answer to these dilemmas or quarrels or tensions, the priority has to be on Our Lord's teaching and then we use our reason and we look at the way the Church has interpreted and grappled with these sorts of problems over 2000 years. We are a religion that is incarnated, we are a religion that has tradition and history, but it is a tradition that continues to grow. It is difficult to know where the genuine growth is. Sometimes we use the metaphor of the baby and the bathwater. We can throw the baby out with the bathwater but we certainly need to be rid of the bathwater so that the baby can be cleansed. Everything is not up for grabs, everything cannot be explained away. We stand under the Word of God, and because we are followers of Christ we have to grapple with the truth of the teachings contained in today's gospel.

Faith is an essential element. Religion has to do two things: it has to try to protect us, it has to give us standards or norms or ideals, but it has also to be able to cope with our failures and our weakness.

If we could sum up in a few words: the commandments are necessary, absolutely necessary, but insufficient. They are a little bit like railway lines, a little bit like a great highway; they make it so much easier if we stay on those railway lines or that highway to get from one spot to the other, but love is the motor. We do not reduce religion to morality.

Our Lord said that the two central commands are the commands that we love God above all things, and we love or we try to love our neighbour as ourselves – that is the hard business.

And a necessary corollary of that love is forgiveness – God's forgiveness. Quite a number of adults find it hard to believe that God can or would forgive them. That probably was Judas' biggest mistake. But faith means that we believe in God's forgiveness. It is one of the two biggest differences between us and people who have no faith.

Of course Christian living is just not a question of understanding. It is not something that is just intellectual. It involves acting and praying and believing. Over time we slowly become what we are through our repeated decisions and actions.

The distinctive belief of Christians is our belief that ordinary everyday activities have eternal consequences. When we arrive at heaven we will bring the strengths and the weaknesses we have slowly accumulated in following the Commandments, in our daily living. We often speak of God as light. So at the end time I guess the crucial fact for us will be this. Are we able to come into God's presence happily, into that light, or will we be, because of what we have become, unable to cope with that light and have to turn away into the darkness, probably cursing and blaspheming and absolutely affronted by the pure goodness of God?

In this sense, across all our days we are choosing life or death, love or hate, darkness or light.

14 February 1999, St Patrick's Cathedral, Melbourne

2

The Great Feasts of the Liturgical Year

The Narrow Doorway to Salvation

Readings: Is 61:1-2, 10-11; 1 Thess 5:16-24.
Gospel: John 1:6-8, 19-28 (St John tells of how John the Baptist prepared the people for the coming of Christ – 'the one who is coming after me, whose sandal strap I am not worthy to untie'.)

Third Sunday of Advent – Year B

AT Christmas we celebrate the coming of the Son of God. Advent comes from the Latin word *Advenire* – to come. You might say that we are celebrating four comings: when Our Lord was born 2000 years ago (probably a few more in fact); the coming of Jesus into our hearts – our accepting Him in faith; and the coming of Christ to us at the moment of death, and then at the end of time.

Each of them brings blessings, good news to the poor — spiritually poor, materially poor. But all of these comings also bring an obligation to choose and consequences follow from our choice — consequences for this life and for the next. Christ is the narrow gate, Christ is the doorway to that narrow path that leads to salvation. God is good, God is interested in us and God is a spirit, neither man nor woman, neither flesh nor mineral nor anything material at all.

Basically, we must understand the Son of God's coming among us as something that is beautiful and useful. A relief, it takes away a burden, not just the burden of guilt, but the burden of not knowing what the whole show is about. Many, many Christian writers have used the image of light to explain God and we all know about that. We know how children can fear the dark. We know how people who are sick and awake at night welcome the rising of the sun in the morning. That beautiful Old Testament image — the people living in darkness have seen a great light — like the beauty and majesty of a sunrise. God is light and truth and love.

In the Gospel today we have a passage about John the Baptist, who says he is not the light, he is not the Messiah, the anointed one, whom the Jews were waiting for, but he is a witness to the light. It is interesting that when they asked him he said, 'No I'm not Elijah', and yet later Our Lord said that John was Elijah who came among you and you did not recognize him. Always, especially with issues that are important (and knowing God is really important), the evidence is not mathematically clear. Jesus has told us though that the truth is more obvious to those people with good-will.

John the Baptist is a strange and exciting figure. He was quite fierce, and he was certainly an ascetic. A lot of his background was quite inexplicable to us until 1947 when a shepherd boy near the Dead Sea at Qumran stumbled upon a cave full of old texts. Many of those texts belonged to a small group of Jews called the Essenes. We've heard of the Pharisees, and we've heard of the Sadducees in the New Testament but here was a small, exclusive, secret, and very strict sect called the Essenes.

For a long time people thought the find at Qumran was the library of the monastery. That is now disputed, but a link with such a group provides a lot of useful background for explaining John the Baptist. You know John the Baptist's parents were old, his mother was Elizabeth, Our Lady's cousin, and the Essene communities used to welcome boys as students, much like the old-fashioned minor seminaries. It is very likely that John went to such a community. I was once in the hill country where, so I was told, John lived in the desert until he appeared in the scriptures. It would be a perfect setting for the formation of such a man, although John the Baptist's call was open to all, unlike the call of the Essenes.

The Essenes were waiting for the Messiah. Their preachings, many of the quotations from the Old Testament, and the quotations of John and in the Essene literature, overlap with one another. The Essenes were celibates, they were unmarried as John was. They were ascetical and penitential.

Their diet was similar to that of John the Baptist, locusts and wild honey. Even today I am told that it is common to eat locusts among the Arabs and it's a very good source of vitamins. The Essenes also had ritual washings, which were not too common at all among the rest of the Jews, and these ritual washings were a symbol of their search for purification and coming closer to God.

John, of course, took that over for the baptism we

know as a sign of our repentance and belief; and our Lord Himself took that from John and was baptized by him. So I think that with this background, we can understand a little bit better where John the Baptist came from. It is not certain but highly likely.

While God writes straight through crooked lines, God does work in human history. John's contribution to sensitizing people to the presence of Christ among them also reflects this.

John the Baptist made it quite clear he wasn't the one they were waiting for; he wasn't worthy to undo the Lord's shoelaces. So let's pray this morning that we will understand better this simple call to conversion, this call to try to believe more deeply and more strongly, this call to try to follow Jesus more closely, that was first explained to us in this fascinating figure, John the Baptist.

John the Baptist was saying that Christ's message is a call to duty. It is a promise of immense benefits if we choose well and there is also a promise of real trouble if we persist in turning our back on God and on love. Repent and believe, the same priorities for the Church today as they were 2000 years ago.

Sunday, 12 December 1999,
St Patrick's Cathedral, Melbourne

A Simple, Beautiful Story

Readings: *Is 9:1-7 (foreshadowing a 'great light', the birth of a son upon whose shoulders dominion rests, who shall be called Wonderful Counsellor, Mighty God, Eternal Father, Prince of Peace.) Titus 2:11-14.*

> **Gospel:** Luke 2:1-14 *(telling the story of Christ's birth in a manger in Bethlehem).*
>
> Christmas – Year A

EVEN the youngest among us could probably recount the basic facts of the Christmas story: a young woman and her husband caught away from home because of the census, giving birth to baby Jesus in a stable, being visited by the local shepherds and the angels, rejoicing and singing 'Glory to God in the highest heaven, peace to men who enjoy His favour'.

This simple, beautiful story has brought many of us to this celebration every year of our lives. Even those uncertain of the importance of religion, or at least uncertain of the importance of regularly practising their faith through prayer and worship, will come each year for Christmas Mass.

Are these Christian claims true? Have the people walking in darkness seen a great light? How has this helpless child shone a light into the lands of deep shadow, lifted the yoke weighing people down?

Just recently we have heard more about myths and magic, fairy stories, beautifully woven make-believe worlds than we have for years. My short *Sunday Telegraph* article on *Harry Potter* received more praise and criticism than any other short article I have written in Sydney. On Boxing Day, Tolkien's *Lord of the Rings* will be in the theatres.

We know all cultures have theories to help their citizens to behave well and to acknowledge the powers beyond human control. Usually these teachings are presented in stories as myths. Some claim that the Christmas account of God becoming man, born to a virgin, is only another beautiful myth which the gospel writers dreamed up. Others claim that to get to the truth of the matter all the gospel stories have to be demythologized.

We should remember that a myth is not false simply because it is a myth. Myths are often beautifully expressed, sometimes in the finest poetry. They can awaken in us a longing for mysteries beyond our grasp; they can be expressions of a yearning for the Infinite.

Many myths can reveal a hint, an unfocused gleam of divine truth falling on the human imagination.

One writer who was fascinated by myths was the Englishman CS Lewis, author of the *Narnia* books, of science fiction and of Christian apologetics. He became an atheist at a very early age. He thought, as some do today, that the Christian story of God becoming man, dying for us, was just another recasting of the old pagan myths of a dying God, like Osiris, Cybele, Adonis.

He was first shaken in his scepticism when one of his acquaintances remarked that the evidence of the gospels was pretty good; that it almost looked as though all that stuff about a dying God actually happened in Jesus Christ.

CS Lewis had long believed that myths were not poets' deceptions; not demonic delusions, not even priestly lies, that they were often blurred intimations of important truths or events. He then made the crucial breakthrough and saw that the heart of Christianity is a myth which is also a fact. It actually happened 2000 years ago in Palestine. As Lewis wrote, 'by becoming fact, it does not cease to be myth: that is the miracle'.

Christ is the highest myth because myth has become reality. For a Christian, in faith and in truth, the lights of Christmas reflect the radiance of the one eternal Light; the Word was the true Light which enlightens all people.

In the Christmas story, pagan poetry and common sense are stood on their heads. The Word was with God and the Word was God. The birth at Bethlehem is not another piece of charming poetry, it is the truth to which all the good myths aspire. It is the linchpin, the key to meaning. The Christ child did grow to become the 'Wonderful Counsellor, Mighty God, Eternal Father, Prince of Peace', our Saviour and Redeemer.

Christmas is a celebration of Godly love. We ponder the mystery of God sending His only Son to us, as a baby, to show us the importance of love.

Suffering is real even in our lucky country. The love we receive from others when we are suffering makes all the difference. An awareness of God's love brings strength and consolation. Our love can lighten the burden of suffering for others. Without love suffering is much worse.

Santa Claus, Christmas trees, turkey or prawns, plum pudding, nice presents; none of these can save us. The Christian claim is that Christ does save us. And if we are not saved, we are all lost or damned. Let the beautiful Christmas poem of the Englishman John Betjeman have the last word.

> And is it true? For if it is,
> No loving fingers tying strings
> Around those tissued fripperies,
> The sweet and silly Christmas things,
> Bath salts and inexpensive scent
> And hideous tie so kindly meant,
> No love, that in a family dwells,
> No carolling in frosty air,
> Nor the steeple shaking bells,
> Can with this simple truth compare –

That God was man in Palestine
And lives today in Bread and Wine.

> *Midnight and Christmas Day Masses,*
> *St Mary's Cathedral, Sydney 2001*

Turning Point of All History

'In the beginning was the Word and the Word was with God and the Word was God' and this Word was *'made flesh and lived among us and we saw His glory, the glory that is His, the only Son of the Father, full of grace and truth.'*

(opening stanzas of the Gospel of St John)

THIS is what we celebrate today. Put simply it is the turning point of all history – not just the religious history of the Jews and the various Christian families, but the turning point of all human striving and of the long evolutionary history of the universe.

We can say these words only in the confidence of faith. They defy rational proof and, in some ways, they are a challenge to 'common sense', that cliché we use to describe what was intellectually fashionable one or more generations ago and has now been taken up by large numbers of ordinary people.

If we pull back a bit from these immense challenges (and comforts), what do we see? A young baby boy, born of a young mother (almost impossibly young by our contemporary standards), with a much older man (so tradition tells us) as foster father; the birth was in a stable or a cave and the Christ-child was visited by shepherds, the wharfies of that time and place, in their reputation for toughness and occasional knavery and three foreign philosopher types, who claimed to have followed a star.

A pretty ordinary event among the poor of the world, slightly different perhaps only because of the poverty and muddle and the variety of the visitors.

This child was poor and powerless and this child was God made visible.

God can seem very distant, at least on some occasions, to those of us called to follow Him closely, responsible for too many people (I have just returned from China!), too intelligent (think of those formulas which help explain the workings of our physical world), the source of too much beauty, human and natural, the source of a love that is too powerful and unpredictable, but an all powerful and all loving God who tolerates and turns to good the immense seas of human suffering. This God is almost too much, or too little, to grasp.

We can cope much better with the God-child. The powerlessness of the new born is an invitation to love and service; Christ calls out our love and our service and we must welcome the Christ-child into our hearts and the hearts of our community.

Educated Australia, the Australian world of ideas, often tries, consciously or unconsciously, to ignore Christ. Dedicated priests and religious imitating Christ Himself are not just a call to service, but an intellectual challenge, a stimulus to the weakened Australian religious imagination.

Part of our challenge is cultural – explaining the eternal truths of Christianity in a contemporary accent, not just through schools, but in the media and at tertiary level.

The Christian cause as lived out in the Catholic tradition is a sign of hope, not so much because we are sincere, or good people, or playing a useful role in society, but because God has spoken to us through the Christ-child, who is 'the radiant light of God's glory and the perfect copy of His nature, sustaining the universe by His powerful command'. In some real way, we have the truth and those not knowing this are either in the shadows or in the darkness.

*Christmas Day sermon 1988
to the De La Salle Brothers, St Bede's, Melbourne*

The Transfiguration

Readings: Gen 12:1-4 *(The covenant with Abraham is the foundation of God's covenant with the Chosen People. All future generations are blessed in this covenant.)* 2 Tim 1:8-10.
Gospel: Matthew 17:1-9 *(Jesus took Peter, James and John to a high mountain where He was transfigured before them, His face shining like the sun, His clothes becoming 'as white as light'. Then they saw Christ speaking with the prophets Moses and Elijah who had lived many centuries earlier. God the Father spoke to the three disciples from a cloud, 'This is my beloved Son, with whom I am well pleased; listen to Him.' Terrified, the three fell to the ground, but Jesus came and touched them and said: 'Be not afraid.' And when they raised their eyes, Jesus was there alone.)*

Second Sunday of Lent – Year A

Even we Catholics can be tempted to think like many of the people around us, that our religion exists to keep society decent and to stop individuals hurting one another. In other words, that our religion is entirely about morality, right and wrong, social justice.

This is a mistake. God is of first importance. Therefore if Lent is a time of renewal, it is a time to deepen and purify our faith as well as battle against selfishness.

It is not enough just to nod towards the Transcendent once in a while.

We are children of one God, as was revealed first to Abraham. The Catholic Church constitutes the central line of progeny in this tradition, which began with the Jews (of course) and contains other Christians, especially the Orthodox Churches. Moslems too are children of Abraham.

Abraham lived around 1900 BC, and God's promises of descendants for him are fulfilled in us nearly 4000 years later on the other side of the world.

God's revelation was continued through Christ the Son of God. Jesus was not just the most saintly human and not just a prophet or poet, but the Second Person of the Trinity. The opening words of the prologue to St John's gospel tell us that: 'In the beginning was the Word and the Word was with God, and the Word was God … and the Word was made flesh and lived among us.'

Our claim is not that at heart all the great religions have the same spiritual message. Certainly, there are similarities but also great differences.

We are in the monotheist tradition – the tradition that holds there is only one God (not just the God of our tribe!), who is adored in other monotheist religions. Buddha is silent on God; the Hindus have many gods, but there are gestures in their literature towards one great God.

Moslems do not believe in the Trinity, nor in the Incarnation.

The incident of the transfiguration is told in all three synoptic gospels, and in Matthew's account follows Peter's confession that Jesus is the Christ and Christ's subsequent prediction that He will have to suffer and die. For Matthew, the Messiah is one who will suffer while the title 'The Son of Man' is a figure of glory.

There is no evidence of any inter-testamental tradition of a suffering Messiah, although there is the Isaiah figure of the suffering servant. The images of the suffering servant and the Messiah had not been connected. Therefore the shock and dismay of the apostles at Our Lord's predictions of His death, especially that of Peter, are more easily understandable.

It is interesting to look at the details of the transfiguration. Peter, James and John formed the inner core within the apostles, like the organization of Qumran where there was also an inner circle of three and twelve.

Moses and Elijah symbolize the Law and Prophets. Moses led the exodus from Egypt and received the ten Commandments. In the duel on Mount Carmel, Elijah fought off the prophets of the pagan god Baal. (He is a good model for us today.) The symbolic return of Elijah is not a promise of reincarnation! He is usually seen in the figure of John the Baptist.

The shining clothing described in the gospel account is used regularly in the Book of Revelations as a sign of heavenly Being.

The Cloud of Glory is a sign of God's presence among man in, for example, the book of Exodus. When the magnificent beauty of the Transfiguration had vanished from sight the apostles looked up and saw no one, only Jesus. In their hearts and minds they carried the word of the Father: 'This is my Son, the Beloved. Listen to Him'. The three disciples were not merely spectators. The voice of the Father spoke to them also, as it does to us because we too are the beloved children of the one great God and Father of all.

When the disciples came down from Mount Tabor they were left wondering about what they had seen and heard. It was only after the resurrection that they understood fully what they had experienced.

Their mission to be heralds of the Good News would take them to the ends of the known world. In this way they witnessed to the power of the Risen Lord and so transformed their world.

We have to keep moving to follow Christ; to do God's will; for example, by giving up sin or occasions which lead us to sin. It is a law of life that we are getting older! We leave school, leave university, children grow up and leave home. So Abraham had to leave Chaldaea; Moses and the Jews had to leave Egypt.

So too we have to leave behind our childish ideas of God, our childish ideas of right and wrong, of justice, and how to follow Christ. As we do the right thing, confront our problems, regularly say our prayers – our understandings change, or should change. There should be a slow transfiguration.

24 February 2002, St Mary's Cathedral, Sydney

Healing the Eyes of our Heart

Gospel: *John 9:1-41 (Jesus made a blind man see, incurring the wrath of the Pharisees for doing so on the Sabbath.)*

Fourth Sunday of Lent – Year A

THIS is a beautiful incident in today's gospel, beautifully told by John the Evangelist.

It is a story which moves at many levels. There is an emphasis on the unpredictable nature of God's choice. It uses the symbolism of light in contrast with darkness. It is a story of stress and conflict; of the good getting better and of ill-will dragging Jesus' opponents deeper and deeper into hostility. It is a story of courage, perseverance and developing faith; of a dawning recognition of the importance of Jesus in one man's life. And at its centre is a great miracle, a demonstration of God's power in Jesus.

Jewish society 2000 years ago was very different from Australian society today. There were no hospitals worth the name; no homes for the blind; no schools. The streets of the city were narrow, piled with rubbish, thronged with people of every sort, especially the unemployed. The Jews suffered foreign rule by Romans, partly administered through Herod Antipas, a puppet and tyrant. There was only a limited rule of law. There were no social security payments, so the blind man at the centre of the story was probably a beggar to supplement family support.

Jesus began by denying the common Jewish belief that misfortune struck those who were sinners, or the children or grandchildren of sinners. But while Jesus denied that thesis, he did not claim that the blind man was a saint or unusually deserving among the many with serious afflictions.

Jesus made a paste from mud and spittle, rubbed it on the eyes of the blind man, who was cured. And then the trouble started.

Our Lord was a controversial religious figure, regularly followed by friends and foes, the curious and the bored.

First of all Jesus' opponents queried whether the miracle man really had been blind, was really the one whom they had known. He replied that he was the man, explained what had happened, that he could see and did not know where Jesus was.

Then he was taken before the Pharisees. They were disputing among themselves over the incident. Some objected that the miracle was performed on the Sabbath; some suggested an evil power was behind the miracle and others denied this. What did the miracle man think? Jesus is a prophet, he replied.

The Pharisees next collared the miracle man's parents. They were frightened of being excommunicated from their community, so they prudently said, 'Our son is old enough to speak for himself. Ask him.'

Still unsatisfied, probably more and more frustrated, the Pharisees summoned the blind man again to tell him Jesus was a sinner. As someone who spent a lot of time on the streets, the blind man was well able to look after himself. He was honest, courageous, persistent and able to express himself.

'I've told you once. Are you deaf? Or perhaps you want to become his disciples too?' This provoked another outburst, marginally less offensive to Jesus: 'We don't know where this man comes from.'

By this stage the miracle man was on the front foot and drove them for four: 'What an extraordinary reply. No person in history has worked a cure like this, and you don't know where he comes from. If this man wasn't from God, he could not have done anything.'

By this time the Pharisees decided to cut their losses. They were not going to be lectured to by a sinner and sent him away.

Later he met Jesus who asked if he believed in the Son of Man. 'Who is he?' he asked. 'The man you are speaking to,' was Jesus' response. Then came the finale, the beautiful act of faith: 'Lord I believe.'

Lent should be a time when we strive to deepen our faith, because it is possible to become spiritually blind.

In the Beatitudes we are told that the pure in heart will see God. St Augustine (+430 AD), the greatest theologian in the first Christian millennium, wrote: 'Our entire task in this life consists in healing the eyes of our heart so that they may be able to see God.'

We all know that eyes and ears are needed to hear and see effectively. To see God 'the eye of the soul needs to be opened'. Some cannot see God, and they are like people with cataracts or those who are colour-blind. The God-like sun still shines, but God is not seen there.

With old metal mirrors it was necessary to keep them polished in order to use them to see. Lent is a time for polishing our spiritual mirrors.

Theophilus of Antioch once said that 'purity, holiness and righteousness' are necessary to see God. Spiritually we can become like a run down battery in a transistor radio, or like a dying tube on a TV, with very poor reception. A minimum of purity, holiness and righteousness are necessary to see God.

The man born blind came to see physically and spiritually. Because he was honest, courageous and

persistent he started on that journey, unaware of its final destination, but he arrived at Jesus, the Son of Man and Son of God. So may we all.
10 March 2002, St Mary's Cathedral, Sydney

Jubilee Year 2000 Chrism Mass

ONCE again we come together in this Chrism Mass to celebrate the unity of the ministerial priesthood, that profound unity which unites the priests of yesterday, today and tomorrow throughout the Catholic world, founded in the person of Jesus Christ, the eternal High Priest.

We do so in this year of grace, the Jubilee Year 2000, when we celebrate the anniversary of the birth of the Lord. As is my usual custom, I will take the basis of our meditation from the annual letter of the Holy Father, which he addresses to us from the Upper Room in Jerusalem (which he visited in his recent successful pilgrimage to the Holy Land); the Upper Room where Christ gave us the immense gift of the Eucharist and where our priesthood was born. This last claim is not a linguistic conceit, not a beautiful mythology to justify the human origins of the ministerial priesthood but a sober historical claim that lies at the heart of our priestly self-awareness. Christ made the apostles priests at the institution of the Eucharist, on the night before he died.

In this Jubilee Year of the Incarnation the Pope reminds us also of the essential link between the mystery of Christ's person and His priesthood. Christ's priesthood, which we share as ministerial priests in a particular and unique way, is not incidental, not a task He might or might not have assumed. Our Lord's priesthood is integral to His identity as the Incarnate Son of God, because now the relationship between all mankind and the one true God passes wholly through Christ the High Priest. Christ is not only the alpha and omega, the beginning and end of all history, but the unique axis around which the struggle between good and evil is worked out.

In contemplating the Last Supper, Pope John Paul muses on what would have been the emotion and amazement of the apostles at this first Eucharistic celebration, on the burden of frailty which they bore just as we do today; a frailty soon to be apparent in the weakness of Peter despite his earlier bluster and bravado and already at work in the treachery of Judas. The Last Supper was one of the high points in that still unended struggle between the mystery of unlimited love and the '*mysterium iniquitatis*', the baffling and horrifying mystery of evil.

Especially at this Mass of the Chrism each of us is called to rededicate himself again to the struggle against evil – in our hearts, in our parishes and in the wider society.

In the Upper Room the Holy Father imagines all the priests throughout the world, young or middle-aged or old, some joyful and enthusiastic, others suffering, weary or discouraged. He honours the image of Christ in us all, urging us to move ahead joyfully or to make a fresh start.

Each of us can make this prayer his own, especially for those priests who inspired us to follow the priestly vocation and whose example, support and friendship have sustained us in good times and bad. All of us have known and know among our brother priests heroes and saints, who have lived up to the gift and mystery we receive at ordination. It is certain that the last century saw more martyrs for the faith than any other century. Just as certainly there was a similar number of twentieth-century priest martyrs, who shed their blood in imitation of Christ.

None of this denies our human weakness or the dark presence of sin occasionally found among us. This has been brought home as never before in Australian history by the hostile publicity surrounding the clerical sexual scandals in the last decade.

Christ knew well the human weakness of his priests, but it was still here, on this human weakness, that he set the Sacramental seal of His presence; and the Catholic faithful today still place their trust in the power of Christ shining through the weakness of their friends and helpers in the priesthood. Above all this is a tribute to the faith and service of our predecessors.

Francis of Assisi never tried to become a priest, but he always recognized the power of Christ present in the priest. He explained that 'the only thing I see of the flesh of the Most High Son of God in this world is His most holy Body and Blood which (priests) alone consecrate and they alone administer to others'.

For 2000 years all the Sacraments, but especially the Eucharist, have given nourishment to countless believers. The Eucharist remains the richest source of Christ's great river of grace or spiritual energy. It is the priest's joy and responsibility to be so closely linked to this Eucharistic river nourishing faith and goodness, as day after day he celebrates the Mass following the Lord's command to 'do this in memory of me'.

The Holy Father prays that we priests may always attend and learn from the 'school' of the Eucharist, finding there the consolation Jesus promised, the way of overcoming loneliness, the strength to cope with suffering, the inner food to remain faithful and the energy to begin again after disappointments and discouragement. Nor should we forget that just as there is no Eucharist without sacrifice, so an element of sacrifice, doing God's will against the grain, is also one essential dimension of priesthood.

The Church is a great mystery of love – as much needed in our society today as in any age. Within this communion and mystery, the ministry of the priest remains unique, indispensable and irreplaceable.

For these reasons, while conscious of our inadequacies, we still, once again, thank God for our vocation; and pray that the Lord will continue to send labourers into the harvest as we rededicate ourselves to our priestly vocation and duties.

18 April 2000, St Patrick's Cathedral, Melbourne

Good Friday

Readings: *Is 52:13-53:12; Heb 4:14-16; 5:7-9; John 18:1–19:42*

Sing my tongue of warfare ended
of the Victor's laurelled crown;
Let the Cross, his trophy splendid
Be the theme of high renown;
How a broken world was mended
Life restored by life laid down.

THIS verse from an ancient poem captures two of the truths which are fundamental to the celebration of

Good Friday, and it is the second truth which explains the strange title of this feast day.

First of all Jesus really died. God cannot die, but Jesus was also true man and shared the fate of us all. He died on that cross in Jerusalem nearly 2000 years ago.

The readings chosen for this afternoon demonstrate this, especially the section from the Old Testament prophet Isaiah. The crowds were appalled by the suffering; they could not look at him, screened their faces, he was like a lamb led to the slaughterhouse.

What is the second basic truth of Good Friday? I often retell Jesus' story to the Year Six confirmation candidates. Jesus was a good young man in his thirties, doing great work teaching, healing, forming communities. Not only did He die young but He was murdered. I ask why the anniversary of such a sad and terrible event is called 'good'? Always there is someone, usually after a moment or two of quiet, who explains that Jesus died for us, Jesus died to save us.

Once again Isaiah captures the second truth: 'On him lies a punishment that brings us peace and through his wounds we are healed.' That was the text at the start of Mel Gibson's film *The Passion of the Christ*.

Paul's letter to the Hebrews also explains this second dimension: 'Although He was Son, He learnt to obey through suffering; but having been made perfect, He became for all who obey Him the source of eternal salvation.'

Time magazine of 12 April is out early but devotes eight pages of text and pictures to discuss 'Why did Jesus have to die?' listing three of the classical theories or explanations of redemption and atonement; that Jesus died to defeat Satan and rescue humanity from evil; to make amends for sins against God and finally that he died as an exemplar, to inspire people to live in obedience to God's ways.

Books have been written to explain these theories and explain why some are better explanations than others, more in conformity with the Scriptures and what we know about God.

This afternoon I would like to follow one of these threads and discuss the reactions of the two thieves crucified with Jesus and Jesus' response to the good thief.

All the gospel accounts of the Passion recount that some at the foot of the cross, soldiers, passers-by, opponents mocked and abused Our Lord. Luke's gospel, which we are following this year, gives a fuller account and is the only one to mention the good thief's defence and prayer.

The bad thief joined the others in abusing Our Lord. 'Aren't you the Christ? Save yourself and us as well.'

Then the good thief had his say, rebuking the first, 'have you no fear of God at all?' He added that they deserved their sentences because of their crimes. They were paying for their mistakes, but Jesus had done nothing wrong. Then he turned and asked 'Jesus, remember me when you come into your Kingdom.'

Jesus' reply is one of the most beautiful moments in the whole New Testament: 'Today you will be with me in paradise.' It should be a consolation to every one of us in those moments when we feel weighed down, worried that God will be too strict, that we will always be unworthy. Whenever we are tempted to doubt, to wonder whether God will forgive, those beautiful words to the good thief should run like a refrain of mercy through our minds.

Neither should we conclude that Jesus was not thinking clearly, that He was confused being so near to death, that He was touched and uncharacteristically moved by this unexpected kindness and support.

The good thief had explicitly acknowledged his sins, he had asked for help, recognized not only Jesus' sinlessness but His spiritual authority. He was also undergoing a hideous punishment in reparation for his sins.

But Jesus' kindness is also completely at one with other sections of the New Testament; with His treatment of the woman accused of adultery and threatened with death by stoning: 'I do not condemn you, but go, sin no more'; completely at one with the parable of the prodigal son welcomed back by his loving father after years of debauchery and wasting his inheritance. This incident is like the good shepherd leaving the ninety-nine sheep to seek out and save the one that was lost.

The reactions of the two thieves are not the only examples of the different paths sinners might take. We also have the story of Judas and Peter, which is captured so dramatically in Mel Gibson's film and filled out with non-scriptural material.

After Peter denied Christ three times he realized his mistake, repented and wept bitterly. The film has him going to Mary and asking forgiveness.

On the other hand Judas could not bring himself to ask for forgiveness. With the bad thief we have no evidence that he acknowledged his wrongdoing, one way or the other. We know that Judas did, recognizing that he had betrayed innocent blood for thirty pieces of silver.

Gibson's film graphically traces his descent into madness and despair, hanging himself next to the rotting corpse of a donkey. It was a grim portrayal of a man overwhelmed by his sin and unable to reach out for the warm hand of God.

Another non-biblical incident in Gibson's film told

me something about my own unconverted self, about the untamed and unchristian subconscious. After the bad thief had abused Christ, a large black raven descends onto his cross and begins to attack his right eye.

Instinctively I was delighted. The 'baddie' was getting what he deserved; that would teach him to be a bit more respectful next time.

With embarrassment I realized that this was not a Christian response, not an example of a disciple practising forgiveness. Years ago I remember hearing the story of a barbarian chief, being instructed for conversion with his followers. As the story of the Passion was recounted to him, he asked where these enemies of Jesus were. Were they nearby? He would ride with his men and deal with them!

I remember, too, smiling in a superior way at this primitive response, but my rejoicing with the raven was moving in the same direction. He who stands must always beware lest he fall!

In the Eucharist we celebrate the death of the Lord until He comes again, and I like to link the *Agnus Dei* prayer, the prayer to the Lamb of God who takes away the sins of the world with Christ's act of forgiveness on the cross. Through the Mass and Sacraments Christ's forgiveness is available to us. Therefore we pray 'Lamb of God, who take away the sins of the world, have mercy on us all and grant all of us peace'.

Good Friday, 9 April 2004,
St Mary's Cathedral, Sydney

Easter

Readings: *Rom 6:3-11; Matthew 28:1-10*

EASTER is a strange feast. Some unbelievers would say that most or all of our feasts are strange; but Easter has a strangeness over and beyond the celebration of a birth, or the remembrance of those who have died before us, or the presence of the Transcendent among us.

On Good Friday we celebrated the death of the Son of God. In the Easter Vigil we celebrate the resurrection of this same Son, who was also the human son of Mary. Immediately we are plunged into the mysteries not just of the Incarnation and Redemption, but of the Trinitarian God Himself, Father, Son and Spirit.

Jesus Christ is only one single person, with a human nature and a divine nature; fully God and fully man, fully human. These two natures are united in the one person of Jesus Christ unconfusedly, unchangeably, indivisibly, and inseparably as the great Ecumenical Council of Chalcedon (the Fourth) defined in the year 451 AD.

This does not mean that Jesus had a human nature through all eternity before His birth in Bethlehem from his mother Mary.

Just to make it more complicated it is not really accurate to say that God exists in time, because for time we need matter and space. As the Creator Spirit, God is and exists beyond our categories. God is not the best footballer in the team. God is offstage, interested and involved, but the mastermind and sustainer of everything.

His Son came among us as a human; God's Son was and is a player, but in His Divine nature the Son, the Word, had been from all eternity. While there is no past or future to God, the Son of God has always existed and always will. The Word of God always was; or perhaps more accurately, always is.

I make this point about the humanity and divinity of Jesus, Our Lord, because it is a mystery beyond our understanding and we are always tempted to lose one half of the story. Different ages, indeed different people, are tempted in different ways. Some find it easier to disregard the fact that Jesus was human (and remains human, in some mysterious way in eternity, where we too hope to join Him in eternity, not as ghosts, or disembodied spirits, but as human persons, in some changed and developed form of flesh and blood).

Others, especially today, are tempted to reject Jesus' divine nature. Some say that all creation is a part of God, somehow divine; and that because Jesus is the most perfect human being who ever lived, He can be called divine because of this human perfection. This is not enough. We mean much more when we talk of God than to reduce God to human dimensions; and Jesus was much more than simply another saintly human like the Buddha.

Jesus Our Lord and Saviour is a mystery, whose components are always in tension, but we come to know Him through His human life, death and resurrection as Jesus of Nazareth, born of Mary in Bethlehem, who died, was crucified in Jerusalem and then rose triumphantly to life on the third day.

As always, now at Easter there were newspaper and journal articles claiming it is impossible to believe all this today. They often do not spell out why it is more difficult today than it has been for 2000 years and usually disregard the fact that billions of people believe in God and that there are one billion Catholics and hundreds of millions of other Christians.

But to struggle for faith, to struggle to retain our faith is now the lot of many people, especially in our type of society.

We should not forget that the first disciples were men and women of flesh and blood like us; perhaps of stronger faith; not as well educated as many here tonight and certainly not as prosperous, comfortable or well cared for as most Australians.

Pope Leo the Great, preaching in the middle of the fifth century, emphasised the fact that when Jesus was killed His disciples had thought that was the end of the story. They were numb with shock and sorrow; so much so that when the women told the apostles and disciples that the sepulchre was empty and the stone rolled away they thought their words to be 'pure nonsense' (Luke 24:11).

Pope Leo said that one good consequence of their doubting is that it helps us to confront our own slowness of heart. We were being instructed and strengthened against the slanders of the wicked and the arguments of earthly wisdom. Their slow start, their surprise, then their enduring courage and conviction after meeting the Risen Christ and putting their hands in His wounds, eating with Him – all this now helps us to dissipate the mists of doubt which can surround us from time to time.

The Easter ceremonies, especially on Holy Saturday night, are spectacular in deed and word as we hear of God's mighty interventions through His chosen people, the Jews and now the Christians. Once again all the traditional symbols are employed: the fire which reminds us of the burning bush; the Risen Christ as the light of the world, a single light in this darkened Cathedral which spreads and spreads and spreads until this huge beautiful space is full of light. We hear of the water of life, which vivifies and cleanses and heals and then the central symbols of bread and wine signifying the Body and Blood of Jesus sacrificed for us on the Cross.

All these symbolic words and actions are to bring home to us what happened then in Jerusalem and what Jesus accomplished for us.

What did Jesus accomplish? How did Our Lord's death and resurrection change things for us? What are the enduring consequences for us 2000 years later, on the other side of the world, where there is still much evidence of terrible evil and suffering and where our Australian way of life is far ahead of many other parts of the world?

Let me conclude by answering these questions in the way I believe St Paul did. What did Paul mean writing to the Romans that we too have a new life through baptism? That we shall imitate Christ's resurrection and never die again? That death has no more power over us provided we ourselves are dead to sin?

As a good Jew, Paul had long believed that God had made a special pact with the people of Israel (called a covenant) to deal with sin and bring salvation to all the world.

He seemed to think of this as a great legal showdown, a cosmic and universal type of court case before the Great Judge, where Israel would be vindicated and her opponents judged and punished.

Jesus changed the understanding or content of this framework. As the Jewish Messiah, His life and activity were a turning point for all of history. His death on the Cross represented a new stage in God's dealings with the world. Jesus had already done through His cross and resurrection what will be completed at the end of time for Abraham's people.

But Abraham's people are no longer defined by their physical membership of the Jewish race; but through their recognition of Jesus Christ. They do this by hearing Christ's message, joining the Christian community through baptism and sharing in the worship and common life of the community. This is how we and our ancestors came to be included.

When Jesus died He healed the world. The final age has already dawned.

Paul did not believe that the good news for the pagans lay in telling them that they were more or less all right as they are. Paul believed that the pagans were going about things in a basically wrong way; that the God who had made them loved them and longed to remake them.

This is the Easter message for us, especially when we sin, and for the whole world.

Holy Saturday and Easter Sunday, 3–4 April 1999,
St Patrick's Cathedral, Melbourne

The Third Eye

Readings: *Acts 1:1-11 (St Luke's account of Christ's Ascension, being lifted up on a 'cloud that took Him from their sight'.) Eph 1:17-23 (St Paul tells the Ephesians that he prays to God to give them a spirit of wisdom and revelation.)*
Gospel: *Mark 16:15-20 (Jesus tells His disciples to proclaim the Gospel and that those who believe will be saved and those who do not believe will be condemned. He is then taken up into Heaven*

> *and continues to work with the Church on earth through what St Mark calls 'accompanying signs'.)*

Feast of the Ascension – Year B

THE Ascension is the last appearance of the Risen Christ. He had used the period after His death and resurrection to instruct His apostles and disciples on what was going on. We heard in the Acts that some of them were still hoping against hope that Our Lord might have now finally been going to set up His political Kingdom on this earth. 'Are you now going to set up the Kingdom of Israel?' And He said, 'No, no, no, I am about something else.'

We are told there that He ascended into heaven, into the skies. It is a way of speaking, the only way we can describe it, but we should not conclude automatically from that, that heaven is upstairs and hell is downstairs. It is a way of thinking, a way of speaking. When I studied in England I used to do some chaplaincy work at a Catholic primary school. The kids there of course knew that I was Australian and they sometimes would ask me why we did not fall off because we were on the other side of the world and on the bottom of the globe. And it is a similar way of speaking that describes the Ascension.

At the Ascension, Our Lord told His disciples to go out everywhere and preach the Gospel and here we are 2000 years later. If we start from the Holy Land, we are almost as far away from there as you can possibly be, all at the end of that long succession of witnesses, that long tradition, bringing us to faith today.

So what is the significance of this feast of the Ascension? It is not simply the going up of any good person to be with God. It is rather the return of the Son of God to the Father. It is a re-affirmation in a different way that Jesus, as well as being the Son of Mary, is also the Eternal Word, the second person of the Trinity. Jesus is going back to being (as we say) at the right hand of the Father.

Secondly, it emphasizes that Jesus is the Lord of the whole cosmos, the whole world of nature. Jesus is not just the head of the Church. As the saints and some of the New Testament writers said, not just the Lord of history, but part of the one true God who created the entire Universe.

And thirdly, with the departure of Jesus we know that the Holy Spirit will come, and we celebrate that next week at Pentecost, that completely spiritual Being who can work anywhere and everywhere, but is sometimes so difficult to recognize.

In the Letter to the Ephesians, Paul prays that the Spirit of wisdom and perception might be with us to bring us to the full knowledge of Christ our Lord and he uses a very useful image: he prays that the eyes of our mind might be enlightened.

I remember reading years ago Aleksandr Solzhenitsyn, the great Russian Christian writer, and he spoke about the third eye. A third eye, metaphorically speaking, helps us to understand what is going on at some depth around us. It is useful, indeed necessary, to understand what is happening in the hearts of those who are closest to us or those working with us. We also need this sort of third eye sometimes, perhaps often, to understand what is happening inside our own hearts, and of course we need this deeper level of understanding to try to work out where God is acting in our daily lives, especially when the unexpected or the sad and sorrowful occur.

But to grasp all this we need real humility and we need persistence. Very, very few important things are understood in the flash of an eye, especially by men. In these days it is not at all difficult not to believe and sometimes, good people – genuinely good people – can find it very hard to believe. Speaking more broadly, the Australian poet, Stan James, penned a few lines which I think will help us understand what I am trying to say. He said:

> Sometimes we are at our lives the same way dogs are at a concert – we hear all the sounds and none of the music.

That is quite possible and it happens and we men are sometimes accused of being worse at that than the women. It is a stereotype, which I suspect is sometimes, perhaps often, true. For example, the husband can be the last to realize that the marriage is in trouble and perhaps in crisis. It might be Dad who is very slow to realize that one of the children is in trouble and really agitated or sad and needs to be helped. But whatever about that, both men and women can travel on the surface and refuse to go underneath the surface, because we fear that there we might find things that will upset us.

So we have to pray that in our pilgrimage as Christians – whether we have been at it for a month or so as full members of the Church, or returned to the Church, or whether we have spent a lifetime at it – we will strive to understand the supernatural, to follow the call of faith to an ever deeper level of understanding and decision.

Some truths of science and maths we may understand and accept, but they do not really touch us personally at all. It is very, very different when Jesus says, 'come follow me' and we have to decide to try to organize our lives, our basic values around His teaching.

4 June 2000, St Patrick's Cathedral, Melbourne

Pentecost

> **Readings:** *Acts 2:1-11; Rom 8:8-17 (St Paul tells the Romans that the Spirit of God will give life to their mortal bodies and urges them to be concerned with spiritual matters.)*
> **Gospel:** *John 14:15-16, 23-26 (Christ tells His disciples that the Father will send the Holy Spirit to teach us everything and to remind us of all Christ has told us.)*

Pentecost Sunday – Year C

ON Pentecost Sunday we celebrate the reality of God among us; the fact that the one true God sends His Spirit to be in our hearts, our families, this congregation, our enterprises – unless we expel the Spirit through evil, through hate.

It was this conviction that the Spirit had come upon them that transformed the apostles and disciples from good, frightened believers into preachers and miracle workers of courage and initiative; the first of many generations who suffered persecutions off and on for 300 years; and who survived, and expanded during these long years. The passage from the Acts of the Apostles today tells us of that turning point, that transforming miracle.

We think of the Spirit in terms of wind and air, 'the breath of God', as a lifegiving flame, something alive and enlightening, being different from and greater than matter. If we are to recognize this immanent and often anonymous presence of God, then we have to be sensitive to the reality of that part of the universe beyond the realm of our physical senses.

We know that the Holy Spirit is the third Person of the Trinity; we know too that Christ promised to send the Spirit to be with the Church through all ages.

It is of course the Spirit who gives authority to decisions taken in the name of the Church; through the Spirit sins are forgiven, the Church has increased, multiplied and survived during the 2000 years of her history despite the best efforts of our opponents and all the sin and stupidities committed by Christians, sometimes even in the name of Christ Himself.

To say that the Spirit is with the Church does not mean that she cannot make mistakes, and adopt courses of action which are fruitless and even dangerous. The Spirit is with us in our lean years as well as our good years.

For this, we have to realize that the Spirit works through our weaknesses as well as apparent strengths; that He is certainly at work in the other Christian Churches and in fact wherever good is being performed.

Paul writing to the Romans instructed them that they must not be interested only in unspiritual things, like money, possessions, holidays, even our work. What are the spiritual things which should concern us? Worship, prayer, love, forgiveness, thanksgiving.

There is an eternal conversation in the heart of the Godhead between Father and Son, which we call the Holy Spirit. While the Spirit is among us, the Spirit is beyond us; the Spirit is the beyond in our midst. A personal presence of love for us beyond our imagining.

We need to tune into these divine sound waves; it is not difficult to be deaf in our busy, noisy, pleasure seeking society. Therefore regular prayer is important to maintain and deeper our sensitivity to the Spirit. This is regularly difficult, and not always pleasurable. We have to persevere and ask the Spirit for help.

Prayer helps us drive away that fear, which is so regularly the opposite of faith. We love a personal God, the source of energizing love and interest in each one of us; not those vast impersonal forces, the relentless laws of nature which rule the universe and sometimes strike us unfairly. The Spirit of God is beyond all this, greater, infinitely kind and healing especially when we are wounded. Prayer helps us realize this and continue to realize it.

There is no doubt that the Spirit is at work in the hearts of all individuals, prompting us to reflection and insight, urging us to be prudent, not to be rash or foolish, to sleep on it because 'morning is cleverer than evening'. It is the Spirit who sharpens our readiness to help, who jogs our goodwill. But this is not the whole story.

As well as the Spirit of God there are the spirits of the evil in the world and in our hearts, the personal conflict between our feelings of inferiority and arrogance, our urges to serve or to dominate, the bewildering and complex struggle between the beast and the Spirit, the frustration, guilt and suffering that always attend the interplay of good and evil.

The story of the Fall, the doctrine of original sin which explains the presence of evil in the world (an evil presence which God does not want) not only separates Christianity from religions of the East such as Hinduism, but also from many contemporary pagans who deny the existence of evil in men's hearts and place it somewhere else, outside in the structures of society.

The presence of the Spirit therefore means a struggle against evil, personally and communally. Because of our weaknesses the Spirit brings the pain of judgment on our past as well as the promise of future glory. Judgment and promise go hand in hand as there is no birth without pain, no death and dying without suffering. To quote

English Bishop John Vernon Taylor, author of *The Go Between God*, 'the resurrection will not set us free for the future unless the cross also sets us free from the past'.

We are called to God and to wholeness, but innocence is not an available option. This is why today's gospel from John has Jesus insisting, 'If you love me, you will keep my Commandments'. These are essential signposts, pointing out the best way to travel to God. We need the Spirit of wisdom to recognize the beauty of these commands and to have the courage to follow them.

It should be a special task for the Catholic Community to help all Australians approach the Divine Power, hidden so effectively in our society, with a sense of reverence and love.

3 June 2001, St Mary's Cathedral, Sydney

3
Mary, Mother and Role Model

Our Lady Help of Christians

Readings: Eccl 4:11-18; 1 Cor 1:18-25.
Gospel: John 19:25-27 (Mary was standing at the foot of her Son's cross with John when Jesus turned to her and said 'Woman, behold your son.' To John He said: 'Behold your mother.')

THE Cathedral Church of the Archdiocese of Sydney is dedicated to God in honour of the Blessed Virgin Mary Immaculate, Help of Christians.

This wonderful church was built by your ancestors without any government money. They were poor and there were not many of them. It shows what they thought was important, and the strength of their faith.

In the year 1821, the pioneer missionary priest Fr John Joseph Therry, recently arrived in the Colony of New South Wales from Ireland, began construction of the first Catholic church to be erected in Australia.

The government of the colony granted the land for this building in a spot away from the city and close to the jail, the army barracks and the rubbish tip. This sacred edifice was named in honour of the Blessed Virgin Mary, and was known as 'St Mary's Chapel'. It was therefore known as the 'Mother Church' for all Australia, because it was first.

With the arrival in Sydney, in 1835, of the Most Reverend John Bede Polding OSB, Vicar Apostolic of New Holland and later Archbishop of Sydney, the Catholic Chapel became known as 'St Mary's Cathedral'. A Cathedral is where the bishop's teaching chair is placed. 'Cathedra' is the Greek word for this chair. Most of your priests were ordained here, and some of you were here for the blessing of the oils for baptism, confirmation and anointing of the sick.

The devotion to the Mother of God of the Catholics of the Australian colonies was reaffirmed by the First Provincial Synod of Sydney in 1844, which elected as Patroness of Australia, the Blessed Virgin Mary under the Title of 'Help of Christians'. This Act of the Synod was confirmed by the Holy See in 1847.

With the tragic destruction by fire of the first St Mary's Cathedral on 29 June 1865, Archbishop Polding and the Catholic people of Sydney began the task of raising a new and more noble Cathedral on the site of the old building. William Wardell, the great English Catholic architect was commissioned to build the new Cathedral and his brief was simple: to build 'Any style, any plan, anything that is beautiful and grand to the extent of your power'. The foundation stone was laid in 1868, and is dedicated under the patronage of the Immaculate Mother of God, Help of Christians.

The Cathedral was opened for worship by Archbishop Roger Bede Vaughan in 1882, while only partly built; the spires were completed in the Jubilee Year 2000.

During your years in Catholic schools we want you to learn and understand some important and beautiful truths. Only a few are of first importance. The most important truth is that God, the invisible Spirit, is love and God loves all His creation, every person, every one of you, me too.

However, among the many different races God chose one group in particular to do His work and explain His teaching, the Jews. Jesus was born a Jew and His teachings built on all the good news in the Jewish writings we call the Old Testament. As Catholics we are now part of God's people.

The Old Testament prophecy tells us this, that Yahweh, the Jewish name for the one true God, is coming to look after the Jews, and that later, other people, like us Aussies, will know God too. The second reading from St Paul tells us we are God's sons and daughters. The first truth is that God loves us, especially when we are in trouble.

The second truth has been mentioned already; that Jesus is Mary's son, but that He had no human father, as He is the only Son of God. He was born in a stable, not a palace, had a hard life with many attacking Him and died, crucified on a cross when He was about thirty-three years old.

He saved us through his death and resurrection so that our sins can be forgiven and so we can go to heaven to be happy forever. This is the second truth. Jesus is God's Son and redeemed us.

The gospel passage shows us that when Jesus was dying He gave His mother Mary to the apostle John, who represents us, as our mother.

I know how you love your own mums. With your

father she is the most important person in your young lives. Mary is our heavenly mother. You must learn to pray to her, Our Lady, regularly, each day, even if for some reason you do not always get to Sunday Mass. That is why we have prayers each day at school. But that is not enough. You yourself should always pray a Hail Mary every day, with the Our Father, so that Our Lady will ask God to protect you and your loved ones.

Nearly all children turn to their mother when they are sick, or in trouble, or in need of help or advice. I want you to turn to Our Lady, to pray to her, when you are in trouble.

The stained glass window behind the altar shows Our Lady Help of Christians. Her statue is there. The windows around the Cathedral show the Mysteries of the rosary. Get your teachers to explain this to you.

Many centuries ago, Pope Pius V gave the title Help of Christians to Our Lady after a European fleet in an immense battle defeated the Turkish fleet at Lepanto in 1571. The Turks were pressing on many points to conquer Europe. Those of you from Malta would have heard of the heroic deeds of the knights and people defending Malta in the siege in 1565.

The Australian bishops chose this title Mary Help of Christians in 1844 at their first official meeting together, because two successive popes, Pius VI and Pius VII, had been imprisoned by the French leader Napoleon some thirty or forty years before, and the Catholic people prayed to Our Lady Help of Christians to protect them.

We too should pray for one another, our country, especially the soldiers who died for us and pray for peace, now and especially during your lifetimes.

Sermon preached to primary school children at St Mary's Cathedral, Sydney, 24 May 2002. Feast Day of Our Lady Help of Christians, Patroness of Australia

The Immaculate Conception

Readings: *Gen 3:9-15, 20; Eph 1:3-6, 11-12; Luke 1:26-38*

FOR centuries people believed that the earth was the centre of the universe. The unfortunate disagreement between Galileo and the Church in the early seventeenth century resulted in all educated opinion recognizing that the sun was the centre of our system of planets.

Today, through our radio and visual telescopes we know that neither the earth nor our solar system can be usefully described as being at the centre of the universe. In fact our planet earth, and even the entire solar system in our universe, can be compared in size to something like a grain of sand or a pebble on a beach (or more accurately as one grain of sand on all the beaches and deserts of the world)!

Yet we know that human life is of unique importance when we consider the role of Jesus the Christ, the Palestinian son of Mary, Pantocrator (creator of the universe), Redeemer of the world, the only Son of God.

Leaving to one side any question, appropriate or otherwise, about the location of the angels and the holy souls, we have the most precious elements of Creation hid in an unlikely corner of the universe, battered by the green-house syndrome, the depredation of the ozone layer and acid rain!

When we consider purely human history we have a parallel irony or oddity.

Teilhard de Chardin wrote of the axis of hominization passing through Rome. Today the Catholic Church is an immense world-wide body, politically and intellectually more influential in many other countries than it is in Australia; but even in our world the Church is visible through Popes and cathedrals, local churches and schools. Our origins were very different.

The intelligent outsider would expect the greatest religious teacher to come from one of the ancient, high civilizations such as India, China, or Egypt, or the briefer stars such as Persia or the Greco-Roman world. Such a teacher could be expected to come from the best elements in such a society, to have received every human and educational advantage in life.

The truth leads us in a different direction. The revelation of monotheism was given to a group of nomadic Semites (shepherds were often regarded as we regard wharfies today!), a quarrelsome rump of a nation, the Northern Ireland of the Middle East then as now, regularly squeezed and sometimes submerged by more powerful neighbours. It was not regularly successful in its politics and certainly not always faithful to its traditions.

Within this intellectual backwater, a young lad was born in a stable to a young woman married to a carpenter. This baby was and is the Son of God and His mother we revere as the mother of God and the Immaculate Conception.

In cosmology, in the history of nations and religions, in our personal story, what is important is rarely as clear even as the nose on our faces! Truth, beauty and significance are rarely at centre stage. We need effort to find them and retain them.

Many contemporary Christians see today's celebration of the Immaculate Conception as a magnificent anachronism, suitable perhaps to the peasant religion of Bernadette Soubirous of Lourdes in mid-nineteenth century France, but having no relevance today.

The incongruity is blunted because many Catholics and most Australians have no idea what the feast of the Immaculate Conception celebrates and not much more interest to discover its meaning. But the feast still has a message for us, and the history of this doctrine shows us how the Church works, and how we shall have to work.

The dogma was defined on 8 December 1854 in Rome by Pope Pius IX, about a week after a small uprising had been put down in a rough mining town on the other side of the world called Ballarat. It declared that Mary, the Mother of God, was conceived free of any stain of original sin, and that she was in a spiritual sense totally beautiful and perfect and full of innocence and holiness – full of grace.

The Immaculate Conception is *not* the same dogma as the Incarnation (Christ's being conceived of the Holy Spirit) or His being born of a virgin. Nor does the Immaculate Conception mean that Mary's own conception and birth was different physically from others.

Naturally such a belief predates its solemn definition, as it is based on the Scriptures and logically connected with the doctrine that Our Lady is not simply the mother of Christ, but that she is, using the very apt Greek word, 'Theotokos' (i.e. the God-bearer or Mother of God).

The first evidence for the celebration of the feast of the Immaculate is found in the East in the seventh century, spreading from there through Naples and Ireland to England in the eleventh century. However the feast also provoked strong opposition.

In the twelfth century even St Bernard, the preacher and enthusiast for the Crusades, opposed the doctrine, as of course did many of the intellectuals, including St Albert, St Bonaventure and St Thomas Aquinas. Strangely enough the defence of Our Lady was led by an Englishman, Blessed John Duns Scotus, an Oxford philosopher born around 1270!

Gradually after this, opinion hardened in favour of the doctrine, which the Council of Basle recognized as a pious opinion in 1439, while Pope Clement XI declared the feast universal and obligatory throughout the Church in 1708.

This is not exactly a story of triumphal progress and universal acclaim, but a story of doubt and division during more than a thousand years. We should be heartened by this.

Being so much influenced by the Irish we are often tempted to romanticize history; to admit that things might have been harder then but that at least they seemed to see the issues clearly; they knew what to battle for, or at least (and this is often easier) what to battle against.

This is a mistake. St Paul told us that only in heaven shall we see things as they are, and that we are condemned on earth to see things darkly and with difficulty. Issues are always clearer in hindsight, as usually priorities are clarified and convictions deepened only through prayer and thinking and experience.

Devotion to Our Lady is a vital element in the Catholic tradition and it is more important than ever in a society that has a heightened consciousness and radically different views about the proper place of women in society. Until a few years ago our age was confidently permissive in its attitudes to sexuality. The permissive society in this sense is now crumbling, although financial interests and the world of advertising will battle ferociously to preserve the façade.

The model of faith, Mary, a family woman, innocent and pure, could never be described as relevant for us, but she is a sign of challenge and contradiction, like her Son.

Mary is a symbol in another important way as the first reading from Genesis explains. There will be enmity between her offspring and the children of the serpent. In other words the important tension must be between God and the World; between the followers of Christ and those who do the work of the anti-Christ.

We must not be distracted from this. We must use our energies to build, and if we have an urge to destroy let us exercise it, in charity, on the works of the anti-Christ.

Factionalism, in politics and in religion, is a symptom of decline. Ecumenism now hinders us from being rude to non-Catholic Christians. Unfortunately a small minority of Catholics now feel the work of the Kingdom is advanced, if they can disadvantage their Catholic opponents. It is as though the old sectarian energies threaten to burn themselves out in intra-family antagonism, while those outside use these public differences as an excuse to ignore Christ's message.

As Australian poet Kevin Hart wrote in the last two verses of 'To Our Lady':

> ... you take from us
> the mounds of darkness we bury inside of us
> and make from them a night of stars
> where we can see your Son;
> Our Lady,
> Withheld from death,
> Mother of all things that must die,
> Speak for us,
> Do what we cannot do ourselves,
> Help us to hold in our hands the bird in flight,

To pull from our feet our heavy shadows, to walk your way.

Sermon preached at St Mary's,
East Malvern, 7 December 1987

The Assumption of our Blessed Lady

Readings: *Apocalypse 11:19; 12:1-6, 10; 1 Cor 15:20-26; Luke 1:39-56*

MARY occupies a special place in the Church. She is the First and perfect Disciple who believed, and hoped and loved with every part of her being.

St Augustine said of her that she first conceived Christ through faith in her heart before she conceived Him in her womb. Her obedience to the word and will of God is a reflection of the same obedience of Christ to His Father. Her place in the mystery of our salvation is equal to her desire to co-operate with God. Her faith was unimpeded by sin from the first moment of her existence. Her conception of the word of God was, on her part, an act of faith. Her divine motherhood is the elevation of all discipleship to its crowning glory: 'My mother is (she) who hears the word of God and acts on it.' (Mark 3:35) Her assumption is a pledge of the glory that is promised to all God's children.

In the last chapter of the Constitution on the Church (*Lumen Gentium*) of Vatican II, Mary is addressed as the Mother of believers. In the same way that she brought Christ into the world by her faith and charity, so all Christians are called to make Christ present by their faith-filled service of their brothers and sisters. This unique place of Mary in the history of our salvation was recognized at a very early stage in the Christian tradition. This recognition was not only intellectually expressed. It can be identified in the devotion that was given her not only by the theologians but by all the faithful over 2000 years.

The feast of the Assumption is the oldest feast of Mary in the two millennia of reflection on and devotion to the holiest of human beings. The celebration of the Dormition or falling asleep of Mary was held on this day as early as the fifth century. It is the principal Marian feast in the Church's year. There are many different strands held together in the liturgy of today's feast. We celebrate the great things which God achieved in Mary, and praise Him as she did in her *Magnificat* which we heard in the gospel. In the second reading we are promised a share in the resurrection of Christ, even as Mary shares already in the blessings promised to those who believe and are faithful.

But it is in the mysterious image of the Woman, bright with the sun, crowned with twelve stars and standing on the moon whom John saw in his vision of the Apocalypse that we have a key to understanding the significance of the feast of the Assumption in our own time.

It was in the Holy Year of 1950, after the whole world had been ravaged by a war unequalled in history for its savagery and violence, that Pope Pius XII solemnly defined the dogma of the bodily assumption of Mary into heaven. It was not a new teaching: it had been a consistent feature of Catholic teaching and devotion for centuries. But Pius added something new to the meaning of this ancient belief. A story about the Pope and the Second World War can help us understand what the Assumption means.

On 14 July 1943, Rome was bombed for the first time by the Allied Forces as they moved northwards through Italy. That morning, the Pope could see the bombing of the railroad terminal from his window in the Vatican Palace. He telephoned his secretary, Monsignor Montini (who was later to become Pope Paul VI) and ordered him to draw out all the cash that the Holy See had in Rome. Montini put this money, about two million lire, in a sack, and found a car parked in the Vatican grounds. The Pope came down alone, and the two of them drove through the deserted streets of Rome to the ancient basilica of St Lawrence outside the walls of Rome. That quarter had sustained the worst of the bombing. On one side of the square before the ruined church there was a long line of burning railway carriages. On the other side were the tottering walls and smoking timbers of burning houses. People were furiously digging through the rubble, directed by the cries of those buried alive. In the square were laid out rows of the mangled remains of men, women and children. In the surrounding confusion, the wounded were being tended.

The Pope stepped from the car and the people rushed to him, clinging to his clothes, and bloodied his white cassock. A workman threw his jacket on the cobblestones, and the Pope knelt with his people and asked them to pray for those who had died.

When calm had been restored, Pius stood up and directed Montini to distribute the money to those in the greatest need. As the Pope moved through the crowd, a distraught mother placed the body of her dead baby into the Pope's arms. The Holy Father continued to clasp this child while trying to console the many people who clung to him. The Pope stayed until there was no more that could be done, and he drove back to the Vatican, tearstained and bloodied.

When the Second World War had exhausted itself, and the whole world with it, and as the scene outside St Lawrence's had been repeated in practically every country in Europe, Pius saw the need to give a broken world a sign of new hope. It was then that he pointed to the Woman of the Apocalypse who had triumphed over the angry dragon. Mary's Assumption was proof that death and destruction were not to be the fate of humanity.

Therefore, in defining the bodily assumption of Mary into the glory of the resurrection of her Son, Pius was reminding the world about the dignity of the human person and the infinite value of every human life. It was materialism and greed that had unleashed the dragons of war. If we are to prevent that from happening again, Pius said, we have to become as Mary was, totally open to God and to the needs of our neighbour. In Mary, we are promised and shown the glory that belongs to all the children of God. This hope brings the obligation to guard and defend the integrity of each person and of the created order.

In our own day, we are faced not so much with the ugliness of open warfare (even though it is a reality for so many people and countries) but with a situation where the small and weak are disregarded and sometimes despised. Unborn life is not cherished, families are not given the opportunities to grow and develop, the elderly are out of sight and so out of mind, drug addicts are vilified – the list can go on. In short, people are valued for what they produce, not for what they are. The unfortunate are, in Christ's own words, His brothers and sisters, and to fail in charity towards them is a failure to recognize Christ.

One of the great countersigns to the disrespect for

human life is the work that goes on in communities such as parishes. Church buildings are important because they reflect our belief that the worship of the One True God is an essential part of our faith. The other aspect of our faith is to serve as Christ did, as Mary did, as those who have gone before us did.

We believe that we have the supreme advantage, as St Paul called it, of knowing Christ our Lord. We need to put that faith into action, as Mary did, as those who have gone before us did.

Mary, from her place in heaven, continues to show us the same loving care with which she held the Christ Child to her heart, and we are to hold to our hearts those who need to experience the dignity we believe they have as the children of God. In her *Magnificat* she acknowledged herself as one of the little ones who long for God's justice. Let us ask Mary to intercede for us, and after this, our exile, to show us the fruit of her womb and her faith, Jesus, our Risen Lord.

Sts Peter and Paul, South Melbourne,
Vigil Mass, Saturday 14 August 1999

The Rosary

Reading: *Luke 1:26-38*

WE find in our Blessed Lady the most generous example of dedication to God and to the needs of the children of God. In Chapter 1 of St Luke's Gospel we hear the wonderful story of how Mary placed herself in God's hands and accepted His call to be the Mother of His Son. St Bernard described the meeting of Mary and the Archangel Gabriel as the most important conversation that was ever held on earth. It is, he said, as though the whole of humanity was waiting for the response of the humble maiden of Nazareth. Her 'Yes' to God was the beginning of the mystery of our salvation in Christ. When Mary said: 'Behold the handmaid of the Lord', our faith tells us that the only Son of God began His human journey among us. In a real way we can say that Jesus took from His mother not only His body, but also many of her attitudes: His concern for the poor and the weak, in exactly the same way that many of our own ways of acting were taught us by our own mothers.

In the month of October, the Church traditionally recalls the importance of one of our most beautiful traditions: the Rosary. It is a unique and incomparable prayer. In the Rosary we have a complete summary of the principal truths of our faith. We proclaim our belief in the Incarnation of the Son of God in the joyful Mysteries. In the sorrowful Mysteries we recall the events by which Christ saved us and gave us the gift of new life. In the glorious Mysteries we anticipate the truth that one day we will share completely in the risen life of Christ.

Legend has it that it was St Dominic who first spread the Rosary as a popular devotion. He was accustomed to asking his listeners to seek Our Lady's intercession each time that he explained a mystery of the Catholic faith. The Dominican family has been associated with the devotion to the Rosary for many centuries. It was a Dominican Pope, Pius V, who established the feast of the Rosary in 1571, as a thanksgiving to Our Lady for her protection during the Battle of Lepanto – one of the three great victories of Western Christendom against the threat of the Turks. I know that the Maltese are also devoted to Our Lady for her intercession in the great Siege of 1565 which ended on the feast of Our Lady's Birthday, 8 September 1565, the first of the victories.

Today, perhaps more than ever, we need the intercession of our Mother Mary in the struggle against those forces which would deny God and His plan for us. One of the bigger struggles is the issue of euthanasia, which would have us believe that human life is no longer a sacred good, and that an old and sick person loses the right to live when he can no longer contribute to society. In this area in particular, the Church, through such places as this Rosary Home, proclaims the truth that all people, regardless of age or health, are precious to God and are a sign of the suffering of Christ. My prayer for all of you is that you will always, whatever the difficulties you face, be confident of God's love for you. You, in your turn, can be a great source of good for your families and for the whole Church.

I know that many of you pray every day for your families – that God will bless them and protect them. May I also ask you to pray for the Church – for the holiness of our priests and religious, for an increase in vocations to the priesthood, and for the Church in the many difficulties she has to face both here and abroad. And perhaps, when you say your Rosary, which I know is a part of the community life here, you might spare a prayer for me as your bishop, that I might be supported by the intercession of Mary, Mother of God.

Homily at Rosary Home for the Aged,
Keilor Downs, Melbourne, 10 October 1997

Update: In the month of the Holy Rosary in 2002, Pope John Paul II announced the creation of a new set of Mysteries to be used in praying the Rosary. The

Luminous Mysteries, or the Mysteries of Light, centre on important events in the life of Christ: His Baptism; His presence at the wedding feast at Cana, His call to conversion; His transfiguration, and His institution of the Eucharist.

The Holy Father called for the **Joyful** Mysteries to be said on Monday and Saturday, the **Luminous** on Thursday, the **Sorrowful** on Tuesday and Friday, and the **Glorious** on Wednesday and Sunday (except for Sundays during the Christmas season when the Joyful Mysteries are said, and the Sundays of Lent when the Sorrowful Mysteries are said).

4
Heroes through the Centuries

25th Anniversary of Election of Pope John Paul II

You are Peter and on this rock I will build my Church. And the gates of the underworld can never hold out against it. I will give you the keys of the Kingdom of heaven: whatever you bind on earth shall be considered bound in heaven; whatever you loose on earth shall be considered loosed in heaven.

Matthew 16:13-19

THESE words from St Matthew's gospel, spoken by Christ just after Peter's confession of faith in Jesus as the Son of the Living God, are written around the dome and walls of St Peter's Basilica in Rome and are one of the classical biblical texts about Peter's leadership and the Papal line of successors, the oldest surviving institution in human history.

Today we celebrate the election twenty-five years ago of Karol Wojtyla, Archbishop of Cracow as the 264th successor of St Peter, Pope, Bishop of Rome, Vicar of Christ, leader of the Catholic Church.

We rejoice at the blessings God has brought to the Church and world through our Pope, through whom the Lord has consoled His people and bared His holy arm in the sight of all nations.

Karol Jozef Wojtyla, Lolek to his friends, was born in 1920, the son of a professional soldier, also Karol, who first served with the Austro-Hungarian Army and then as a Captain with the Polish Army after Poland's national re-emergence in 1918. A gentleman of the old school, multi-lingual and respected for his integrity, he was the most important influence on the young Lolek, whose mother died when he was nine.

Karol junior attended the local elementary school at Wadowice, and was goalie in a soccer team largely made up of Jewish boys. When he was twelve, his only brother Edmund, a medical doctor, died after catching scarlet fever from a patient.

He never attended a minor seminary, a secondary school reserved for boys aiming at priesthood, but received a sound classical education, taking both Latin and Greek at the local state high school. Professor Jerzy Zubrzycki, a contemporary, has written that their final 1938 matriculation exam was demanding, focused on the study of ancient Western civilization, especially Aristotle and Greek tragedy. They were told that the vital question for them, as in the past, was how to define a good human life. They were soon to be confronted with violently opposed definitions.

Karol was the outstanding student in his last year, chosen to give the address to the visiting Archbishop of Cracow, Cardinal Adam Sapieha. When informed that this impressive young man was going to study Polish literature, in which he was already saturated, at the Jagiellonian University, he replied, 'a pity'.

On 1 September 1939, the Nazis invaded Poland and seventeen days later the Russians struck from the East. Six million Poles died during the Second World War and the Poles suffered a double defeat; first from the Nazis, then from the Communists.

Under Hans Frank, Nazi rule in Poland was a nightmare. The Poles had no rights, their culture was to be destroyed, secondary schools and universities were closed to them, leaders in every walk of life were to be imprisoned, often killed, while Nordic looking Poles were to be assimilated, the others allowed to die out. Chopin's music was forbidden.

For years Wojtyla's friends had told him he would become a priest, an idea he strongly resisted. It was only in the autumn of 1942, three years into the War and eighteen months after the death of his father, that he offered himself and joined the underground seminary of Cardinal Sapieha. There were frequent Gestapo raids and some of these seminarians were jailed or executed. In April 1944 Jerzy Zachuta, also a secret seminarian, who served the Cardinal's daily Mass with Wojtyla, was arrested and executed. He began to study philosophy.

Earlier he had joined the Rhapsodic Theatre which gave twenty-one illegal performances during World War II. It was a small part of a broader movement of hidden cultural resistance which espoused Christian moral principles and Catholic social doctrine. This movement also covered a military section of 20,000 members (there were some sharp exchanges between the Theatre group and the partisans on the best way forward) and a council to help the Jews, which, among other activities, prepared 50,000 false passports for them.

What this young intellectual, as an illegal part-time student and then seminarian, attempted with his friends in this tiny circle, he was to develop in the much wider world of Communist Poland as an archbishop and then throughout the world as Pope.

George Weigel is the American author of the best biography of the pope, *Witness to Hope*. His claim is that John Paul came to realize that history is driven by ideas, ideals and the moral commitment of people to their versions of culture, which are always more powerful in the long run than politics or economics or armies.

John Paul also believed that at the heart of every enduring culture is an acknowledgement of the Transcendent, preferably the worship of the one true God and His only Son, Jesus Christ. This was not an enthusiasm for abstract, impersonal forces.

He was always a disciple of Jesus Christ, Catholic and Polish, as he attempted to explain and relate eternal truths to the tragedy and muddle of twentieth-century life. He began to teach regularly, in season and out of season; that there are truths about the human situation, which can be known; in them is found human flourishing.

His 1979 visit to Poland is the most spectacular example of the changes he wrought in human hearts. The truths he preached gave hope to millions in 'the evil empire' and the mute acceptance of Communist lies and violence became no longer possible.

As his friend and ally, the priest sociologist and chaplain to Solidarity, Professor Josef Tischner, explained, the 1979 pilgrimage convinced the Polish people to 'stop lying' about the world they inhabited and the Solidarity movement grew like 'a huge forest planted by awakened consciences'.

Most Western commentators missed the significance of this Polish visit at the time, but Aleksandr Solzhenitsyn, the Russian writer who exposed the Gulags for what they were, and Yuri Andropov, then head of the KGB under Brezhnev, made no such mistake. They knew the likely consequences of the waves the Pope was creating. In 1981 there was the attempted assassination by Mehmet Ali Agca and in February 1984 the Pope sent Dr Jerome Lejeune, the French geneticist who had lunched with him before Agca's failed attempt, to represent him at Andropov's funeral in Moscow.

John Paul II repeated and developed his central theses in every type of teaching from short homilies to solemn encyclicals, as he explained the scandal of the Cross and how the Church must be a sign of contradiction, while emphasizing the power of reason to know the liberating effects of truth.

Some of the Holy Father's teachings were predictable and uncompromising, especially his consistent opposition to artificial contraception. Perhaps this will come to be seen in a new light once the implications of negative population growth sink in.

Some of John Paul II's encyclicals especially on morality were highly controversial far outside Catholic circles, particularly *Veritatis Splendor* (1993). The powerful affirmation of moral truth provoked every leader-writer in the Western world into print, with newspapers such as *Le Monde*, *The Times* (London) and *The New York Times* discussing it at length. Less controversial but just as politically incorrect was *Evangelium Vitae* (1995), which vigorously reaffirmed the value and inviolability of every human life, solemnly condemned abortion and euthanasia, and declared the death penalty permissible only when it would not otherwise be possible for society to defend itself, effectively ruling it out as an option in Western nations.

The great body of John Paul II's teaching in faith

and morals and on social questions forms a powerful and coherent whole, drawing on the dynamic of tradition and development that has made the Catholic Church one of the most robust and longest-surviving institutions in the world. There is no easy courting of popularity and no shirking of challenges, but despite this – or indeed because of it – it will continue to have an important effect on public thinking and discourse well into the twenty-first century. For at the centre of his work is the question of the meaning of human life, and in particular, of suffering. A principal point of difference between secular humanists and Christians is the value accorded life and suffering. The radical secularist view that suffering is meaningless, that a life of suffering is without value, is no longer enough for people. We know there is more to the story than this, and John Paul II has addressed this intellectually and through the public performance of his duties at such personal cost.

The Pope has seen his task as proclaiming Jesus Christ and His message to all who are prepared to listen.

To do this, he has shown time and again, that he is happy to suffer for us, to do what he can to make up all that still has to be undergone by Christ for the sake of His Body the Church. This is why, today, he struggles wearily on, helped only by Christ's power driving him irresistibly.

We thank God for his presence and witness, his teaching and courage and pray, yet again, as we did as children, that the Lord preserve him and give him life and deliver him not into the hands of his enemies.

Anniversary Mass to mark the Silver Jubilee of Pope John Paul II, St Mary's Cathedral 16 October 2003. In March 2004, the Holy Father overtook Pope Leo XIII's longevity as Pope, making him the third longest-serving Pope in history behind St Peter himself and Pius IX

Saints Peter and Paul

Readings: *Acts 12:1-11; 2 Tim 4:6-8, 17-18; Matthew 16:13-18*

THE joint feast of St Peter and St Paul has been celebrated in the city of Rome from at least the time of Constantine, the first Christian Emperor of the Roman Empire in the early fourth century. In the East the feast was often celebrated on 28 December, as evidence from Syria in the fifth century and Egypt in the sixth century demonstrates; but gradually the date of the Roman commemoration took precedence.

We now take this apostolic partnership for granted; the apostle to the gentiles and the apostle to the circumcised; the greatest theologian of the New Testament (just nosing out St John for the honour) and the rock man on whom Christ promised to build His Church. Both travelled to Rome, the centre of power and administration in a mighty Empire which endured in the West for 400 years after their death and in the Christian East for another 1400 years. Both were martyrs there in the sixties. Both made spectacular and public mistakes. Peter denied Christ three times and Paul was a persecutor of Christians.

They represent different threads in the Christian tradition. Peter had been a Galilean fisherman, poorly educated. Paul was from Tarsus, a Pharisee of the Pharisees, a student of the famous rabbi Gamaliel and a Roman citizen to boot. They were probably in different theological schools, as Peter would have lined up closer to James than to Paul and they clashed publicly and deeply over the necessity (or otherwise) of circumcision for non-Jewish converts. Their unity in faith across these differences has important lessons for us in at least a couple of ways.

Our age today, dominated by science and technology, is geared to the future. We like novelties, strive to be modern and up-to-date.

In ancient times the majority appealed instinctively to the authority of the past, to precedent, as often as we now strive to clinch an argument by showing we are up-to-date, perhaps even relevant!

One of the strangest aspects of Christianity is that Our Lord left no writings. We cannot even be sure that He could write; the only direct evidence being that He drew something in the sand when defending the woman accused of adultery. As the first generation of personal contacts with Our Lord aged and died, the New Testament scriptures were written. But no written documents can completely answer changing contemporary problems and who was to define what the Scriptures actually meant?

Especially in the second century the Church was shaken and almost destroyed, not by the imperial persecutions, but by a vast and various movement, which we lump together under the label of Gnosticism from the Greek term for knowledge. It had a bit of everything, in different ways in different sects; philosophy and Eastern mystery religions, puritanism and promiscuity. The mood was for individualism and syncretism and many of the Gnostic sects had secret traditions which were passed from master to chosen pupils, kept from the masses, from the unenlightened, those who did not know.

This was the second-century background which saw the rise of the doctrine of the apostolic tradition and the apostolic succession of bishops, which went back to the apostles themselves. The faithful could be sure that they had access to what Our Lord had taught, because the Church drew up a list of genuine new scriptures (the New Testament for us), distinguishing these from the many other writings claiming this status (which we now describe as apocryphal), and because the bishops became universally recognized in the orthodox communities as the prime guardians of the teachings of Christ and the apostles.

Among those bishops and communities churches founded by the apostles themselves had a special authority as defenders of the tradition and arbiters in doctrinal disputes. The special claims of the Church of Rome came from the fact that it was the city where the two greatest apostles taught and were martyred. The bishops of Rome, successors of Peter, came to embody this supreme tradition of orthodoxy, this guarantee of the faithful transmission of Christ's teaching, which Peter and Paul had handed over to the Christians in Rome.

As we remember Peter and Paul, we might firstly thank God for the quality of leadership we have received from the individual popes during the last century and especially for the leadership of our present Holy Father, one of the great popes of history.

Secondly we should pray in thanks for the institution of the Papacy. Conquerors and tyrants have often understood the importance of the office of pope much better than we do. Napoleon imprisoned two popes, Pius VI and Pius VII. Hitler boasted at table that when he won the War he would set up a pope in each country; and in every nation the Communists took over they tried to set up a national Catholic Church and separate bishops, priests and people from the pope.

Despite the bad popes, despite the Great Schism of popes and anti-popes around 1400, the papacy is a miracle of grace.

We remember Peter and Paul together because they founded this Roman tradition. As Pope Leo wrote 1500 years ago, 'we must not make distinctions (between them) because they were equal in their election, alike in their toils, undivided in their death. (It was God who) set them like the twin light of the eyes in the body, whose Head is Christ.'

30 June 2002, Feast of Sts Peter and Paul,
St Mary's Cathedral, Sydney

Mother Mary of the Cross

WHEN Pope John Paul II beatified Mother Mary MacKillop in Sydney in January 1995 he paid a wonderful tribute to Australians when he noted that Mother Mary embodied all that was best in our nation and in its people: 'genuine openness to others, hospitality to strangers, generosity to the needy, justice to those unfairly treated, perseverance in the face of adversity, kindness and support to the suffering.'

Mother Mary was a woman of courage, the Holy Father said, who 'placed the spiritual and material well-being of others ahead of any personal ambition or conveniences'.

Mary MacKillop was a woman of her time and ahead of her time. She had the grit and the stoicism to survive the challenges of breaking new ground in colonial Australia, and the maturity and magnanimity to turn the other cheek to those who sometimes made her task impossibly hard. Mary knew and loved the rugged bush country and colourful characters of colonial

Australia as deeply as the poets who captured that world and its hardships so strikingly – Banjo Paterson, Henry Lawson and Adam Lindsay Gordon and later, our own John O'Brien.

At age twenty-four, she must have thought particularly of Christ's birth as she opened her first free Catholic school in a disused stable at Penola in the remote south-east of South Australia. It was there, too that she put on a black dress as a sign of her religious dedication on St Joseph's Day 1866.

In religious life, her name was Mary of the Cross. No name, she wrote, 'could be dearer to me, so I must endeavour, not to deserve it, for I cannot, but at least I must try not to dishonour it'. The Cross, she wrote, was 'a sweet and dear instrument in the hands of a great and good Father in making His children all that such a Father had a right to expect His chosen children to be'. Throughout her own life, she was to feel its weight and its splinters many times.

Mary was born in Melbourne on 15 January 1842 in Brunswick Street, Fitzroy, the eldest of eight children of Alexander MacKillop and Flora MacDonald, who had emigrated – separately – from the western highlands of Scotland a few years earlier. It is entirely appropriate, I think, in the light of Mary's practical compassion for the suffering, that in 2000, on the site of her birthplace, the Archdiocese of Melbourne opened the Mary of the Cross Centre for the support of families suffering from the effects of drug and alcohol abuse.

Mary was baptised at St Francis' Church, Lonsdale Street, and grew up in the then-fledgling settlement of Melbourne where, local legend has it, she and her brothers and sisters played under the gum tree outside St Francis' after Mass on Sundays. That gum was used to construct the bishop's chair in St Patrick's Cathedral,

Melbourne. Mary's father was a former student for the priesthood at Scots College, Rome, and was neither a practical man nor a good provider, but he taught his intelligent eldest daughter well. After starting work as a shop assistant in Collins Street, Mary left home at age eighteen as governess to her cousins on Penola Station.

In colonial Australia in the 1860s, often the most basic education was a privilege reserved for those whose parents could pay for it, an appalling injustice that troubled Mary and the English-born priest/intellectual/geologist whose job it was to care for the souls scattered throughout a 57,000 sq km parish which stretched across much of south-eastern South Australia. Father Julian Tenison Woods was a gentle, kindly man who incurred the wrath of local doctors when he cared for the local Aborigines when they were sick. Father Tenison Woods became Mary's friend, confidant, inspiration and practical support as she set about creating a new order of nuns, the Sisters of St Joseph of the Sacred Heart. He was Mary's spiritual director, wrote the order's Rule and conducted retreats.

The Sisters' highest work priority was to provide poor children, both in cities and in isolated rural settlements with a basic education, a good grounding in the faith and a love of God. Higher learning it was never meant to be, but it was invaluable at a time when the vast majority of children would otherwise have grown up illiterate and without basic Catechetical instruction. Time and again, Church history shows that religious orders meeting the spiritual needs of the people of their time and place are blessed with vocations, and the Josephites were no exception. Within eighteen months of the foundation, ten more members had joined Mary in her work. Just a year later, by the end of 1869, the number had increased to thirty-nine and new schools were opening. At age twenty-seven, however, Mary had begun to be afflicted with the severe headaches and ill health that plagued her throughout the rest of her life.

By the time of Mary's death at North Sydney on 8 August 1909, she had established 109 houses, staffed by 650 Sisters teaching 12,400 children in 117 schools in New South Wales, Victoria, South Australia, Queensland, Western Australia and New Zealand. The 'Brown Joeys', as they were affectionately known, were welcomed and respected across the country as requests for sisters to start and run schools flooded in from parish priests and bishops. In a hard age of sectarianism, Catholic schools received no Government funding from the 1870s to 1963, and without the dedication of the Joeys, many Catholic schools would never have opened and those that had would have closed. The Sisters also ran orphanages and refuges, but teaching remained their priority.

Mother Mary's vast achievements were forged in the face of intense opposition both from within and outside the Church. Undoubtedly, her lowest point was from September 1871 onwards when the ailing Bishop Sheil of Adelaide, acting hastily on bad advice, excommunicated Mary over a conflict about control of the Order. She languished until February the following year when the Bishop rescinded the decision, acknowledged the injustice of his action and apologised. Even as the victim of such a bad mistake, Mary remained charitable, accepting that the incident had been permitted by the will of God. She was deeply conscious of this and summed it up eloquently: 'To me, the will of God is a dear book which I am never tired of reading, which has always some new charm for me. I cannot tell you what a beautiful thing the will of God seems to me.'

Life was not always smooth sailing, either, for Mary in other dioceses with inevitable tensions among the

Sisters themselves and also, on the odd occasion, with Father Tenison Woods as his health failed.

Mary was a prodigious letter writer – to her family, to Father Tenison Woods, to friends and to her Sisters – and her precise turn of phrase and clarity of expression provide invaluable insights into her thoughts and feelings as her work unfolded. The letters reveal a woman of keen intelligence, practical initiative, honesty, and above all, faith. Without these letters we would know Mary only from second-hand accounts, which raises important questions as to how historians of the future will dig out the essence of today's leaders who rely so heavily on email, so often deleted, to communicate.

Beatifying Mother Mary in 1995 Pope John Paul II acknowledged that the Church faces a challenge in finding fresh and creative ways of recognizing and integrating the specific charisms of women, essential to building up the Body of Christ in unity and love. Through the centuries, the Church has encouraged the soaring spirits of strong female leaders who sought to make a significant difference to the souls they served. In this, Mother Mary of the Cross belongs in the stellar company of Catherine of Siena, Joan of Arc, Teresa of Avila, Lady Margaret Beaufort, Mary Ward, Catherine McAuley, Nano Nagle, Mary Aikenhead, Mother Mary Martin (the Irish founder of the Medical Missionaries of Mary), the great American educator Katherine Drexel, Mother Marie Adele Garnier who established the Tyburn sisters in London, Edith Stein, Eileen O'Connor and, in our own time, Mother Teresa.

How ironic then, that in the 1960s and 1970s, when women across the secular world began taking on wider roles in public life, business and the professions, that the major nursing and teaching orders of the Catholic Church in Australia withdrew from positions of leadership and the classroom, where they had wielded such a positive and important influence for decades.

Whatever the merits of the alternative paths they now pursue, the Church in this country faces challenges in the classroom, in terms of evangelisation, every bit as daunting as those faced by Mother Mary in the Victorian era. We're more prosperous, more comfortable and have facilities she never dreamed of, but the sad truth is that only a fraction of the students leaving our schools do so with sufficient love of Christ or sufficient understanding that He loves them, to give Him an hour a week at Sunday Mass.

Righting this serious failing will require the kind of faith, determination and grit Mother Mary showed in abundance when she established so many of our schools. Perhaps it will also require new teaching orders or lay members of new movements, willing to take up where the others left off.

Like the work of Mother Mary, the new evangelization will need planning, tenacity and a strong capacity to withstand internal criticism. We need to be channels of grace; or, to use another image, we must be determined not to hinder the Spirit of God when it blows, as it surely will if we persevere. But most of all, we will need prayer and faith, because as Pope John Paul observed when declaring Mary MacKillop, Blessed Mary of the Cross, she worked not only to 'free people from ignorance through schooling or alleviate their suffering through compassionate care'. Her main task, he said, which is ours also, was to 'satisfy their deeper, though sometimes unconscious longing for "the unsearchable riches of Christ" (Eph 3:8)'.

Expanded version of sermon preached at North Sydney Shrine, 8 August 2003, Feast day of Mother Mary

Edith Stein

AT different times in her extraordinary life, Edith Stein was a devout Jew, an atheist, a radical suffragette, a feminist rightly appalled at the lack of opportunities for women to use their intellectual talents in the early decades of the twentieth century and a nurse in an Austrian field hospital during World War I. From a young age, Edith was a fine scholar, philosopher and writer and remained so until, at age fifty-one, as Sister Teresa Benedicta of the Cross, she was wrenched from the Carmelite Monastery at Echt in Holland, herded into the infamous Nazi 'cattle trucks' and gassed in Auschwitz on 9 August 1942. She died a saint and a martyr.

In May 1987, Pope John Paul II, whose own suffering at the hands of the Nazis is well-known, beatified Edith Stein in Cologne paying tribute to 'an outstanding daughter of Israel and at the same time of the Carmelite Order', a personality who 'united within her rich life a dramatic synthesis of our century. It was the synthesis of a history full of deep wounds that are still hurting … and also the synthesis of the full truth about man. All this came together in a single heart that remained restless and unfulfilled until it finally found rest in God.'

The Holy Father canonised Edith in October 1998, and the following year declared her co-patron of Europe along with two other outstanding Catholic leaders, Sts Catherine of Siena and Bridget of Sweden. In an age of spiritual confusion, Edith Stein, who was a rigorous and relentless seeker of truth, was an inspired choice as patron of Europe where secularism is increasingly obscuring a rich Christian heritage.

Human nature everywhere needs heroes and role models, people to be admired and sometimes followed or emulated. One only has to consider the adulation given to sports stars, rock stars and movie stars — of varying values and virtues — to recognize this fact. The Church also needs to be producing exemplars and leaders who can show us the way to God.

Edith's canonisation, which some of the Stein family attended in St Peter's Square, sparked controversy and also curiosity among the European Jewish community, who, correctly, saw that she was killed primarily because of her race and not because of Catholicism.

However, she was also killed as a result of the forthrightness of the Dutch Catholic bishops in formally protesting the policies of the Nazi occupation troops and the treatment of the Jewish peoples in July 1942. The day after the bishops' letter was read in Holland's churches, all Catholic Jews, around 700 in number, were ordered to be deported. Edith and her sister Rosa, who had also converted to the faith, were among them.

'Come Rosa, we are going for our people,' Edith said to Rosa as the SS led them away. The girls' conversion had deeply distressed their mother, Auguste Stein — a deeply religious Jew and from all accounts, a great mother and excellent businesswoman who ran the family timber firm after her husband died when Edith was just two. However, Edith's exploration of Christ and His teachings had, in fact, drawn Edith closer in mind and heart to her race. 'We know from the Gospel accounts that Christ prayed as a believing Jew and faithful follower of the Law …' she wrote.

She was proud of her race, and, feeling that the weight of the Cross was being laid upon them, was prepared to share their suffering as one of the 6,000,000 Jews who perished in the Holocaust. She can also be counted, of course, as one of 41,000,000 Christians who died across the world in World War II.

So who was Edith Stein? She was the youngest of a large family, born while her family was celebrating Yom Kippur, the Jewish feast of atonement, on 12 October 1891 in Wroclaw, a medieval university city 300 kilometres south-west of Warsaw and 200 kilometres east of Dresden. From its origins in the tenth century, Wroclaw was ruled in turn by Polish kings, Germans, Bohemians and Prussians, and it was Frederick the Great of Prussia who changed its name to Breslau about 150 years before Edith was born. It has now reverted to its original Polish name and is Poland's fourth largest city.

Edith was an outstanding student, and as Pope John Paul said when he named her co-patron of Europe, she 'travelled the arduous path of philosophy with passionate enthusiasm'. Although brought up religiously, from the age of fourteen she 'had consciously and deliberately stopped praying', determined to rely exclusively on herself and assert her freedom. Years later she came to the surprising realization that 'only those who commit themselves to the love of Christ become truly free'. [1]

Parents saddened by their own children's religious indifference at a similar age may well take heart from Edith's youthful attitudes and pray that, like her, their children will continue to sift for truth, and find it. In this sense, Edith was a true *radical*, someone seeking the *radix*, or root, of truth. When she found it, she embraced it.

At University in Breslau, Edith studied German and history and joined the Prussian Society for Women's Franchise. She recalled she was a 'radical suffragette'

---

[1] From Pope John Paul's declaration of Teresa Benedicta of the Cross as co-patron of Europe, 1 October 1999.

before 'I lost interest in the whole issue'.[2]

Increasingly fascinated with philosophy, Edith transferred to Gottingen University to study under Edmund Husserl, the leader of an influential philosophy movement known as *phenomenology*, a forerunner of existentialism. Phenomenology sought to explore the relationship between the visible world 'of things' and the world of ideas and values.

Edith Stein's books take thought and study to absorb. As a pupil and assistant to Husserl, she completed her doctorate on empathy *summa cum laude*, 'with highest praise' after her studies were interrupted by a period of working as a nurse in a field hospital in Austria during World War I, an experience which brought her face to face with suffering and death, mainly of young soldiers with typhoid.

Back in academia, encounters with a number of Bavarian Catholics played on her mind, helping her to realize that their goodness and faith was a sign that 'truth wears human features'. She was also deeply impressed by the faith of a friend, the widow of a fellow professor, who had been killed in World War I.

However, it was only by chance, in 1921, when she was thirty, that Edith picked up the autobiography of St Teresa of Avila from a friend's bookshelf. Unable to put it down, she completed it in a single night, and from there, her life changed irreversibly. I too, have read this autobiography, but unaccountably, I was little moved and struggled to finish it.

In a 1952 essay, Evelyn Waugh relates the story, as told by one of Edith's fellow Carmelites, Sister Teresia de Spiritu Sancto of how the life of St Teresa prompted Edith to move on to study the Council of

---

[2] Zenit biography of Edith Stein.

Trent Catechism and Roman Missal then to attend Mass, where she understood every phrase and gesture.

'After Mass she followed the priest to the presbytery and asked for baptism,' Waugh wrote. '"Who has instructed you for how long?" "Test my knowledge." He did, and a full discussion ranging over the whole field of Catholic theology ensued, and Edith was baptised, to the sadness of her Jewish friends and family, on New Year's Day 1922.'

From there, Edith became a keen student of Thomas Aquinas, translating his treatise *On Truth* into German. But in an era when full professorships for women at top universities were unknown, Edith left her appointment as Husserl's assistant and taught for eleven years at a Dominican teachers' college in Speyer, Germany, becoming well known throughout the Catholic world in Europe for her lectures to women's groups on the education and role of Catholic women.

Ahead of her time, and even ahead of many of today's feminists, Edith recognized that the special charism of women to bear and nurture children was compatible with their intellectual lives.

However she realized that her own calling was not to motherhood or even to the continuation of a career in the wider world. Edith postponed her entry into religious life out of kindness to her mother, who remained distressed by her conversion. At age forty-two she entered the Cologne Carmelite Monastery in 1933, an important year in Hitler's rise to power.

After Kristallnacht (8–9 November 1938) she and her sister, Rosa, wearing their Yellow Stars, took refuge over the border in Holland, where, sadly, evil followed them.

As a nun, Edith chose to be known as Teresa Benedicta of the Cross – out of deference to Teresa of Avila who inspired her, Benedict, founder of Western monasticism and St John of the Cross whose theology of Christ's suffering she embraced.

As Pope John Paul reminded us when he declared her patron of Europe, many of our contemporaries would like to silence the Cross, which, because it is a mystery, can never be understood by reason alone.

'Through the experience of the Cross,' the Pope said, 'Edith Stein was able to open the way to a new encounter with the God of Abraham, Isaac and Jacob, the Father of our Lord Jesus Christ. Having matured in the school of the Cross, she found the roots to which the tree of her own life was attached.'

Facing the Nazi's final solution, what mattered most to Edith was that she was 'a daughter of the chosen people' and that she belonged to Christ 'not only spiritually, but also through blood'.

St Mary's Cathedral, Sydney, 11 August 2002

The Forty English Martyrs

NEXT Sunday at St Peter's Basilica in Rome, the Pope will canonize the Forty English and Welsh Martyrs – forty men and women who died for their faith during the Reformation.

I thought that I might say a few words on the general significance of this event; and on its significance for you all in a college such as Eton, whose fortunes since the Reformation (but not originally) have been so closely linked to Anglicanism.

Canonization is the public recognition by the Church that certain men and women are saints; by this ancient ceremony, the Church puts forward these people as models for us to admire (and imitate?!).

It is not an irrelevant piece of show business; and there will be tens of thousands of English men and women present at the ceremony to show how importantly they regard the occasion.

We cannot escape from our past; and there is no more certain sign of a superficiality of character than the tendency to despise all those who went before us, in the Church, or in the history of our countries. They made mistakes, terrible mistakes, but they built on a scale quite beyond our capabilities.

We should be proud of these men – as Englishmen, and as Catholics; but this pride must not degenerate into a tribal rejoicing, which despises others, rather than rests content in its own achievement.

No longer do we think (if we ever did) that Catholics are completely right, and the others are completely wrong. We admit sorrowfully that Catholics also persecuted; and we admire the Anglican and other martyrs who died at our hands.

But we firmly believe that the Catholic martyrs died for a fullness of faith, which is not found elsewhere and which was and is worth preserving. In Oxford the right note will be struck with a special Catholic Mass in the Anglican Chapel at Campion's old college, St John's, where the Master of St John's, an Anglican, will preach.

Of the many English men and women who died during the religious persecutions, these forty have been chosen for canonization partly because there is no breath of suspicion of political activity. One who is perhaps better known than others is Edmund Campion, whose biography, written by Evelyn Waugh, is worth reading if you are interested in Elizabethan history and especially if you like Waugh as a writer. Perhaps it is a bit romanticized, but is none the worse for that!

Campion, an Anglican, was born into a London business family just before the middle of the sixteenth century, and as far as we know had all the advantages of education, good family and material comforts. He went very early to St John's College in St Giles in Oxford, and at the age of seventeen was a Fellow of the College – think of it. These were wonderful times, and he was a very popular lecturer, with a group of devotees. At age twenty-six he gave one of the two addresses of welcome to Queen Elizabeth I at Christ Church, and she, by all accounts, was extremely impressed by him.

As a friend of Sir Philip Sidney, the Elizabethan poet, courtier and soldier, the world lay at Campion's feet. For men of ability, Elizabethan England was an exciting place.

He was obviously no ignorant peasant, who had been brainwashed or bullied by his parish priest into believing all this superstition. Nor was he a religious fanatic, like some of the saints of pious memory who decided at the age of five and a half to be virgins and martyrs, and whose images on holy pictures make them look likely candidates for a sex change!

Campion was intelligent, with a good job and excellent prospects. As we say, the world was at his feet. He clearly realized this and was attracted by the prospect; but he was uneasy.

The rest of the story is well known; he left St John's and fled to Catholic Ireland. He converted to the faith and travelled to Rome where he became a Jesuit, and was ordained in Prague. Campion risked his life returning to this country in 1578 to 'cry alarme spiritual against foul vice and proud ignorance' as he put it (not without a touch of melodrama). He was caught just outside Oxford, tortured in the Tower of London (and apparently came close to recanting) and was executed at Tyburn Tree, near where Marble Arch now stands in London, on 1 December 1581.

It is worth remembering the state of the Church in Elizabeth's time; it was already finished, persecuted out of existence, with little future. And it was for this lost cause that Campion and friends gave their lives. They could only have dreamed of the present 'flourishing' state of the Church here in England, due largely to the Irish but also to converts, especially from intellectual circles.

One of the first Catholics to be martyred by Henry VIII exclaimed 'let us die for our integrity'. This is their message for us, that in our lives we remain faithful to our principles.

Preached to the Catholic boys of Eton College, Windsor, 18 October 1970

St Patrick's Day Mass

THIS year we are celebrating the bicentenary of European settlement on the Australian continent. Later in the year we shall remember the twenty-fifth anniversary of the death of Dr Mannix, Archbishop of Melbourne, one of the greatest figures in Australian history and, without doubt, the greatest Irish Australian.

I therefore regard it as a special honour this evening to concelebrate and preach at this Mass of St Patrick's Day because although I am an Australian, who owes no allegiance to any land across the seas, I am also an Australian who is proud to acknowledge the debt of the

Catholic Church in Australia to St Patrick, to the nation of Ireland and particularly to the Irish Australians who, almost single handed, planted the faith among us.

It is a long journey from the time of St Patrick to the Australia of 1988. Most scholars now believe that Patrick was born about 390 AD and died about 460, rather than in 493 as given in the Irish Annals.

It was a period when the Roman Empire, which never included Scotland and Ireland, was being attacked and penetrated by the outsiders, the barbarians, Goths, Vandals, and Huns. Rome itself fell to Alaric and the Goths in 410, the first such occupation for 800 years and the Irish pirates, known as Scotti, were active in these chaotic and terrible times.

Patrick's birthplace is still controverted, although he probably came from southern England or Wales. For many centuries the good Catholic answer to this question was to insist that Patrick was born in France, apparently as the lesser of two evils, but there is little evidence for this.

Background

Patrick's father and grandfather were clerics. Patrick's grandfather was a priest and his father Colpurnius was a deacon and well-to-do landowner at Bannaven Taburniae, the site of which is unknown. His family was not strongly religious.

At the age of sixteen Patrick was captured by Irish pirates and spent six years as a slave and shepherd in either County Mayo or County Antrim where his religious convictions deepened. He escaped across Ireland, perhaps to the port of Wexford or Wicklow and then returned to Britain, with a raiding party. In some ways he never recovered from the trauma of his early capture.

He was ordained priest, visited Gaul and it was

decided to send him to Ireland as a missionary bishop, probably by Pope Celestine, who sent Palladius as the first bishop in Ireland between 422 and 431.

Patrick travelled much, made many converts, ordained many clergy and set up monasteries. He provoked strong opposition, some attacked his character, which provoked the writing of his *Confession*. He was imprisoned at one stage and feared martyrdom.

Myths

Many of the stories about him are either not true or, at least, without evidence. We first hear of him banishing snakes from Ireland 300 years after his death; his explanation of the Trinity through the three leaves of the shamrock first appeared 1000 years after his death. There was no High King of Ireland then for Patrick to encounter at Tara; no evidence that he climbed Croagh Patrick to commune with God. The bishop's mitre, which appears often on his head in paintings, was not used for another 600 years. He does not need these stories; his achievement and those of his Church are on record.

The *Catholic Encyclopaedia*, however, does recount Patrick's arrival at the hill of Slane, near Tara in the Irish midlands, on Easter Eve 433 and credits him with kindling a Paschal fire, beginning an important tradition and drawing fierce opposition from the pagan druids whose incantations failed to stop his spectacular progress.

It is a sad fact that most Australians, and this includes most Irish Australians, are ignorant of Irish greatness, influenced by the historical stereotypes first coined by Ireland's enemies and stemming from those centuries when the Irish people were systematically brutalized.

The great missionary expansion of Irish Catholicism in the nineteenth and twentieth centuries which took the faith not only to Australia, but to the United States,

New Zealand, Canada and many parts of Asia and Africa too, is only a rerun of Irish missionary activity in the sixth to the eighth centuries, which saw the conversions of Northern Europe, e.g. St Columba in Scotland and St Columban on the Continent. *The Book of Kells*, that four-volume masterpiece of the gospels, is testament to this period of faith and scholarship.

We should not forget this period of high achievement, when we thank God for the contribution of the Irish Australians to the building of our nation.

In many ways the Irish Catholics in Australia were the first European Australians, they never called Ireland home; they were adamant that England was not home, that there would be a place for them and their ways here in Australia; and they succeeded.

Vincent Buckley, the Australian poet, has written beautifully about how life in Australia changed the Irish. They escaped from their stereotypes. They adapted Australia to Irish ways, so that Australia became another homeland for the Gael.

> There is no Australian patriot more ardent than an Irish Australian', he writes, 'who not only knows how much reason they have to be grateful but feels deeply at home here. (Australia) is now in many respects an Irish kind of place.

The conviction of many Australians that religion is important and an everyday thing, our irreverence 'making affectionate fun of sacred matters' (Les Murray), our humour, the democratic spirit, our sympathy for the underdog, the fire and energy we sometimes bring to bear on issues; all of these Australian qualities might not be exclusively Irish, but they certainly contain a large dose of Catholic Ireland.

The greatest achievement of the Irish in Australia, brought about through the leadership of men like Archbishop Mannix and the good sense of the majority of Australians, has been to ensure that the tragedy of Irish history, and more particularly of Northern Ireland, has not been repeated here in the Great South Land. This is no small thing.

Times are now changing. The Catholic primary school in Springvale now has pupils from more than fifty nationalities. There are now more Italian Australians in Melbourne than the number of Irish Australians, when Mannix arrived here.

There might be more Irish Australians than there ever were who want to learn about Ireland, but I am also convinced that the faith of Irish Australians is under greater threat now than at any time since education was secularized in the 1870s.

We are not threatened with assault, but with erosion; not threatened so much by agnosticism or atheism as by a diminished interest in the things of God and the call of Christ. It is as though those Irish instincts which preserved the faith for centuries against direct assault have been weakened by prosperity and are less able to cope with guerrilla attacks from the flanks and the rear!

Faith in Christ is the core of Irish tradition and the motivating force of all her achievements in Ireland or overseas. We must never forget this.

We pray in thanks for those who passed on the faith to us and we pray for the wisdom and strength to inspire our young people so that they too will be bound and strengthened by the faith of our fathers, 'the strong name of the Trinity', the 'Three in One and One in Three'.

17 March 1988, St Patrick's Cathedral, Melbourne

Isidore the Priest

Of all evil suggestions, the most terrible is the prompting to follow your own heart.

THIS sounds strange. They are not the views of some modern-day fundamentalist, but written by Isidore the Priest, a fifth-century Egyptian Christian, and I found them in a recent book by the Anglican Archbishop of Canterbury, Rowan Williams, *Silence and Honey Cakes: The wisdom of the desert*.

In the third century AD during the anti-Christian persecutions of the Roman Empire spiritual men and women fled into the Egyptian desert to pray and to fast, so they could come closer to God. When the Empire gave freedom of religion to Christians in the next century, more and more people joined them and eventually there were thousands in loose local communities. Sometimes these are called 'the fathers of the desert', although there were also women.

They left a considerable literature of sayings, but they were people of prayer, healers, rather than theologians or writers. Many visited them, not so much as religious tourists, but rather as pilgrims, seeking advice or consolation. Often they wanted to know how to come closer to God. 'Give me a word', they would ask the holy man.

The attack on following the promptings of our heart is one such piece of advice, a thought to chew on, perhaps a meditation topic.

Today we are regularly exhorted to get in touch with our feelings. A 'stiff upper lip' is even more unfashionable, as we are encouraged to follow the promptings of our hearts, to feel comfortable with our decisions. A few even claim that we decide what is right or wrong from our emotions.

But Isidore the Priest was onto something of value.

The truth about ourselves can be complicated and unpleasant. We are often quite unable to accept the whole truth. Searching for the promptings of our hearts can be like peeling an onion and failing to find anything much at all at the core.

Often when we go to friends for advice, perhaps even when we pray to help us decide (or discern), we can be seeking justification for our preferences, our feelings. Friendships have been broken by unacceptable advice.

Isidore was not urging self-hatred or psychological scourging, but he was clear that all of us, to different degrees, need to be coaxed into honesty, towards belief that faith in God and prayer can be healing.

To know one's own heart is the work of a lifetime, because evil is often fascinating and disguised.

Cardinal Henri de Lubac, a great Jesuit theologian last century, wrote that 'It is not sincerity, it is truth which frees us … To seek sincerity above all things is perhaps, at bottom, not to want to be transformed.'

Sincerity or truth? Instinct or duty? Freedom or the tyranny of fashion? Each of us chooses.

The Sunday Telegraph, *23 May 2004*

Frederic Ozanam

(Founder of the Society of St Vincent de Paul)

Charity must never look backwards but always to the front, because the number of good deeds accomplished is very small, while present and future hardships remain infinite. (1835)

It remains to be seen which will win: the spirit of selfishness or the spirit of sacrifice. Will society merely develop into a means of exploitation for the strongest members to make huge profits, or will everyone devote themselves to the common good and the protection of the weak? (1836)

THESE words could easily have been written in the last five years in Australia, so well do they fit our situation. In fact, they were written by Frederic Ozanam before he was twenty-three years of age. As well as being a saint, Ozanam is a remarkably interesting man and sympathetic personality.

Therefore, today we are not simply celebrating the beatification of a French Catholic layman from the nineteenth century; not merely celebrating the fact that once again the Holy Father is revindicating the wonderful work of the St Vincent de Paul Society. We are also rededicating ourselves to the type of Christian work which Ozanam so brilliantly organized and inspired. Unfortunately, there is no sign that the need for this activity is becoming less. Most signs point to an increase of misery.

In the nineteenth century, along with Britain and

Germany, France was one of the world's great powers. The Church there prided itself on being the oldest daughter of the universal Church, but French society had been undermined by the eighteenth-century Enlightenment and then convulsed by a series of revolutions in 1789, 1830 and 1848, punctuated by the Napoleonic dictatorship and the Napoleonic wars waged under the banner of Liberty, Equality and Fraternity.

The Church was a central part of the old order. Many of the revolutionaries were explicitly anti-Catholic. In the 1790s a statue to the goddess of Reason had been installed in Notre Dame Cathedral, Paris. There were Catholic martyrs too and later Napoleon, who was not unsympathetic to a 'co-operators' Church, imprisoned two popes, Pius VI and Pius VII.

Many French Catholics were passionately committed to a restoration of the Bourbons to the throne (this is still a small recognizable current in France today) detesting the republicans with an equal passion. Distracted by these struggles we would now say the Church was slow to adapt to the new situation with millions crowding into city slums from the countryside.

The French Church had for centuries been one of the chief centres of Catholic learning, a proud intellectual tradition in a society where there were many public conflicts over the reality and nature of God, over what was truly human, what constituted a 'good life'. Ozanam grew up in this fascinating world.

Frederic Ozanam was born in Milan, Italy on 23 April 1813. In 1829, at the age of sixteen, he underwent a 'crisis of doubt' which he overcame with the assistance of his teacher, Abbé Noirot. This experience consolidated the intellectual basis of his faith and imbued him with a deep charity in controversy with unbelievers.

In 1831 he went to Paris to study law and met the leaders of the Catholic revival including Chateaubriand, Montalembert and Lacordaire. He was concerned to refute the attacks on Catholicism which were widespread at the Sorbonne. In May 1833 he and a few fellow students formed a 'Conference of Charity' to undertake practical work among the poor. This is accepted as the foundation date of the Society, named after the seventeenth-century saint, St Vincent de Paul.

Ozanam insisted that the Society should not restrict its charity to Catholics and that countries should assist each other. Thus, the Paris Society aided Dublin during the Irish Famine and Dublin reciprocated during the 1848 Revolution. This helped to show their opponents that they practised what they preached, which is always the beauty of faith. By 1840 there were 2000 members of the Society in France, and in 1854, the year of the Eureka Stockade in Ballarat, the first St Vincent de Paul branch was founded in Australia in Melbourne. At this time there were 2000 branches of the Society throughout the world. Today, the Society has approximately 900,000 members and 50,000 branches in 180 countries. The Society enjoys continuing and extraordinary growth.

During the late 1830s Ozanam was active in the Society of St Vincent de Paul, the Society for the Propagation of the Faith, Catholic journalism and many Catholic causes. He became the first to hold the chair of commercial law at the University of Lyons in 1839, but returned to Paris the following year to teach foreign literature at the Sorbonne. He was elected professor in 1844.

Ozanam advocated that Catholics should play their part in the evolution of the democratic state, a controversial idea at that time. Archbishop Mannix's message was the same. Ozanam unsuccessfully stood for election to the National Assembly in 1848. He denounced economic liberalism and any form of socialism. Lecture 24 of his course of commercial law is a brilliant exposition of Catholic social teaching, foreshadowing *Rerum Novarum*, the 1891 encyclical of Pope Leo XIII, by over forty years, and antedating the Communist *Manifesto* in its attention to the social question.

Ozanam married Amélie Soulacroix in 1841, and they had one daughter, Marie, who was born in 1845. He died in Marseilles from tuberculosis in 1853 at the age of forty. Frederic Ozanam was a man ahead of his time, and certainly a man for our times. He demonstrated the central importance of Christian love expressed in hands-on practical help and sympathy.

God has intervened in history on a number of occasions, especially through the redeeming activity of His Son Jesus Christ. The object of our faith is part of human history, just as surely as God and His Son transcend history also. Christ did not write a philosophy. There is a deep symbolism, especially for those who are well educated, in the fact that Our Lord left no personal writings at all. The Scriptures are primarily important as testimony to the works of God, and the activities of God's favourites and His enemies.

Our everyday activities have eternal consequences as the Gospel about the separation of the sheep from the goats, the saved from the damned, makes frighteningly clear. God is not like an indifferent clockmaker, who wound up the world and then let it go, on and on, alone and unaided. God creates and reveals, especially in the resurrection and ultimately at the Last Judgment. The crucifixion is not the end of the story, but a prelude to the resurrection and the cause of our resurrection.

As Christians we are called to lives of active worship and service. Many times Ozanam wrote of the importance of hard work. Hard work 'rendered people useful and nations worthy'. The One who redeems us, he also wrote, 'hid for thirty years in the workshop of a carpenter'.

Above all, he believed that when we preach and when we work, we must 'go to the poor'. For Ozanam the poor are ambassadors sent from God, to be treated with respect, not only as equals but as our masters. If we do this, our own wounds will be healed and we shall shine like the dawn as the Old Testament prophet Isaiah promised. We shall also make the grade in the Last Judgment.

Ozanam realized the radical difference practical Christianity made in the fiercely divided and stratified society of the Roman Empire. Christianity 'never hesitated', he wrote. It 'never regretted helping them (the barbarians) from the beginning, when they were still considered as no more than fodder for slave markets and as victims for gladiatorial displays. St Paul had declared them equal to the Greeks.' If our society continues to slide into paganism, then as surely as dark follows day, we shall see society's divisions widen and deepen.

Ozanam was also an intellectual, in a Catholic society, unlike Australia's, which understood the power of ideas to influence people for good or evil. Ozanam understood the romance of orthodoxy. The power of his vision and his work rose out of his Catholic fidelity. The unbelievers do not have the best lines, because they are out of tune with the Eternal Harmony. It comes as no surprise to an adult believer to realize that those who listen to too much pagan teaching, too much pagan music, find their teeth set on edge, that they become uncomfortable and ill at ease, sometimes, even often, deeply unhappy.

Ozanam is also important because he is a saint and a Catholic leader who was a married layman. Bishops, priests and religious cannot do everything and neither should we try. It is much more important to have lay faithful involved in the world, especially in the service of the poor and the suffering, than it is to have a large liturgy committee or social committee. These examples are not alternatives; indeed all three can be useful, but service of the world is a primary duty for the baptised.

Following Ozanam's inspiration and example, may the work of St Vincent de Paul groups continue to thrive; may they win many new recruits, especially among the young. God needs this work with the poor, who represent Christ Himself, and the whole Church, if she is to remain faithful, needs it too.

Sunday 24 August 1997, St Patrick's Cathedral, Melbourne – Mass to mark the beatification of Blessed Frederic Ozanam by Pope John Paul II in Paris

Mother Teresa of Calcutta

IN the illustrious history of the Nobel Peace Prize, the world had never seen an acceptance speech of the kind delivered by the 1979 winner.

Mother Teresa of Calcutta reminded her audience that Jesus died out of love 'for you and for me and for that leper and for that man dying of hunger and that naked person lying in the street not only of Calcutta, but of Africa, and New York, and London, and Oslo – and insisted that we love one another as He loves each one of us.'

He Himself becomes the hungry one, the naked one, the homeless one, she told the audience, and whatever we do in response He says: 'You did it to me.'

Mother Teresa also spoke about a different kind of poverty that was harder to solve. She spoke of loneliness, of well-cared-for elderly people in nursing homes, their eyes on the door hoping that a son or daughter will come to visit them, feeling hurt because they are forgotten. And of young boys and girls whose parents are so busy they have little time to spend with them. 'These are things that break peace,' she said. In Australia, time-poor, 'successful' working parents, too busy and exhausted to enjoy their children, or to chat to their ageing relatives understand only too well.

But the greatest destroyer of peace, Mother Teresa went on, was abortion, because it was a direct war, a direct killing by the mother herself. 'And we read in the scripture, for God says very clearly: "Even if a mother could forget her child, I will not forget you. I have carved you in the palm of my hand."'

Outstanding people invariably attract trenchant critics, and in this Mother Teresa, like Christ Himself, was no exception. Her forthright comments on subjects like abortion drew strong opposition from commentator Christopher Hitchens and others, who complained that Mother Teresa had an agenda that extended far beyond helping the poorest of the poor. In this, if in little else, Hitchens was right. Mother Teresa's most significant work was not relieving suffering, but bringing souls to God and vice versa. As she told the Nobel Prize audience: 'I believe that we are not really social workers. We may be doing social work in the eyes of people. But we are really contemplatives in the heart of the world. For we are touching the body of Christ twenty-four hours.'

Widely admired as a beacon of selflessness in a materialistic and often brutal world, Mother Teresa can only be understood in terms of her own self understanding. Her motivation was overwhelmingly religious; her prayers and actions reflected her love of God through Christ His Son.

To me she regularly appeared as serene and compassionate and in her lifetime she attracted thousands of nuns to join her. Saints are not people who always perceive the Transcendent clearly and pleasantly, without a veil of ignorance and suffering or always feel God's love intensely; much less are they individuals who pass through life in a state of sentimental euphoria. They do have a passionate conviction of the importance of God's love and work.

And like many saints, Mother Teresa could be pragmatic, blunt and tough. In Victoria, when her nuns were given a closed-down hotel as a residence, she personally took down the curtains because they were too expensive, inappropriate for the poor lifestyle required of her nuns.

Agnes Gonxha Bojaxhiu was born in Skopje, Macedonia, to Albanian parents in 1910. Her father, a businessman, died when Agnes was eight, leaving her mother to support the family with embroidery and sewing. Agnes left home at eighteen to join the Institute of the Blessed Virgin Mary (Loreto order) in Rathfarnham, Dublin, her ambition being to serve the poor in India where the Irish Loretos worked. It was in Dublin that she received the name Teresa after St Therese of Lisieux, and the following year, 1929, she left for India where she completed her training, taught religion and geography and became principal of St Mary's School in Calcutta in the 1940s.

From all accounts, Mother Teresa's years as a Loreto nun were happy and productive, with her students – some of whom later joined her in the Missionaries of Charity – inspired by her ability to fire their interest in the supernatural.

On 10 September 1946, on a train journey from Calcutta to Darjeeling, Mother Teresa received a 'call within a call' from God which was to give rise to a new order of sisters, brothers, priests and lay workers to work for 'the salvation and sanctification of the poorest of the poor'. The new congregation, the Missionaries of Charity, officially began in 1950. Their work continued quietly until the late 1960s when a British Broadcasting Corporation producer in India, Malcolm Muggeridge, began asking why so many young women were leaving secular life to don the white sari with blue trim.

His documentary, *Something Beautiful for God*, brought Mother Teresa to world attention and Muggeridge was later to attribute his conversion to the faith at age seventy-nine to Mother Teresa.

For her, fame, notoriety, awards and donations to her order followed, but often she would insist that the attention must stop, and she would withdraw to focus on her work. Mother Teresa's Sisters numbered almost 4000 and were established in 610 foundations in 123 countries, including the Soviet Union, by the time of her death on 5 September 1997.

As the *Washington Post* recorded in its obituary: 'For a time, it seemed that no matter where people suffered, the tiny nun from Calcutta was lending a hand. She helped feed the starving masses of Ethiopia, comforted the radiation victims of Chernobyl and worked for the relief of earthquake-stricken Armenia. In 1982, during the bloodiest siege of Beirut, she persuaded Israelis and Palestinians to stop fighting so thirty-seven children trapped in a front-line hospital could be rescued.'

Aged eighty-seven, Mother Teresa died just one day before the funeral of her friend Diana, the Princess of Wales. Diana's former butler has confirmed that he ensured that the ivory rosary beads Mother Teresa gave Diana, which she treasured, were placed in the Princess's hands in the Paris hospital where she died. While the friendship of these contrasting twentieth-century 'icons' was unpredictable, they shared a genuine love of sufferers, and a willingness to co-operate in helping the down and out. Public esteem for their work suggests that happily, our age is still deeply influenced by Christianity and that we retain a sympathy for the battlers.

Both Diana and Mother Teresa also understood, from vastly different experiences and standpoints, the pain of emotional and spiritual emptiness.

An intensely private person in terms of her personal relationship with God, the details of Mother Teresa's motivation in founding the Missionaries of Charity emerged only after her death, during the collection of documents to support her Cause of Beatification. In late 2002, a detailed study of Mother Teresa's life, written by the postulator of her cause, Missionary of Charity Father Brian Kolodiejchuk, was published by the Vatican news service, Zenit. The woman who emerged was no plaster cast saint, but a woman of flesh and blood, fear, humour, and even, at times, doubt.

In *The Soul of Mother Teresa: Hidden Aspects of her Interior Life*, Father Kolodiejchuk reproduced the writings of Mother Teresa where she described the call she heard from God: 'Come, carry Me into the hovels of the poor. Come, be My light. I cannot go alone. They don't know Me so they don't want Me. You come, go amongst them. Carry Me with you into them. How I long to enter their holes, their dark, unhappy homes. Come, be their victim. In your immolation, in your love for Me, they will see Me, know Me, want Me.'

Like many called to a genuine religious vocation, the young Loreto nun was reluctant to respond. 'The thought of eating, sleeping, living like the Indians filled me with fear,' she wrote. 'How can I? I have been and am very happy as a Loreto Nun. To leave what I love and expose myself to new labours and sufferings which will be great, to be the laughing stock of so many, especially religious, to cling and choose deliberately the hard things of an Indian life, to loneliness and ignominy, to uncertainty – and all because Jesus wants it, because something is calling me to leave all and gather the few to live His life, to do His work in India. These thoughts were a cause of much suffering, but the voice kept on saying, "Wilt Thou refuse?"'

Mother Teresa's private papers also shed light on a startling secret. That is, from the time she began her work among the poor of Calcutta, 'a long period of interior darkness' settled upon her, depriving her of spiritual consolation similar to renowned Christian mystic, St John of the Cross's concept of the 'dark night of the soul'.

As Mother Teresa wrote to her spiritual director: 'I am longing with painful longing to be all for God, to be holy in such a way that Jesus can live His life to the full in me. The more I want Him, the less I am wanted. I want to love Him as He has not been loved – and yet there is that separation, that terrible emptiness, that feeling of absence of God.'

As the darkness became 'thicker' she wrote of feeling '… not wanted by God, repulsed, empty, no faith, no love, no zeal. Souls hold no attraction. Heaven means nothing; to me it looks like an empty place. The thought of it means nothing to me and yet this torturing longing for God. Pray for me please that I keep smiling at Him in spite of everything. For I am only His, so He has every right over me. I am perfectly happy to be nobody, even to God.

'They say people in hell suffer eternal pain because of

the loss of God; they would go through all that suffering if they had just a little hope of possessing God. In my soul I feel just that terrible pain of loss, of God not wanting me, of God not being God, of God not really existing.' As terrible as these feelings were, her surrender to the will of God remained strong: 'The darkness is so dark and the pain is so painful, but I accept whatever He gives and I give whatever He takes.'

By 1961, Mother Teresa's letters suggest she had come to a different view, writing to a Jesuit priest friend that 'I have come to love the darkness, for I believe now that it is a part, a very, very small part, of Jesus' darkness and pain on earth. You have taught me to accept it as a "spiritual side of your work", as you wrote.'

We can be quite confident that Mother Teresa's sensitivity to emotional and spiritual suffering and her capacity for compassion were drawn, at least partly, from her own interior experience. Even when this pain was most acute, she showed us how to focus on others instead of ourselves as she communicated the truth that 'God wants you, God loves you, God is with you, God cares for you'.

Mother Teresa was beatified by her devoted friend Pope John Paul II on Sunday 19 October 2003, St Peter's Square, Rome
Missionaries of Charity Chapel, Surry Hills,
4 September 2004, feast of Blessed Teresa of Calcutta

The Faith and Devotion of St Therese

Readings: *Acts 2:42-47; 1 Pet 1:3-9.*
Gospel: *John 20:19-31 (St John relates the story of 'doubting' Thomas who was absent when the risen Christ appeared. Thomas told the other apostles*

> *that unless he could see the mark of the nails in the hands of the Lord, and put his hand into His side he would not believe they had seen Jesus. Jesus reappeared a week later and told Thomas to feel His wounds and 'do not be unbelieving'. Thomas replied 'My Lord and My God.' Jesus said 'Blessed are those who have not seen and have believed.')*

THE account of Thomas defiantly doubting the reports of the other apostles, and then of Our Lord appearing before him are a beautiful reminder of how the Risen Christ brings peace and forgiveness to all of us, no matter how weak or foolish we might be.

The story of St Therese is the opposite of Thomas' story. It is a story not of doubt but of the most fervent faith and devotion.

In many ways these relics of a French Carmelite nun represent some of the strangest aspects of Catholic life. Why give reverence to a box of bones, even if it is a beautiful container? What is the relevance to Australians today of a young middle class woman, who locked herself away from the world in a convent at the age of fifteen and died in 1897 at the age of twenty-four?

What is beyond dispute is her continuing popularity. These relics have been taken around the world since 1997. Fifteen million came to pray before them in Mexico alone and more than two-thirds of the entire population of Ireland.

Many of us too have mementos of our loved ones. We care for their graves. Venerating relics is an ancient pagan practice taken over by the Church, which provides a tangible link with the deceased and points beyond the materialism of everyday life to the sacred and the spiritual, to life beyond death. Sacred sites can perform a similar function.

Two years after her death Therese's autobiography *The Story of a Soul* was published. Now translated into many languages it has never been out of print.

This small classic records her searching for love as a teenager and then a young woman. Unusually this love is centred on Christ as the Son of God, although her struggle for perfection is based on overcoming the small everyday imperfections and anxieties which surround each one of us. Few writings have equalled her vivid appreciation for God.

Unusually, Therese is grieved not so much by the suffering around her as by that suffering caused by human sin; that is, the conscious human opting for evil. She recognized too that people can turn explicitly against the light. Some are unable to believe in the good God, but some choose not to believe. It brings too many constraints!

Like Mother Teresa of Calcutta she made her own the words of Christ dying on the cross, 'I thirst'. She saw her task as pouring the dew from Christ's suffering onto human souls; not from on high, but as a fellow human being who shares with compassion the suffering of sinners and unbelievers.

The Little Flower's memory has suffered through romanticizing, although this sentimentality also appeals to many. I remember playing tennis with a friend, who claimed that as a child he had been taught to pray silently 'Little Flower, in this hour show your power', when he risked serving a double fault!

But this is only part of the story. Dying from tuberculosis Therese lost all the consolation of religion; she could no longer feel God's presence or love, only a black hole, dark night. Without her faith, which she retained through this trial, she claimed she would have suicided 'without hesitating a moment'.

There are many areas of Church life in Australia, where we might seek St Therese's intercession, especially in the struggle for faith, to explain the need for God and the importance of regular prayer.

One task in particular could be mentioned – the struggle to defend human life, to explain the importance of protecting human life at the earliest stages.

Many people do not understand what happens in an abortion and do not suspect the guilt that often follows for those involved. So too on the complicated issue of stem cell research, we should work to understand what is at stake and then strive to explain these principles.

Therese was one of us, a modern woman who knew the void of unbelief and triumphed through expressing her love in small successes and failures.

7 April 2002, Low Sunday (Divine Mercy Sunday)
St Mary's Cathedral, Sydney, ahead of the arrival
of the relics of St Therese which drew tens of thousands
of people all over Australia

St Thomas Becket

DEVOTION to Thomas Becket is not strong in Australia but the life and death of this twelfth-century Archbishop of Canterbury continue to fascinate many moderns, principally through Eliot's masterpiece, *Murder in the Cathedral*, but also through biographies and a good film of some years ago starring Peter O'Toole and Richard Burton.

We often forget how strange the cult of martyrs is to most Australians today when we celebrate the fact that men and women died not to retain their personal integrity, nor to follow their conscience ('as Robert Bolt, quite erroneously, presented Thomas More as doing); they died in defence of the Catholic Christian faith and the community and institution of the Catholic Church.

In an Australian survey a few years ago, 67 per cent of non-practising Catholics and 59 per cent of practising Catholics believed nothing was worth the sacrifice of one's life. Naturally when religious attitudes were considered the situation was worse. No non-practising Catholics believed religious beliefs were worth the sacrifice of one's life, while only 16 per cent of practising Catholics were prepared (or claimed to be prepared) to die for their religion.

The crisis of religion in the Western World today, to which Australia belongs, is not a crisis of authority or even of morals — there has always been plenty of sin. The great threat is not heresy or modernism. The crisis is one of unbelief, radical unbelief, a crisis of faith; many cannot, or will not believe that God is alive and active and loving.

TS Eliot, like John Henry Newman before him, understood this crisis of faith well. In Becket's sermon of Christmas morning, we have Eliot speaking of martyrdom to the doubters, inside and outside the Church, and the unbelievers of our century: 'We both rejoice and mourn the death of martyrs. We mourn for the sins of the world that martyred them; we rejoice that another soul is numbered among the Saints in Heaven, for the glory of God and for the salvation of men.'

Martyrdom is not the effect of a man's will 'as a man by willing and continuing may become a ruler of men. A martyrdom is always the design of God, for His love of men, to warn them and to lead them, to bring them back to His ways.' The true martyr is 'the instrument of

God, who has lost his will in the will of God, and who no longer desires anything more for himself, not even the glory of being a martyr.'

Today, more so even than then, the majority of people would agree that the Church mourns and rejoices over her martyrs 'in a fashion that the world cannot understand'.

Thomas was born in England about 1118, in the narrow, constricted world of feudal Catholicism. The Crusades against Islam had commenced, the break between Byzantium and Rome was over fifty years old, and the Moslems ruled in the Middle East, all of North Africa, and Spain. The great Moslem leader, Saladin, was a contemporary, working to remove the Latin Kingdom of Jerusalem, established by the Normans. Thomas himself was a Norman, at a time when the English and Normans were intermarrying. In many ways he was typical of his race, being hard, direct and fiercely efficient. He was not a poet or intellectual, but possessed a fine memory. He was devout, pure and addicted to sport, especially hunting. He had an aptitude for action, organization, leadership and debate. He received his piety from his mother.

He was educated in Paris, later studying law at Bologna, subsequently joining the household of Theobald, Archbishop of Canterbury. In 1154 he was Archdeacon of Canterbury and in 1155 the young Henry II appointed him Chancellor. In this he proved efficient, often acting against Church interests and in favour of the King to whom he always remained deeply attached. He was generous, extravagant and although a deacon, saw active service in France for Henry. While never one of those incapable of co-operation he was always admired, but from a distance, and few loved him closely.

In 1162 Henry ensured Thomas' nomination as Archbishop of Canterbury, an appointment he strongly resisted as he foresaw the tensions and some of the likely differences between Church and State.

Many regard Henry as one of England's greatest kings. Intelligent contemporaries marvelled at this complex man, so richly endowed with natural gifts. Through his legal and his administrative reforms he asserted a national authority at a time when England could have chosen to remain in feudal anarchy. It was a time of economic expansion. It was Henry, too, who brought law and Church reform to Ireland, annexing the Emerald Isle to the English crown at the behest of the Papacy and so beginning that tragic love-hate relationship between the two peoples which continues till today.

The stage was set for the clash of two mighty men in the service of great institutions and high principles.

The ostensible cause of conflict was the Church's right to deal with 'criminous clerks'.

But with the dispute over the Constitutions of Clarendon the issue became the freedom of the Church in England in its relationship with the Papacy. Finally it broadened into a defence of God's rights against Caesar.

Thomas made mistakes during the quarrel and his six years of exile. At one stage he weakened and temporised; at other times he was harsh and provocative. But with time his understanding of the issue deepened and spiritualized.

The crisis, the turning point, was in October 1164, when Becket was alone, deserted by friends and Henry had become implacable, bent on Thomas' ruin.

His confessor, Robert of Merton, told him that he could easily escape: 'Mitigate the king's anger and make him your friend. You refuse to do so. Therefore you choose rather to seek the will of God. The affair, then, is no longer in your hands, but in God's and He will be with you. Stand fast in your just cause.'

Becket is often accused of misreading the situation and overstating the issues. It is one of the ironies of history that Becket chose to die for those very issues which most of the churchmen in the time of Henry VIII chose to dismiss as harmless: the restraint of appeals, the submission of the clergy, the diversion of Peter's Pence to the royal benefit and the oath against the papacy.

We all know the rest of the story, Henry's impatient remark about the 'meddlesome cleric', of the triumphal return of Thomas to Canterbury, of his assassination by the four knights in 1170, his canonisation by the Pope less than three years later and the immense devotion and centre of pilgrimage which sprang up at his tomb in Canterbury.

Thomas died for God, for the Pope and the independence of the visible Catholic Church. He was an imperfect instrument in a violent age.

His task is part of our task. However inauspicious the omens, however hostile the clime, the task of each one of us is to preserve the Catholic tradition, the centrality of God, of Christ's love in the Church that is led by the Pope, the Bishop of Rome.

I suspect that Christ does not expect us to be 'successful' in a numerical sense, not even perhaps in a qualitative sense, but he does expect us to retain the tradition, to hold onto the faith.

As TS Eliot concluded *Murder in the Cathedral*:

Forgive us, O Lord, we acknowledge
ourselves as type of the common man,
Of the men and women who shut the door
and sit by the fire;
Who fear the blessings of God, the
loneliness of the might of God, the
surrender refused, the deprivation inflicted,

Who fear the injustice of men less than the
justice of God;
Who fear the hand at the window, the fire
in the thatch, the fist in the tavern, the
push into the canal,
Less than we fear the love of God.
We acknowledge our trespass, our weakness
we acknowledge
That the sin of the world is on our heads;
that the blood of the martyrs and the
Agony of the saints
Is upon our heads.
Lord, have mercy on us.
Christ, have mercy on us.
Lord, have mercy on us.
Blessed Thomas, pray for us.

*Preached at St James Church, Gardenvale
Melbourne, 29 December 1987, Feast of St Thomas*

Our Lady of Lavang and the Vietnamese Martyrs

AS a believing community, we look to Mary and to the saints for example and guidance in our journey to Christ. For the Vietnamese people, this journey has been made on a long and difficult road and we celebrate how those who have gone before us have remained faithful and true to the words of Christ and His Church.

The history of the Church in Vietnam is one of struggle and persecution, from the early days of the Spanish and Portuguese Dominicans who first preached the Gospel there in the sixteenth century. Since then, the faith in Vietnam has been nourished by the witness of many ordinary men, women and children who willingly laid down their lives in witness to their faith. Initially, the Catholic faith spread throughout the country with little opposition. But from the seventeenth century until the nineteenth century, political leaders declared that to be a Christian was to be under the domination of a foreign religion. This was viewed as subversion and civil disobedience. Thus began three centuries of bloody persecution, which was as severe as that 1500 years before in the time of the Roman Empire. It is estimated that as many as 300,000 people were either executed or made to suffer because of their religious convictions.

As happened in other places including Japan, anyone suspected of being a Christian in Vietnam was forced to trample on a crucifix. If the person refused to do so, he or she would be tortured in the most painful ways, or their villages and homes would be destroyed. On 19 June 1988, Pope John Paul II canonized 117 of these martyrs, the largest single group ever in the Church's 2000-year history. The group included bishops, priests, religious, seminarians, laymen and women and even children. The oldest is thought to have been eighty, and the youngest, Joseph Tuc, was only nine years old when he was beheaded in 1862.

It was during the darkest days of the persecution at the end of the eighteenth century that many Christians fled from the forces of King Canh Thinh. They hid in the deep forests of Lavang, near the city of Hue. There was a special tree under which they would gather to say the Rosary. It was during such gatherings that Our Blessed Lady appeared to console them in their sorrow and anxiety. She promised to help them with these words: 'I have heard your prayers. From this day on, whoever comes here to ask for help will have their prayers heard, and I will grant them their desires.' When the persecutions ended, a shrine was built at that place. In 1963 Pope John XXIII declared it to be a minor basilica. In 1972, during another dark period in the history of Vietnam, the Church was destroyed, and it remains so today.

The days of active persecution are behind us, although some hostile pressures remain in Vietnam. For many of you it is impossible to forget how hard it was to live in a country where you were not free, where you did not have the right to practise your faith and to bring up your children in that faith.

Earlier this year I celebrated Mass for the Vietnamese community at Keysborough. It was a very clear and still night. At the end of Mass I saw one of your beautiful customs, where the people turn to face the north, where Vietnam is, and to pray in silence. It was a very beautiful moment, to see so many people in a country so far removed from their home, remembering things that most Australians cannot imagine. In the middle of the congregation at Keysborough that night there was a beautiful gum tree which sheltered many people. It was a symbol of how the Vietnamese community has found shelter in a free country.

It is important that the next generation of Vietnamese Australians do not forget their history. It is very easy in a peaceful country such as Australia to think that the stories told by older people from Vietnam are only stories, and that it could not have been that bad. Young people need to know the truth of their history so that they, in their turn, will not forget the lessons that all of us need to learn.

The most important thing that we need to learn is the importance of our faith in living a truly good life.

The martyrs of Vietnam did not offer up their lives for no reason. They did so because they believed that God's way is different from the way of the world. It takes great courage to believe in Jesus, the one true God, and to be prepared to give up your life for this truth.

Our great example is Mary, the Help of Christians, who was the first to hear the Word of God and keep it completely. From the moment that the angel Gabriel asked her to be the Mother of the Saviour, Mary was faced with a dark and uncertain future. She was confronted with something of unprecedented magnitude, something that required a trust in God reaching into the darkness far beyond human imagining. She gives her answer: Let it be done to me as you have said. In the manner of a great leader, she puts all she has at the disposal of the One she serves.

From that moment until her death, Mary's destiny was shaped by that of her child. This is soon evident in the hardships of the birth of her child in a manger, the threat to her Son's life, which meant that her family had to make a sudden escape and live in a foreign country as refugees. When it was safe to do so, she returned to Nazareth and there worked as any mother does, with all the same cares and concerns.

She would have remembered the disturbing prophecy of Simeon on the occasion of the Presentation of her Son in the Temple. 'A sword of sorrow will pierce your heart, so that the secret thoughts of many will be laid bare.' This sword pierced her heart many times, but she always remained certain that God would be faithful to His promises.

Many years of silence follow. Nothing is recorded of Mary in these years, yet the silence of her heart becomes more profound until that moment when it faced the supreme test. It was in the silence of Calvary that the love of the holiest of mothers was shown. Even under the shadow of the cross Mary still cannot fully understand why her Son should be dying. Like so many mothers in every time and country, but perhaps most especially in Vietnam, Mary suffered with her Son and because of her Son. No one, except a mother, can understand how deep was the wound in her heart. In that way, Mary understands us and our needs. As she said to the little huddle of people under the trees of Lavang, she will never refuse any requests for grace and peace.

In the years ahead, as you come to pray at this Shrine of Our Lady of Lavang and the Martyrs of Vietnam, remember the people of your homeland and of your new homeland and all other people in need, so that we too may know the protection and comfort that comes from the faith, hope and love we share.

Blessing of the Shrine of Our Lady of Lavang and the Vietnamese Martyrs, St Joseph's Springvale, Melbourne, December 1999

5

The Faithful of Tomorrow

For Senior Secondary Students

> *Readings: Ezk 47:1-6, 8-9, 12.*
> *Gospel: John 4:1-38 (Jesus met a Samaritan woman at the well who had had five husbands and told her the man she had now was not her husband. He said whoever drinks the water He would give would never thirst but have a spring of water welling up to eternal life.)*

WE Australians understand the importance of water, the difference it makes. We stand in awe of the outback, a vast desert, usually bone-dry, relentless. But we also appreciate the other side of the coin. We have often seen how the brown, parched countryside greens up, responds to good rains; the dust settles and the bushfire danger recedes.

The Old Testament prophet, Ezekiel, who wrote when the Jews were in exile in Babylon in the sixth century BC, also understood the difference water makes.

The gospel today tells us God is spirit, neither male nor female. We worship an unseen God. The qualities we admire, such as faith, hope and love, or honesty and honour are spiritual and invisible, so spiritual writers have often used images, metaphors such as living water, to explain what genuine religion, the worship of God means in daily life.

Ezekiel spoke of a huge river coming out of the Jerusalem Temple, God's dwelling place at that time, teeming with fish and producing every type of fruit tree in the surrounding countryside. Good, faithful people have this sort of effect on their families, friends and their communities. Fountains of water are a symbol of what we all should be doing, of what you as young adults are now called to do.

Ezekiel also knew that the effects of bad religion can be very different from streams of living water, which can become dangerously polluted. He also has another famous image of a valley full of dry bones; dead, without flesh or sinew or skin. Religiously, they were people whose hope was gone; they were as good as dead.

These are the alternatives, which confront every adult. Not one of us can avoid choosing life or death, love or hate, good or evil, the waters of life or drought and the desert.

Water is also central to the fascinating encounter in St John's Gospel between Jesus and the Samaritan woman at Jacob's well in the village of Sychar.

The Samaritans too were worshippers of the one true God, followers of Abraham and Moses, but there was bad blood, strong mutual prejudices between them and the Jews. The Samaritans would not worship at the Temple in Jerusalem and did not accept the writings of the great prophets, such as Ezekiel. They had also helped the Syrians in their war against the Jews in the second century BC.

What proved to be an important spiritual encounter, a conversion experience for this Samaritan woman and her friends, began with an exchange of basic courtesies and greetings. If Jesus had not spoken, if she had broken off the conversation, none of the spiritual gains could have occurred.

Even by our contemporary standards, the Samaritan woman was interesting and colourful; five husbands and now a partner! Whatever else about her, she liked men!

I wonder though what lay beneath the externals, the confident smile and the banter. We do not know how many of her husbands died or how many divorced her, but those hidden wounds would have been deep. There must have been sorrow and sadness for her, her children, for the men involved. She must have been depressed, perhaps tempted to despair, to believe that in her life nothing worked out. Naturally, she became defensive with Jesus when asked to bring along her husband. 'I have no husband,' she replied.

'You are right there,' Jesus replied, 'because, although you have had five, the one now is not your husband.'

Confronted by this truth, the woman might have lost her temper, abused Jesus for impertinence or simply walked off and left him. She certainly never anticipated being in such deep water when Jesus asked her for a drink.

But she was honest with herself, open to this unusual and spiritual man talking about the living water that takes away our thirst forever. In humility she acknowledged him. 'I see you are a prophet,' she said.

Most Australians today know that right and wrong are important, but many Australians are uncertain whether it is important to believe, to worship our unseen God.

Most of the Jews then had a different approach. To worship God in spirit and truth, to have nothing to do with false gods, was important for them. The Samaritan woman accepted this and knew also that God would send a Messiah, Christ, the anointed one 'to tell us everything'.

It was then that Jesus, Our Lord, said something he never said to His fellow Jews; He acknowledged to her that He was the Messiah. 'I who am speaking to you, I am He.'

This is a beautiful story, which has recurred again and again in history: a wounded person allowing God's love, the cleansing waters of life, into her heart; the person judged least likely to turn to religion being cured and healed by God's love.

Her conversion can be our conversion, if we are honest and open and prepared to pray.

Gladiator

Let us touch on another society, different from our own, but soon after Jesus, where the life-giving waters of Christian faith radically humanized a cruel world.

Many of you will have seen the film *Gladiator* set in the second century under Marcus Aurelius, one of the most enlightened of the pagan Roman Emperors. The brutality of the amphitheatre was mirrored by the brutality of daily life.

My thesis is simple. Christ's teachings were like a river of life-giving water, nourishing and strengthening those who believed in Him in this hostile and savage environment. Christian faith, lived out in daily life, produced a movement of cure and renewal responding to the misery, chaos, fear and oppression of daily life in Rome. They came much closer to a civilization of life

In the beginning was the Word, and the Word was with God and the Word was God.
John 1:1

Jesus Christ, painted by Francisco Argüello, founder of the Neo-Catechumenal Way, in the church of The Most Holy Trinity, Piacenza, Italy.

Through him, all things came into being.
John 1:2

Orion Nebula, about 1600 light years across, photographed by Peter Ward through the telescope of Bishop Chris Toohey of Wilcannia Forbes in outback New South Wales.

The Word became flesh, he lived among us.
John 1:14

Our Lady of Perpetual Help painted by Andrew Molczyk in Corpus Christi Seminary Chapel, Carlton, Victoria.

*His father saw him and was moved with pity. He ran
to the boy, clasped him in his arms and kissed him.*
Luke 15:20

The parable of the Loving Father, or the return of the Prodigal
Son. Painting by Rembrandt Harmensz van Rijn (1606-1669).

They took branches of palm and went out to receive him, shouting: Hosanna! Blessed is he who is coming in the name of the Lord, the King of Israel.

John 12:13

Palm Sunday. Painting by Francisco Argüello, founder of the Neo-Catechumenal Way in the church of The Most Holy Trinity, Piacenza, Italy.

He came back to the disciples and found them sleeping.
Matthew 26:40

The Beginning of the Passion. Paintings by
Mary Anne Coutts in the chapel of Aquinas Campus,
Australian Catholic University, Ballarat.

My God, my God, why have you forsaken me?
Mark 15:34

Mary at the death of Jesus her Son. Painting by
Mary Anne Coutts in the chapel of Aquinas Campus,
Australian Catholic University, Ballarat.

*Till this moment they had still not understood the scripture,
that he must rise from the dead.*

John 20:9

The Resurrection.
Painting by Giotto di Bondone (1266–1337).

Praying to Australia's patron,
Our Lady Help of Christians …
Joseph, Simeon and Rachel Casey in
St Mary's Cathedral, Sydney.

St Therese of Lisieux (1873–1897).
St Mary's Cathedral, Sydney.

Pope John Paul II reverencing the Real Presence of Christ, by carrying the Blessed Sacrament in procession. Typical of a Corpus Christi celebration.

Bronze statue of Archbishop Daniel Mannix,
third Archbishop of Melbourne (1917-1963) by Nigel
Boonham, outside St Patrick's Cathedral, Melbourne.

Mass in the Good Shepherd Seminary Chapel, Sydney.

Gian Lorenzo Bernini's (1598–1680) window and altar
of the chair, in St Peter's Basilica, Rome, where I was ordained
priest on 16 December 1966.

Blessing the Pope John Paul II Building, St Kevin's Parish, Geebung, Brisbane. 20 April 2004.

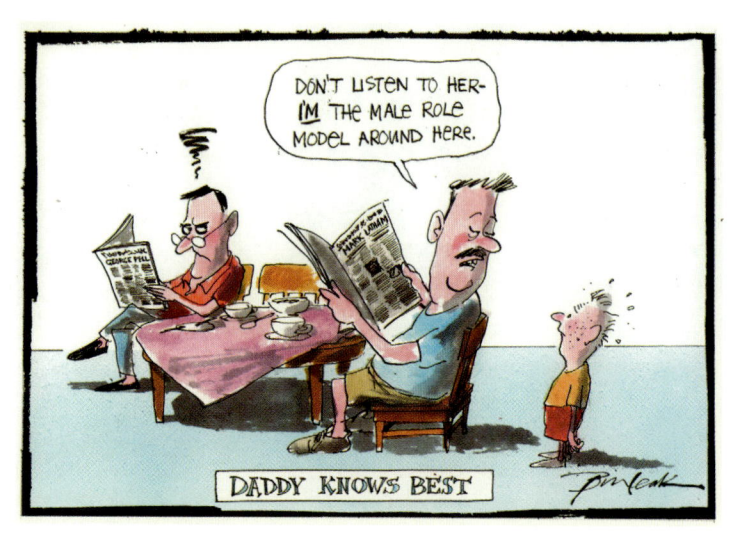

How *The Australian*'s Bill Leak saw the successful opposition to same sex 'marriages'.

and love through Christian living.[1] The improvement was a result of Christian faith.

This was a society where about 40 per cent of the population were slaves, the property of their owners. This was a society where men regularly fought each other, or animals, to the death – and hundreds of thousands of spectators delighted in this spectacle. Rome was a city which rarely produced sufficient babies to keep the population stable and relied on regular migrations. These congregated in mutually antagonistic ghettos and race riots were not uncommon. This was a society where abortion was commonplace, as was infanticide, the killing of the newborn, especially girls who were unwanted in this pagan society where there was such a significant imbalance of the sexes. Life expectancy was less than thirty years; at least half the children died at birth or during infancy and survivors usually lost one parent before maturity!

The main roads were only about 10 metres wide and people lived, often with their livestock, in crowded tenements a few stories high, which often collapsed. Fires were not uncommon and one of the first secular references to Christians was when the Emperor Nero tried to blame them for the great fire there in Rome in 64 AD. Corpses were often dragged from the house and left in the street. For the poor there was no soap, little sanitation and limited dirty water; they lived in filth and stench beyond our imaginings.

Sexual life too was a jungle, where the strong oppressed the weak. We know from the mosaics of Pompeii that nothing was off limits: women, men, boys, girls and animals, and all this was portrayed on the walls

---

1 For a detailed elaboration of this claim, see R Stark, *The Rise of Christianity,* Princeton: Princeton University Press, 1996.

of the bathhouses before the eyes of even the youngest.

What was the early Christians' response to all this? Did they accommodate themselves? Conform to the fashions of the time? Go with the flow, because everyone was doing it?

Enough of them, the best of them, refused to do any such thing. With invincible obstinacy they stuck to Christ's teachings; they sometimes fell, as we do, but they persevered. Christ's teachings sustained, inspired and directed their efforts; gave them life, which spread into the wider community.

To cities filled with the poor and homeless, Christianity offered charity as well as hope. To cities filled with immigrants and strangers, the Christians offered community, friendship. To cities filled with orphans and widows, Christianity offered help and a wider sense of family. To cities torn with ethnic strife and riots, Christianity offered social solidarity. To cities faced with epidemics, fires and earthquakes, Christianity offered effective nursing services. Even Galen, the most famous ancient physician, fled to his country house away from the plague. The Christians stayed and nursed their sick.

The Christians taught a new concept of sexuality, not as an escape, not as recreation, not as another opportunity for the strong to oppress the weak; but sexuality linked to love; the love between a husband and wife, open to fertility, life and children. Therefore, in a society where the male head of the household had a literal power of life and death over its members, where women were oppressed, almost legally powerless, Christianity required men to love and respect their wives as they respect their own bodies. This was a revolution.

Christians taught forgiveness; forgiveness of one another and forgiveness by God for those sins, such as murder, that no human victim can forgive.

And Christianity gave especially to those who suffer, those who mourn, those who struggle for justice in this life, the promise of eternal reward, eternal justice and eternal life.

As young Catholics about to leave school and enter the wider world, the torch is being passed to you. The long twilight struggle, with its hundred-fold reward even in this life, is passing into your hands. Continue to ponder and pray on the strange life of Jesus Christ, whose jubilee we celebrate. Follow His teachings, don't abandon Him simply because you sometimes fail to meet His standards. Pray to Mary His mother and ask her to show you God's love. Take heart from His redeeming death and resurrection. Evil and suffering will not have the last word; that is His message, the meaning of Christ's life. Think on the achievements of the early Christians; of all the good Christians over 2000 years. Remember always that they, like us, got their strength from this same Christ, the living water, which can bring life and health to any spiritual desert. Continue to drink from this stream, work and pray that it continues to bubble up in your heart too, taking you into eternal life.

May God bless and reward you for your enthusiasm and goodness. May you say 'yes' with courage and without hesitation when Christ calls you. May you be able to trust in His promises. May you always choose God and goodness and love.

Homily at senior students' Jubilee Mass,
Rod Laver Arena, Melbourne, 5 September 2000

Seven Rules for 'Fine Young Men and Women'

ONE of the most remarkable characteristics of the Catholic Church is her universality. Today, almost 2000 years after the untimely death of Christ, the faithful gather in all corners of the world, united by His presence and memory. This should also be a consolation to us, as we recognize that the God we serve is not a tribal god of the Irish or the Italians, but the Lord of all history and peoples, who live this same faith in many different ways.

A few years ago, I came across an extraordinary sermon first preached to the university students of Siena, Italy, in 1427. I found it in a collection of letters written for church magazines to characters from history by Archbishop Luciani, when he was Patriarch of Venice, and before he reigned briefly as Pope John Paul I for thirty-three days in 1978.

The sermon was delivered by St Bernadine of Siena (1380–1440), who was born into a noble family at Massa Maritima in Tuscany. His parents died when he was young and he was brought up by an aunt.

Probably the major catalyst for his religious development was a terrible plague which troubled Siena in 1400. At its height there were twenty deaths a day and Bernadine nursed the sick until he himself succumbed. When confronted by sickness – which is one of life's challenges – our response will change us; dry and shrivel our hearts or deepen and enrich us.

On his recovery and after the death of his aunt, Bernadine entered a local Franciscan monastery, which he left after some time for a more isolated monastery of stricter observance where he remained for twelve years. Only after this did he begin his great missionary work throughout Italy. There were 300 members of the Franciscans of Strict Observance when he entered, and 4000 at his death.

In his sermon, he gave seven rules to the students so that they would become fine men and women and I commend these goals to students today for their own personal lives.

> 1. First of all, he urged them to respect learning – knowledge and wisdom – and to love the treasures of their culture. This means lots of reading and discussion. Teachers must love books and introduce their pupils to this world of learning, so that they all come to read well and as many as possible come to love reading and books. Just as certainly we should teach you not to trust books completely, much less our newspapers or the other media, such as television and radio.
>
> But it is especially through books that you will be introduced to the wisdom of the past. It is better to receive great ideas from others than to invent and use ordinary ideas ourselves. A boy on another's shoulders can always see further than any individual, Pascal reminds us. For his part, Bernadine compared a student who won't work to a pig in a sty, who eats, drinks and sleeps.
>
> 2. Bernadine urged as his second point detachment – that is, the ability to give up certain things and stay away from others. Students know the truth of this, but youngsters today probably find it a harder lesson to learn than their predecessors, given the current emphasis on personal fulfilment and

development, the broadening of experience – and doing their own thing.

Bernadine had a long list of things to be avoided, but Pope John Paul I mentioned two in particular, bad company and bad reading. We could all add to the list – drugs, X-rated films, too much alcohol, hard core pornography. But none of us can totally escape the charms of a prosperous, comfortable paganism. Think of a clown selling a piece of string to the peasants so that they won't be kicked by a mule. The peasants were mystified by this useless string until he told them to unroll it and stay that distance away from the mule.

3. Thirdly, Bernadine urges quietness. The mind is like water. When it is still it is clear; if it is always moving it is muddy and unsettled. There is a desperate need for quiet in our society, and as the Pope added, a touch of silence and a pinch of prayer did no one any harm.

4. His fourth point recommended a proper order and balance both in the things of the body and the mind. This is common wisdom, but often forgotten; we recognize it as being true for others, but not applicable to ourselves. But no one can burn the candle at both ends indefinitely.

5. Bernadine next recommended perseverance, contrasting a fly (he would have welcomed the great Australian 'blowie'), rushing noisily to and fro, disturbing and polluting and creating nothing of benefit with a bee buzzing quietly from flower to flower making honey. A weak will is a much greater disadvantage than a low intelligence and

students who are plodders should remember this. Perseverance is much more important in life than intelligence.

6. Discretion is also important, as everyone must suit his aims to his ability. However, for every young person who aims too high there will be four or five who do not aim high enough. Discretion is needed by all of us in other ways, as every adult at different stages in his life is required to decide what he or she really wants and regards as important. However, we should not forget Bernadine's advice: if you chase two hares at once you lose both of them!

7. Bernadine's last rule to his students was that they should enjoy study. Usually when this is mentioned to youngsters today there is a ripple of amazement and nearly always a few laughs. The St explained, however, that this taste or love of study develops slowly and only through overcoming laziness and boredom. It is a prize which does exist and which should be reverenced; it is a prize for the amount of effort that we are prepared to make. Not every student attains this prize, but any true student should work for it.

The Pope when he concluded his article on Bernadine wondered whether the relics of that 1427 sermon would be scattered to the winds or gathered by someone. For better or worse, by reading this far, you have shared them at a place on the other side of the world. Life is like that sometimes.

Bernadine also advised teachers and students: 'Speak clearly so that whoever hears you goes away happy and enlightened, not confused.'

There could be no better advice for now or later.

Adapted from sermons to students in Wagga Wagga, New South Wales, 10 March 1996 and to Catholic teacher Graduates, Aquinas College, Institute of Catholic Education, Ballarat, 13 December 1980

The Parable of the Good Father

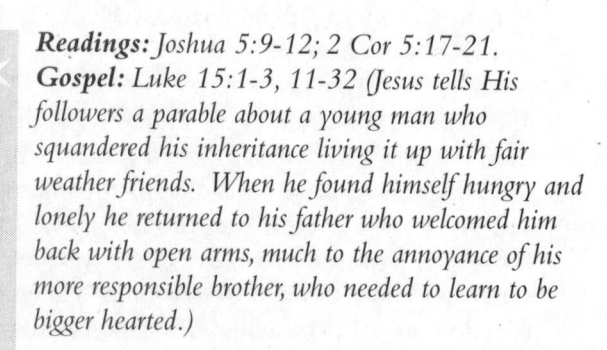

Readings: *Joshua 5:9-12; 2 Cor 5:17-21.*
Gospel: *Luke 15:1-3, 11-32 (Jesus tells His followers a parable about a young man who squandered his inheritance living it up with fair weather friends. When he found himself hungry and lonely he returned to his father who welcomed him back with open arms, much to the annoyance of his more responsible brother, who needed to learn to be bigger hearted.)*

Fourth Sunday of Lent – Year C

WE all know that Our Lord was a wonderful teacher, having more influence than any other teacher in history, and that He was a marvellous storyteller. If we really want to understand what Our Lord is about, the best place to start is in His teachings and particularly with His parables because often they move in unexpected directions.

Probably the best known is the parable of the Prodigal Son. However, it is not really a story about the prodigal son because it is a story about God, about the nature of God. It is the parable of the good father.

The details of the story ring true if we are going to set it in Our Lord's time because the Jews then lived not just in Israel — as we call it today — but throughout the Roman Empire and throughout the Middle East. It is estimated there were about four million of them through the Roman Empire, that is 10 per cent of the total population, and there was half a million at home in Palestine. So the younger brother would have had tons of friends or family, cousins, aunts or uncles, and he would have gone to a Jewish community in some other place.

If we put the story in a contemporary setting we might say that he came from a family which had a good farm in rural Australia. The older brother was very steady, worked at home with his father. A hard worker, he had never given much trouble at all. The younger fellow was a different type altogether, as often happens. He was a wild lad, perhaps he had been up to Queensland for Schoolies' Week, and he wanted to be off. He said to his father, 'Give me my share of the inheritance, I want to go off and make a lot of money and have a lot of fun.' For some reason or other his father agreed, gave him the money equivalent to his share of the farm, and he headed off.

There might have been an economic downturn, it might have been that he could not handle money, was too extravagant with the riotous life that he led; at any rate, he blew the lot. There were no social security provisions then and, as you know, pigs were unclean to the Jews. They do not touch pork. So he sunk as low as a Jew could. The only job where he could get food to put in his mouth was to work with the pigs.

And it was there that the conversion process began. It was not terribly exalted or spiritual, at least initially, because he said to himself, 'I could be home working for

Dad on one of the farms and I would be much better off than I am here looking after the pigs and having to eat their food', and it developed from there. He was able to say, 'yes, I have sinned before God and before my father', and he started to head for home.

The father might have done a couple of things. When he saw him he might have said: 'Lovely to see you son, very strange we never heard from you, not even a telephone call for all those years. Your clearing out and disappearance killed your mother, upset all your sisters terribly and everybody around the house. I will give you a few dollars, I will set you up, but you will have to keep moving. There is too much hurt around here for us to have you back.' Or he might have said: 'Good to see you son. Why didn't we hear from you? Although you hurt many people, I will give you a job on one of the farms at some distance, because if you come back into the family you are going to cause too much trouble. But I will get you a good job and you can make your own way.'

Now the father did neither of those things. He ran out to greet the son. They ate meat very rarely; but he killed the prize calf so that they could have an enormous feast, a great welcome home party. Few people wore shoes; he gave him sandals to show that his dignity had been restored and even fewer people wore a ring and he gave him his ring back to show that he had been restored as a son of the family. It was a very happy return.

Then, as in real life, something goes wrong. The older brother turns up, the steady fellow who had been working at home for years. He says to the servant, 'What is going on, what is all the fuss about?' The servant explains that the young fellow has come home, 'Your young brother whom we haven't heard of for years, everybody is absolutely delighted, we are having a marvellous party.' And the older brother says, 'What are you on about? Here am I, I have been home working for years, never put my foot wrong, day in day out. My Dad's a typical farmer and he doesn't overpay his sons when they are working. He never put on a party like this for me when I had my twenty-first. What do you mean that we are going to have a party for this bloke? The farm is much smaller than it was, he has blown all his money, him and his girlfriends, a life of debauchery, and here we are supposed to be putting on a big party.'

And once again the father did not come out and give him a kick in the tail and say: don't be stupid, get in there and welcome your brother home. He said, 'No, no. Everything I have is yours. The farm is going to be yours. I am deeply grateful for everything you have done. You have done a terrific job, but this young fellow was lost and now he is found. He was dead and now he has come to life.'

It is a most wonderful story about the nature of our loving God, and for older people like myself who were brought up in a world where the Christian teaching was more severe, it is a nice balance, perhaps even a corrective, explaining what God is like. To the young people who have grown up in an entirely different Christian sort of ethos it is also a useful lesson because I am sure that the prodigal son is like many young people today. When things go really wrong their great temptation is to think that they are absolutely worthless, there is nowhere to turn, nobody will welcome them, it is not worth the battling and the striving. In other words, their self-image has been so destroyed by circumstances and their own mistakes, that there is nowhere to go. And this story of the good father reminds them that no matter how many other humans might turn them down, God will always have them back and accept them.

It is a beautiful story and it ties in very well with

Lent. Lent is a time for individual Confession, for a personal celebration of the Sacrament of Penance. For us to follow the example of the Prodigal Son, it doesn't matter whether we are more like the older brother or more like the young fellow, as long as we are battling on trying to do our best, however imperfectly.

Lent is a time for the Sacrament of Penance, of Reconciliation. It is one of the most beautiful services that the Church offers to people. Sometimes it can be a little bit like going to the dentist. I don't think I have ever met anyone who really likes to go to Confession when they are carrying significant guilt, but so many people know and will testify how wonderfully healing and liberating the love of God and the forgiveness of God are in the Sacrament of Penance.

So let us try to move deeper into our heart this image of the God who loves us and always forgives us, the God who welcomed home the Prodigal Son.

Sunday, 25 March 2001,
St Patrick's Cathedral, Melbourne

Remembering to Say 'Thanks'

Gospel: Luke 17:12-18 (Jesus came to a village where he was met by ten lepers who pleaded with Him to cure them. Jesus did so and all but one hurried off without saying 'thank you'.)

Twenty-eighth Sunday in Ordinary Time – Year C

WE have heard the story of the ten lepers many times since childhood. I am pretty certain that we would claim to know what it teaches and am also certain that we have not always practised what it teaches! Before going any further along this line, I might draw your attention to one remarkable feature. The point of the story is not only that one out of ten came back to give thanks; the one who returned was a foreigner, a Samaritan.

The Jews and the Samaritans were divided by history. Although they were like first cousins, the Jews did not speak to Samaritans; it was a little like telling a story here in Melbourne and saying that the only person who came back was perhaps a Crows supporter from Adelaide! All the locals let down the side. Or it is like saying, after the Second World War, though the Samaritan situation was not as bad, that the only person who came back to say thanks was Japanese.

Now what was the point of the story? Can we conjecture that the other nine were not grateful to Our Lord for this colossal miracle? Almost certainly not. Most certainly for the rest of their lives they would have looked back on that miracle with gratitude and regarded Jesus with immense fondness. I suspect though that they were just too busy doing other things. They were racing back to their families, perhaps to tell their husbands or their wives, to tell their children; they were just too excited to say 'thank you'.

So there are many reasons for ingratitude but one of them can be simply that we do not think to express the thanks that are in our heart. I suppose if somebody said to us, those of us who are adults, and adult Christians: 'Are you grateful for what you have?' we would immediately say 'Oh, I hope so!' I hope that I acknowledge all the good things that I have received from so many people. I suppose therefore that the parable of the ten lepers is a story to jolt us into examining our own consciences to see whether we practise what we preach on gratitude.

Many of you would have heard me talk many times about the levels of faith, whether faith is really biting in our lives, whether it is a real force. The first level is whether we pray to God when we are in trouble: in our heart of hearts and in our secret moments do we ask God for help or for strength or to change the situation, 'Give us this day our daily bread'.

The second level of faith is to thank God for the good things that we have, and this is higher and better. So a number of questions: are we grateful to those around us? Do we say thanks to God? Or are we sometimes or regularly like a young child? When a young child has been given a present he is often absolutely consumed unwrapping it, pulling it out, seeing how it works. Then mum or dad has to say to the child, 'Now, say thank you to Aunty Jean (or Uncle Bill or your grandparents) who gave you that present'. The child looks up and quickly says 'Thanks a lot', and then goes back to the present. That is one of the characteristics of being young.

Are we a bit like this? Are we like unpleasant teenagers, our antennae geared primarily to the difficulties and the insufficiencies of those around us, more likely to complain of mum's cooking when she prepares something that we don't like rather than regularly saying thank you for all the care that we receive. What of the things that our father might do for us, running us here, running us there, helping in a thousand ways.

Occasionally you will hear the grotesque example of somebody saying 'I've made it entirely on my own, I owe nothing to anybody, I did it myself'. This is frightful nonsense of course; completely impossible because if all of us received nothing from anybody we would be social and moral cripples. We need love in order to flourish. Those who make their way in the world with some degree of success do it because of the love and the help they receive from their families, their schools, their friends and relations: or from someone. Nobody contributes who is helped by no one.

Are we so absorbed by our little misfortunes (they might be big misfortunes) that we really say on balance, 'Well, I haven't got too much to be grateful for. What's God done for me?' Sometimes we need a shock to recognize the truth; and going around visiting the sick I have frequently received that. You can see people in the greatest extremities but coping with it in faith, marvellously and they will say, 'Of course, Father, I'm so much better off than some others'. You can nearly always find examples of people who are suffering at a greater level.

It is strange that Our Lord Himself never preached too much about the need to give thanks although in His own prayers giving thanks to His Father was certainly one characteristic. But with St Paul it was quite different. St Paul emphasized again and again the need to give thanks. Even the word for Eucharist – *Eucharistia* – is the Greek word for giving thanks.

I want to conclude by mentioning two or three examples which are reasons for immense gratitude. Most of us here in Australia live better at a material level than 95 per cent or 98 per cent of all the people who have ever lived. You have only to take a trip up to Papua New Guinea or Indonesia or the Philippines and see how the great mass of the people live there. Happy lives but much simpler, much physically tougher lives than ours.

The first reason for gratitude, moving from the cure of the ten lepers, is the wonderful medical system that we have. We hear about its problems, the shortage of money, and all that is true. But I have visited hospitals in the Vietnamese countryside, where there was not one piece of equipment and there was not one item of medicine. Many, many countries of the world have nothing like the level of health care that we enjoy in this country.

Secondly, we have been forced to re-evaluate our ordinary everyday way of life by the explosion down in the (Gippsland) gasworks. For many of us the biggest suffering was not to have a hot shower. But thousands of people were put out of work. We usually have the blessing of a hot shower every day, one of the great centrepieces of the Australian way of life. We seem to have better organized showers than they do in many other parts of the world! Getting up on a cold Melbourne morning with no hot water for a shower makes us realize just how dependent we are on luxuries we regard as basic.

The third area which we often take for granted is our political life, the stability we enjoy politically here in Australia. We have an election; both sides accept the result, life goes on. Each one of us is able to vote and choose our democratic masters. I took that for granted until I went as an observer for the Catholic Church to the first free all-race elections in 1994 in South Africa. Three out of the four Catholic archbishops there had never voted; three-quarters or seven-eighths of the population had never voted. It was deeply moving to see enormous queues of people waiting patiently for the opportunity to vote for the first time in their life.

In Australia we should also be grateful for the general level of probity and propriety in our politicians; it is not the same in many other countries. Very few of our politicians become rich while they are in parliament; that is certainly not the case in many other parts of the world.

Children unconsciously are self-centred and have to be trained, to learn to say thanks. One of the characteristics of an adult, one of the characteristics of a Christian adult, is that we are able to say thanks, especially to those who are closest to us. We should also remember in gratitude all our benefactors, and especially God our Father. For whatever reason we should not be like the nine lepers who did not come back to Jesus to say thanks.

11 October 1998, St Patrick's Cathedral, Melbourne

Saying 'Yes' to God in our Hearts

Readings: *Wis 2:1, 12-22 (Writing in Greek, the unknown author of the Book of Wisdom describes how obnoxious a good and just follower of God seems to evil doers.)*
Gospel: *John 7:1-2, 10, 25-30.*

WE are gathered in Rome, the centre of the Catholic world, from many nations to worship the one true God, by remembering and making present again the unique sacrifice of His only Son, Our Lord Jesus Christ. Many of you know Jesus Christ well. Some of you might only be beginning your journey of discovery. Some of you might still be searching, unsure of your path.

As someone who has followed Christ for many years, I can say that it is a beautiful journey, which brings meaning, purpose and peace. I can personally recommend it.

Our unity is built around Christ and as we move closer to Easter, around the mystery of the Redemption. But as a preliminary, I want to share a thought or two on the mystery of the Church's universality and unity.

Universality does not mean uniformity. We

only have to glance at the different national styles in different Catholic countries; to remember the exotic parade through history of hermits, widows, monks, the thirteenth-century Franciscans and Dominicans, the Counter-Reformation Jesuits, the wave of new religious orders in the nineteenth century, and the variety of new religious movements in the late twentieth century. We Catholics are certainly not like peas in a pod.

A controversial French Jesuit priest, palaeontologist and theologian, Pierre Teilhard de Chardin spoke of the axis of hominization passing through Rome, the local Church which was the home of Peter and Paul, and today home of the successor of Peter, our Holy Father the Pope.

It is not easy to maintain unity among religious enthusiasts. Look at the different religious orders who are sons of St Francis of Assisi. Fifteen or twenty years ago I read somewhere that there were 22,000 small evangelical Christian groups in the USA. A few years ago I read that there were now 40,000 such groups.

Our unity founded on Christ, protected by the Pope and the bishops, is a wonderful gift. It explains why Catholics are instinctively universalist. But it can never be taken for granted. It is not an automatic right and entitlement.

Today's readings speak about the struggle between good and evil, in which everyone of us is obliged to join, and which is central to understanding Jesus' crucifixion.

As we contemplate Jesus' suffering and death, we must never forget that He is also the only Son of God, the second person of the Blessed and eternal Trinity.

The one true God is not simply the Lord of history, but the Creator of the universe which began at least 13.8 billion light years ago with the Big Bang (according to most cosmologists). I am told there are all sorts of problems with this. The Hubble telescope has discovered formed stars 13.3 billion light years away. This does not fit the theory, as they should have been soupy, not stars with planets. Perhaps the Big Bang is even further away. Moreover, the galaxies are not moving at a uniform speed.

I am no scientist. The particulars are interesting, but quite subordinate to my principal claim that God is the creator and sustainer of this universe and it was God's only Son, through whom all things were made, who was crucified.

In a recent interview a reporter explained to me that she understood a God of love, compassion and forgiveness, but did I really believe God created the entire universe, all these stars which are more numerous than the grains of sand scattered over the entire earth? Yes, I replied. In fact if God did not create the universe He would not be God. She lapsed into silence.

Life itself is a mystery. In faith we know it is a mystery of love, but it is also scientifically mysterious. There is so much we do not know. All the evidence so far shows that humans are alone in the universe. The Son of God probably had nowhere else He could go except to Planet Earth! But why does God move so slowly? What was the purpose of the dinosaurs?

This is not entirely a self-indulgent digression because the Creator God of the Universe is the Father of Jesus His only Son, who suffered and died for us. We should not forget this.

As I mentioned earlier the first reading captures well that dimension of struggle between good and evil which is at the heart of the redemption.

This Book of Wisdom is among the most worldly-wise, philosophical and somewhat pagan books in the Old

Testament, but the author understood how obnoxious a truly holy person can be to evil doers; 'he is the censure of our thoughts; merely to see him is a hardship for us.'

We even have something of a preview of the discussion between the good and bad thieves on their crosses with the dying Jesus. After the wicked have plotted to put the good man to the test, they boast that 'if the just one be the Son of God, he will defend him and deliver him from the hand of his foes'. 'Let us condemn him to a shameful death; for according to his own words God will take care of him.'

These are like the words of the bad thief, who upbraided Jesus to get them all out of their predicament, if He was who He claimed to be.

We are all called to acknowledge Christ as our leader and teacher. Please God we shall always be among those Jesus described in St John's gospel as 'those who know me and also know where I am from'.

We are also called to accept His teachings, all of them, and join Him in the struggle to proclaim the good news, to live it out in our hidden personal lives and to bear public witness in the myriad ways appropriate to our vocation and personality.

Christ and the Church need young leaders and servants, with hearts on fire for the love of God; not just fair-weather friends, but those willing to enter into the struggle.

Do not conclude that because you are young you can do very little. Yesterday was the feast of the Annunciation, when we remember that a young Jewish girl (whom we would now describe as a teenager, although there were no teenagers then) called Mary, said yes to God and allowed the Incarnation to go forward. All of us, young or old, wise or impetuous, lay person, priest or religious are also called to do God's will. It is the ultimate test.

When we say yes in our hearts and act on it, we do what we should and we cannot know what good consequences will follow from it.

At the beginning of these few words I mentioned the universality of the Catholic Church and as I conclude I return to that theme. In every age and in every continent there have been witnesses to Christ, enthusiastic protagonists for good in the struggle against evil. And in some, perhaps many ages and countries there have been a few who try to kill Christians, as they were trying to kill Christ in Jerusalem before the Passion.

We do not need to go back to the Roman martyrs of the early centuries in this city for examples of heroism. We can find many such examples much closer today. We might begin with the entire families of the Neo-Catechumenal Way, husband, wife, children who leave their homeland to set up a new life for Christ in strange and distant lands, such as Australia. Or the young African priest, a convert from Islam, trained here in Rome not so long ago, who returned home to have his eyes gouged out. There was Father Vincent, a Chinese Jesuit priest now deceased, irrepressibly talking to me in English of Thomas More and Newman, who was jailed for about sixteen years, some spent in isolation, some spent with 6 inches of water always at the bottom of his cell.

And Cardinal Todea from Romania, educated like myself at Propaganda Fide College here in Rome, in his case in the thirties, who was in solitary confinement in jail for many years so that on his release he could not contain his enthusiasm for Christ and the Church (nor his talking). I saw a marvellous photo of the Pope visiting Todea in Romania as he was old and dying.

We are the children of witnesses. We are the descendants of many generations of martyrs, teachers and workers who have followed Christ Our Lord, often at great cost, sometimes paying the ultimate price.

To all you young people I say simply: Go and do likewise.

Homily preached to young people from many countries at the International Youth Centre, San Lorenzo, Rome, 26 March 2004

School Days

FOR 100 years, young Australian boys have been led to Catholic manhood by the Christian Brothers in this College, St Patrick's, Ballarat.

We are gathered here at Mass to thank the one great God for this achievement, to express through these prayers our gratitude to all the staff, religious and lay, who have taught and worked here and to ask God's blessing on this community of learning so that it will always remain a vital source of faith and light for the nation and the Church.

Ours is not a history of easy and confident progress. The comparative financial security we now enjoy through government funding, the fruit of a long and bitter struggle, did not exist for three-quarters of the College's history and the College, and indeed all Catholic schools, only survived through the financial sacrifices of parents and the fact that the brothers, most of the staff then, worked for pocket money and not for anything like real wages. Their workload was often enormous.

St Pat's opened in 1893, the year of the great bank crash, which crippled the colony of Victoria financially and provoked waves of emigration to most other parts of the English-speaking New World. My grandfather was one who moved on to Perth as Victoria lost more people by migration in the fifteen years after 1891 than it had gained in the previous thirty years. Three hundred state schools had to close. It was the worst possible time for a new secondary school – ambitious to prepare boys for Melbourne University and the public service. The first college on this site had been opened by the Holy Ghost fathers and brothers and the first school buildings here, chapel, dormitory, class rooms and refectory, were a replica of their prestigious Blackrock College buildings in Dublin.

The 1880s were also a boom time of extravagance, excitement and financial errors, such that when Dr Thomas Carr, Archbishop of Melbourne, opened Holy Ghost College on 9 February 1889 the Ballarat clergy presented Fr Joseph Reffe, the first rector, with a purse of 1132 gold sovereigns for the school; a fabulous sum for the times. But by the end of 1891 the school was closed and the Holy Ghost Fathers returned to Europe.

St Patrick's College could therefore be described as a second bite at the cherry.

James Moore, the Bishop of Ballarat at that time, was a determined and formidable man and no doubt the Christian Brothers had learned from the previous fiasco as they started again.

Early progress was slow, although of the first three students presented for matriculation, two became priests and the other became Sir Hugh Devine, one of Australia's greatest surgeons. The earliest years of this century saw spectacular academic success and the invincibility at football had begun. The legend was building.

St Patrick's College is now steeped in tradition. Few boys' schools are so aware of their story or have it evidenced so lavishly on their walls. Two great depressions, and two World Wars have come and gone and the College has been enriched and emboldened by the contributions of her old boys in every walk of life. In fact the SPC tradition reminds me somewhat of that misdirected loyalty of so many people for the Collingwood football club in the way both loyalties include people of every age group, every social strata and nearly every level of religious enthusiasm.

While St Pat's has produced sinners as well as Sts (and a larger number of priests than any other school in Australia[1]), from the beginning the College has been unambiguously Catholic and never apologized for the importance it attached to religion, to following Christ. This is a constant from the Annual Report of 1894 where Br Ryan explained that 'education without religion is not sound' to the present emphasis in the school's mission statement on integrating religious faith with everyday living, with the world of the adolescent.

Catholicism is one core element at the heart of the SPC tradition, not just as a religious backdrop for important occasions, but as a freely chosen value which has sustained boys and men in their darkest hours and inspired them to the most noble sacrifices, sometimes visible but usually hidden.

A boys' secondary school is about the making of men, not coarse chauvinists, but real men of strength, compassion and sensitivity. It is about the curbing of aggression, the recognition, commendation and exercise of leadership, about developing an instinct for self-discipline and excellence. It values unselfishness, and prizes courage and cheerfulness in bad times. All this is a tall order, but it is what Catholic boys' schools are about.

For my generation it was Br WT O'Malley who

---

1 310 priests at last count including four bishops.

was the embodiment and the supreme initiator into this SPC tradition. He compared us constantly and unfavourably to our predecessors. Each group was irritated by this; many of us genuinely fearful of being unable to match the achievements, religious, academic and sporting of our 'ancestors'. In many ways we were shamed into 'lifting our game', into a better performance. All of us were touched in some way, while some were branded irretrievably!

However I do not want to idealize any of these years, nor mislead the present generation of students. Few of our teachers wore their hearts on their sleeves and justice until fairly recently was pretty rough and ready. While few of us got more than we deserved, the last time I received a clip on the ears (except perhaps on the football field) was from WT O'Malley in Inter A (now Year 10). My misdemeanour was that I did not stand up quickly enough when the priest came into the classroom. The fact that I was as tall as I am now (although certainly slimmer and more agile) and that I had to extricate myself from a tiny old-fashioned desk availed me nothing against his righteous fury!

Nor do I want to make any inflated claims for the religious enthusiasms of my generation, despite the fact that the retreats were conducted in silence, most day-boys visited the chapel to pray on arriving and leaving school each day, while the boarders went to Mass five times a week and said the rosary together every night.

In those days smoking was not politically incorrect, nor recognized as a health hazard and there was a regular group who tried to escape night prayers for a 'weed' (as smoking was then called). Sometimes too in order to shorten proceedings the Year Nines during the rosary would try to start the 'Glory be to the Father' to end the decade after five or six Hail Marys (rather than the requisite ten). However when the chips were down in some way or other very few of my generation, or the earlier ones, were unwilling or unable to pray and to mean what we said. Our teachers were able to draw on deep reservoirs of popular piety and religious imagery to achieve this although the formal teaching of religion was usually straightforward, and sometimes boring, with few concessions or frills.

What about the future? I am confident that the range of educational opportunity, the pursuit of academic standards, the level of personal care, the sense of community and tradition, the enthusiasm for sport, competitive and recreational, will all remain strong. The fiercest challenge will be to retain devotion to Christ and loyalty to the Catholic tradition among the inner passwords of the student community; real values when the students are completely free to be themselves, one with another, or in the privacy of their hearts. Will religion inspire the old boys of tomorrow to duty and service or will too many of them slide easily into the scramble for money, comfort and pleasure?

I have a short check-list for the present senior students to judge their own level of religious commitment and that of the student community.

• Do you pray when you are in trouble, whether the trouble be from family, or romances, or exams or sport? How regularly do you thank God for the good things you have?

• Do you believe in the power of God's forgiveness; that He can and will wipe the slate clean of your secret shame and guilt, provided you are genuinely sorry? Do you ever go to the Sacrament of reconciliation?

- Do you believe some activities are right and some are plain wrong? Or is the grey of uncertainty the only moral colour?

- Have you a genuine concern for the underdog?

- Do you admire the Christian ideal of life-long marriage? How close have you drifted to the values and practice of our condom culture with easy access to soft and hard porn videos?

- Are the students who regularly practise their religion prepared to defend this and explain their faith, or are they cowed into silence in student discussion?

- Are there still conversations in each graduating year about which year-members might become priests or brothers?

In other words, do you want to see the light?

Homily from the Centenary Mass for my old school, St Patrick's College, Ballarat, 21 March 1993

For Catholic Secondary Principals

YOUR role as principals of big secondary schools is important humanly and academically – but it is also of vital significance religiously. I thank you for your efforts. You are Catholic leaders who are in the front rank of the religious struggle today.

For most of your pupils, you will be the Church leader they know best; your school community will be the touchstone by which they judge the wider Church, as only a minority are likely to be regular members of a parish. It will be in your school communities that the almost universal goodwill among Catholic primary school students will change, as your adolescents are battered by the world around them.

I want to say a few words about the religious situation in Melbourne, to outline the pressures on us. In Melbourne there are 1,000,000 Catholics – 137,000 Catholic school children. Of this number 18 per cent are Mass-goers; made up of 24 per cent above fifty years of age, 11 per cent up to fifteen or sixteen years old and 6 per cent of those in their twenties.

Here lies the explanation of our slow continuing decline in Mass-goers. The logic of these figures is inescapable. The cohort of young people is clearly our greatest religious challenge and you are perhaps the most important agents for the Church in this life and death struggle. A few basic perspectives follow necessarily from all this:

- As Principals, you have to be people of faith;

- As Principals, you have to know that there is a spiritual war going on;

- As Principals, you have to realize that immense consequences for this world and the next life follow from your efforts in this struggle.

In a group recently talking about explaining faith

to young people and to outsiders, the following claims were made:

> The young do not believe in sin.
> The young cannot understand biblical language.
> Youths would reject outright, e.g. the possibility of Lazarus being raised from the dead.

It dawned on me that the problem was less that young people could not believe these claims, the problem was that we Christians did not believe them; or were too embarrassed to express them in the face of opposition, or were intellectually outgunned by the demolitionist scripture scholars.

So here is a list of questions, without answers:

What is the status of our Easter faith?

Are we worried about the moral failures, confusion and scepticism of our pupils – as worried as we are with their academic progress?

Would the students see us as someone for whom the faith matters vitally?

The struggle between good and evil takes place in every age. Peter and Judas are different examples of failure.

In our schools, there are many dimensions to the struggle, e.g. the struggle for justice; community; marriage and family; sexuality and pornography.

Do your teachers know there is a spiritual war on?

Is your Religious Education Co-ordinator a vital ally, fellow leader or someone whose place has to be filled?

Is the religious education area the first to be cut back, postponed or job left vacant for a few months to save a few dollars?

Do we and our students have a vivid belief in life after death? Has it dawned on them that the reward of heaven is not inevitable? That all of us, as we go through life, are choosing between good and evil, faith and doubt, hope and despair? That each of us as we progress through life builds his own heaven or hell?

I wish to commend to you *The Rise of Christianity*, a study of the first 300 years of Christian history under the pagan Roman emperors by a contemporary agnostic sociologist, Rodney Stark. It has important lessons for us today.

Recently, Stark was interviewed about religion today, about our temptation to make the situation easier to attract young people to Christ. He was asked, 'Many churches are lowering the bar to make religion more popular. How would you analyse their efforts?'

Rodney Stark replied, 'They're death wishes. People value religion on the basis of cost, and they don't value the cheapest ones the most. Religions that ask nothing get nothing. You've got a choice: you can be a church or a country club. If you're going to be a church, you'd better offer religion on Sunday. If you're not, you'd better build a golf course. ... If religion gets too cheap, nobody pays the price.'

I believe he is right. May that simple truth also be our conviction.

Address to the Association of Principals of Catholic Secondary Schools of Australia, 18 April 2000

6
Love and Life

The New Age

ALL the great religious traditions are different and teach different doctrines. For example, Christianity, Judaism and Islam differ substantially from Buddhism because Buddha himself did not teach about God. However one ancient way of looking at life has re-emerged, which asserts that the Christian era ('the Age of Pisces') is ending and the Age of Aquarius is beginning.

It claims particular religions, especially the great religions are 'out'; to be quarried for bits and pieces to fit the 'New Age' spirituality.

The 'New Age' claims to offer freedom, authenticity and self-reliance. It celebrates femininity rather than masculine domination, 'right brain' intuitive thinking rather than the exaltation of reason, the 'left brain'. It encourages the revival of ancient pagan religions, especially from the East, and also uses counter-cultural elements from modern psychology, philosophy and science.

The 'New Age' is not a single, uniform religion

or movement, not a sect. In fact it is a re-emergence of the Gnostic movements (from the Greek word for knowledge) of the second and third centuries, which is very different from New Testament Christianity.

The 'New Age' does not accept the existence of a transcendent, personal God and denies the existence of any spiritual authority higher than inner personal experience. The 'New Age' 'god' is not the creator and sustainer of the universe, but the 'life principle', the soul of the world, an immanent impersonal energy, which forms a cosmic unity.

There is no God capable of hearing our prayers, much less capable of answering them in the 'New Age' system.

Often Christian language is retained but given a different set of meanings. So there are many historical figures in whom the 'Christic' nature is revealed, such as Buddha and Jesus.

The 'New Age' universe is a single whole, an ocean of energy and each person is a hologram, an image of all creation. Dualism is rejected, so there is no distinction between good and evil. Nobody needs forgiveness or condemnation, because human actions are the fruit either of illumination or ignorance. Believing in evil creates negativity and fear, to be answered by love, which is energy, a high frequency vibration, tuned into the great chain of being.

The 'New Age' has seen a surge in cosmic religiosity, the resacralisation of the earth. The warmth of Mother Earth removes the threat of judgment by the Father-God of Judaism and Christianity. But it also removes all possibility of justice and redress in the next life for those who have suffered, are victims of history.

Any worthwhile achievement requires us to work hard. The 'New Age' purification through self-awareness costs very little. Conversion from evil is not required and consequently their search for the 'god within' often leaves selfishness unaddressed and the social problems of society untouched.

Jesus Christ is not a pattern in nature, but a human-divine figure who reveals God's love for us.

The Sunday Telegraph, *21 December 2003*

Anzac Day

ANZAC Day is our most important national day. Historically it was a major source of national identity for the new Federation of Australia which had only come into being in 1901. After the First World War those in Australia with English blood, Scottish, Irish and Welsh blood were welded together by a common suffering into a new level of unity. This national feast day deepened in significance during the Second World War which witnessed a titanic struggle against the forces of evil in which the defenders of freedom, the Allies, emerged victorious. Of course many, many people today have no personal memory of that great struggle.

What are we doing on every ANZAC Day? Are we glorifying war? We are doing nothing of the sort. Catholics and all Christians are opposed to war, as we should be opposed to adultery. Few, if any groups, are as opposed to war as ex-servicemen because they know first-hand of the sufferings of body and mind which accompany and follow these terrible struggles.

Once in a while we hear of people espousing peace at any cost, people unable to think of any cause for which they would die. There have been Christian pacifists, heroic Christian pacifists, but it is not my option. From the earliest years the Christian tradition has recognized the right to self-defence. It is completely true that without the people who were prepared to risk their lives, in fact to give their lives for us, especially in the Second World War, we would not have our freedom today.

ANZAC mythology is close to the Christian teaching on redemptive suffering and redemption even through human failure. There was no medal struck for Gallipoli because it is not a British tradition to strike medals for defeats. Yet in some ways defeats are at the centre of Australian mythology – first of all and pre-eminently Gallipoli, but even events like the Eureka Stockade and more controversial subjects like Ned Kelly. Christians believe that unless the grain of wheat dies there is no harvest.

War is always a cancer but like cancer war can sometimes produce heroism and remarkable self-sacrifice. Until we have equalled for a better cause the enthusiasm and the sacrifice of those men and women who died to defend us, we certainly have no right at all to disparage their achievement or to deny our debt to them. So I believe that whether we are young or old, whether we might be tempted to be a warmonger or a pacifist, patriot, nationalist or self-seeking cynic, this epitaph on the cliff-face at Gallipoli is still correct:

> *Bow and listen. This is where an age sank.*
> *This quiet mound is where the heart of a nation throbs.*

Many years ago I was preparing to celebrate a Mass for ANZAC Day and was talking with the young altar servers. One of them said to me, 'Father, I don't think I could hack a war'. It was an honest and beautiful comment. My prayer on every ANZAC Day is that young Australians will never again have to die for our country. I am not sure this prayer will be answered.

The Sunday Telegraph, *Anzac Day 2002*

Harry Potter

LAST Tuesday I saw the film *Harry Potter and the Philosopher's Stone*. I had read the book some time ago and thoroughly enjoyed it. The film was OK too.

One newspaper claimed that the author, an Englishwoman with a young daughter, was the most successful writer in English since Shakespeare. Many other books and films have been marketed slickly, but never succeeded like Harry. What is the secret of his appeal?

I like a good different escapist read, which has to be well written, to take me into other worlds. Would Harry's magic work with me too?

I still read a lot; all sorts of things. I probably owe this gift to a young Christian Brother, my teacher in grade five, who launched us into the many kingdoms of fiction. Being able to read easily is the key to all knowledge and we have to be grateful to any new author who can entice millions of young readers into this adventure, and expand their imaginations.

Eleven years old in the first book, Harry Potter is a wizard whose parents were killed in the struggle against evil. When he goes to Hogwarts, the boarding school for witchcraft, this struggle is resumed. The language is crisp and powerful, the plot is complicated and fast moving, with unexpected turns.

Often when we read a book beforehand, we don't like the characters in the film version, but most viewers seem to have liked the way Harry, and his friends Ron and Hermione (the film taught me how this name was pronounced) were cast. So too with the adults.

The headmaster Dumbledore, a venerable patriarch, the deputy Minerva McGonagall (what a great name), the giant Hagrid, the nasty teacher Snape are all well known English character-types, populating an unusual Gothic school building set in an exotic countryside.

Some Christians have criticized both book and film as giving respectability to witchcraft, to the occult world of good and bad magic. To my mind there is not much danger of this, because the world of fantasy is so extreme, such a clever and unusual stimulation of the imagination. It is clearly unreal; interesting and totally peculiar.

More importantly the book (and the film, which differs slightly) are full of good moral teaching just like traditional fairy stories. Harry learns that his parents were killed by the evil Lord Voldemort, and the story tells how he and his two friends continue this fight, conquer their fears, and put themselves at risk for one another as loyal friends. Ron is prepared to sacrifice his life in the chess game so Harry and Hermione can find the stone, and prevent it being used for evil purposes.

I happen to believe that it is important for all of us, and children, to learn that good and evil are real spiritual forces, that each of us has to commit himself against evil. Voldemort lied to Harry that there is no good or evil, only power, that his parents were cowards; and in a final violent physical struggle Harry triumphed and good prevailed. All of us, and especially the young, need to be reminded good is more powerful and will have the last word.

When Harry was obsessed by the image of his dead parents, his headmaster explained there was neither knowledge nor truth in that apparition. But there is a good dose of moral truth in Harry Potter, book and film. And it is a great yarn.

The Sunday Telegraph, *9 December 2001*

The Return of the King: Parable for the Modern Age

Why is *The Lord of the Rings* so popular?

One youngster told me that *The Return of the King* was twice as good as the first two films. I agree.

What won me over? What in today's world is bringing tens of millions of people to watch this grotesque morality play, more brilliant than anything available in the Middle Ages?

First of all it is a prodigious feat of imagination. Artists can share in the work of God's creation to adorn or despoil it. Tolkien created a whole new world of Middle Earth, coherent in every detail, fantastic and spectacular, brought to us in colour in the savage New Zealand countryside, so unlike Australia's.

The film is also full of enjoyable old-fashioned violence, enormous massed battles between the forces of good and evil. Our choice for good is made easier because the evil are ugly and frightening, often not human.

Tolkien knows human nature, the allure of evil, and the corruption that accompanies power, the possession of the ring. The odious little Gollum, debating right and wrong with himself (Smeagol), is recognized by every one. If evil seems beautiful, ultimately it is ugly, anti-life, hate filled.

Sauron's Mordor was a dying land, where things grew harsh, twisted, bitter and even the buds were maggot ridden.

On the other side, inspired by goodness, we find that honour and courage are valued, required of those beyond the grave and after death; that courage is infectious, that ordinary beings will make sacrifices for great and good causes. Brave and clear headed leaders persuade their followers to fight for good when there seems little chance of victory.

These are grand, age-old themes and most people love them, but there is an unexpected twist.

Frodo, the saviour, is not a hero, not even a man, but a hobbit, a halfling, who perseveres, knows depression, is tricked by lies to distrust Sam his protector. Neither does he administer strict warrior justice, as he spares Gollum, shows mercy. Without Gollum the ring could not have been destroyed.

Many people like to escape their everyday surrounds through a film or a book. *The Return of the King* is escapism, but Tolkien claims it is not an escape without a destination, not 'scientification', using improved means to inferior and ugly ends.

In fact we arrive at the most important point of the traditional fairy story, the consolation of a happy ending, a good catastrophe. A sudden miraculous grace, which will not recur, achieved in spite of sorrow and failure; 'joy beyond the walls of the world, poignant as grief'.

Much modern art is alienated or deeply unhappy, materialist and elitist, designed to appeal only to a few with superior knowledge.

Tolkien's masterpiece (and the film too will be

acknowledged as a classic) is deeply spiritual, hope inspiring, and accessible to all, young and old, educated and less educated.

The Sunday Telegraph, *18 January 2004*

Organ Donors

CRICKET legend David Hookes was buried the day after Australia Day, killed by a senseless act of violence. His family chose to honour his life and respond to his death by agreeing to the donation of David's organs to medicine.

Donating organs isn't like donating clothes or money. Pope John Paul II has said: 'it is not just a matter of giving away something that belongs to us but of giving something of ourselves.' This donation is unique: organ donors offer the gift of themselves. They reverse the tragedy of their deaths by making continued healthy life possible for others. Many people who might have been saved died because no organ transplant was available. Donations have not increased in ten years.

The Church encourages people to consider this selfless choice. We believe that after death the body will rise again. But God does not need all of the body to lie together in one grave in order to perform the miracle of resurrection. The body will rise as Jesus rose – healthy, integrated, restored.

Australians like to think of themselves as great givers, people who won't walk past others when they're down. In fact, I think this Good Samaritan self-image is a bit inflated. Do we really give as much to charity as people do in other affluent countries? In any case, considering organ donation shows we are serious givers, not just takers.

But gifts mean nothing if they're given grudgingly. Nobody should feel pressured into ticking the organ donation box on the driver's licence. This is a sensitive and very personal choice.

Decisions affecting our dying are also decisions which involve our loved ones deeply. People will be grieving, confused, vulnerable. Organ donation is best discussed in the family when we are still hale and hearty. Talking about death is not comfortable; nor should it be. But it gives us a chance to prepare and to support our families' decision-making in the future.

People should also be well-informed about what donation involves. In particular, they should be assured that nothing will happen until we are morally certain death has occurred.

As a Christian, I believe that in death as in life the human body must be respected and treated reverently at all times. It must certainly never be treated as a field for 'harvesting' organs. Respect also extends to family members, who should be encouraged to have as much time and information as they need when a death has occurred.

When tragedy strikes, people want some good to come of it. We all owe a debt to David Hookes' family, to the many families who have responded in the same way previously, and to all donors. We can best repay them by at least considering organ donation.

The Sunday Telegraph, *1 February 2004*

Abortion: Roe v. Wade

WHEN you win a court case you don't normally seek to have the decision overturned. But that's what the winner of one of the most notorious twentieth-century cases has been trying to do.

Norma McCorvey is better known as 'Roe', the name her lawyers gave her in the lawsuit *Roe v. Wade* which ended up in the US Supreme Court and legalized abortion in America.

In 1969 McCorvey was in her early twenties and pregnant. She wanted an abortion but this was illegal under Texas law. She met an activist lawyer who was trying to have the abortion laws overturned, and they sued the local district attorney.

A series of appeals followed, and in 1973 the United States Supreme Court found it was unconstitutional for any state to intrude 'into matters so fundamentally affecting a person as the decision whether to bear or beget a child'.

The decision came too late for McCorvey to have an abortion. She went on to work as an abortion activist. Later, after a conversion in the 1990s, she established her own pro-life group.

As *Wall Street Journal* columnist Peggy Noonan reminded Americans, the abortion toll in the United States since the *Roe v. Wade* judgment stands at around 40 million. Think about it. And think about the total in Australia since the mid-1970s. Proportionally it is also high, with 80,000 Medicare-funded abortions every year and around 100,000 in total in a country with a population of just 20 million people.

In June 2003, McCorvey's attempt to overturn the case she won failed at first instance. It had little chance of success, but it highlights how far we have come in our understanding of the abortion issue.

Surveys show two crucial factors in the public's thinking about abortion. A majority of people accept that abortion means killing an unborn child and think that it should only be available in extreme cases.

But at the same time, most people so far don't want the limits on abortion tightened. They don't want to be responsible for creating a situation where women who find themselves pregnant in difficult circumstances no longer have the way out that abortion provides – even though the 'way out' is in fact a dead end.

The early days of the abortion debate pitched the unborn child against the mother. Although the humanity of the child in the womb is no longer seriously questioned, for many it becomes a secondary consideration when opposed to the idea of a woman trapped in circumstances beyond her control.

Dramatic and unwelcome events can seem like the end of life as we want to live it. There's no doubt that an unexpected pregnancy can look like this, especially for young women.

We need to show that life doesn't end in these circumstances; that there are ways 'out' other than abortion, with its legacy of grief and emotional harm.

Being pro-life doesn't just mean being pro-child. It also means being pro-woman. There are two lives at stake in abortion. As a society we need to do more to save both.

The Sunday Telegraph, *19 October 2003*

Alcohol

LAST year one of our Catholic boys' schools from a prosperous Eastern suburb provoked a wave of public comment and criticism when a Year 12 break-up at Bondi degenerated into a drunken brawl causing $80,000 worth of damage. Ten boys were eventually charged; the seven under eighteen years were cautioned and the three others were given good behaviour bonds. The club which served them the alcohol was closed for seventy-two hours; hardly a drastic penalty.

We have every reason to be worried about the level of alcohol consumption through every age level in society and any criticism of young people involves some level of criticism for those of us who are older and whose example the young ones follow. It is all too easy to criticize generations, any generation except the one to which we belong and that is not my intention. Neither am I prepared to defend the indefensible and the youngsters involved let themselves down first of all, as well as their parents and school.

But we should beware lest we enjoy the lapses and misfortunes of others too much. The media are full of bad news, because there is a greedy market for this. If people consistently showed they did not want too much of this muck-raking, the market would eventually prevail and there would be less of it and more good news. That is not the situation.

About 1600 years ago St Augustine in Christian North Africa wrote about the characteristics of people without hope. He explained that the less attentive people are to their own sins, the more they pry into the sins of others. They seek, he said, not what they can correct, but what they can criticize. And all know that it is much easier to criticize others, often from a lofty moral position than to continue the hard work of self-improvement, correcting our own faults.

At the time last year I did not comment publicly on this sad public lapse, but I am now happy to commend the authorities of this school for a unique contribution they have made to public discussion. They truly are, as Christians must strive to do, bringing good out of bad.

The school commissioned a survey, conducted by two researchers from the National Drug and Alcohol Research Centre, on the alcohol consumption of every student, parent and teacher at the school. This is the first such survey in Australia. Equally brave and equally praiseworthy is the fact that last week they published their findings.

Sixty-five per cent of students reported at least one binge drinking episode, defined as more than five drinks at a session, the medical limit for adult females. Three per cent drink alcohol every day and about 10 per cent drink at least three times a week. All of these, I remind you, are still at school.

All in all the survey found that about one student in five was a heavy drinker and there was a strong correlation between a lot of drinking and the amount of money from work or pocket money available to these young individuals (generally about $30 a week).

The rise of part-time work for secondary and tertiary students is good in many ways, developing a sense of responsibility and independence. But this work is interfering with university studies, cutting into time, energy levels and many of the side benefits that can accompany university life. At secondary school parents should watch how such money is being used and watch what is happening at weekends.

A couple of additional points were also worrying. Nearly two-thirds of the students reported drink-driving (whatever that statistic means as most of the boys were too young to be driving). But it shows that despite the heightened awareness against drinking and driving, that it still does occur.

Secondly, the average age for the first full alcoholic drink for students is now just under twelve years of age, four years earlier than that of their parents and teachers. There is no consolation here, because extra maturity is a great help generally in avoiding trouble.

Many adults of my generation are too complacent about the problems alcohol brings. Few Catholics are wowsers. Our Lord himself instructed that wine be used in the Eucharist. Among Irish Australians there is probably less alcoholism than there was and we are more frightened by drug problems; not around in my youth. But alcohol kills more people than any other drug, even if slowly and silently. All of us need to understand the damage alcohol causes, and young people in particular need this information while they are young and impressionable, so they can learn from their elders' mistakes.

Getting drunk is also morally wrong, because we surrender control of our personalities, making it harder to control our baser instincts. Through drink-driving, aggression, verbal or physical, many other people can be hurt. We should not surrender our dignity or modesty to alcohol. Over the years I have sometimes been struck by the fact that a few young Catholics don't seem to realize that it is morally wrong to get drunk. This useful piece of information should be conveyed to them, with reasons why it is wrong and information about the consequences of alcohol addiction.

The school is to be commended for their survey

and the courage to carry it through to publication. They organized parents' meetings and reorganized the syllabus on the topic.

I hope they provoke wide public discussion because this is not just a Catholic problem.

It is a topic which merits prayer so that there will be wise discussion across the generations of parents, grandparents and children and good example from the adults.

27 July 2003, St Mary's Cathedral, Sydney

Marriage

Reading: *Eph 5:21-32 (St Paul, writing on marriage, urges wives to give way to their husbands, and husbands to love their wives as Christ loved the Church. He also urges children to be obedient to their parents, but tells parents not to drive their children to frustration.)*

THIS lively passage about marriage from the second reading is one that gets St Paul into trouble today. Some only hear the words that the husband is head of his wife as Christ is head of the Church and that wives should submit to their husbands in everything. They go no further than this, often convinced that St Paul was another grumpy old celibate patriarch condoning the oppression of women.

This first point to be made in Paul's defence is to urge that we continue on and read the balancing section, about the duties of a husband to his wife. A husband is to love his wife as Christ loved the Church and sacrifice himself for her as Christ did for the Church. A man must love his wife as he loves his own body; an unambiguous statement of the equal dignity of the sexes; something we take for granted because Christianity has changed the way we regard women.

As in China today, in pagan Rome baby girls were often left to die; the aristocratic families regularly had many more surviving sons. A wife had few if any civil rights. Christianity liberated pagan women into equality and dignity in domestic life and Paul's teaching should be set against this pagan background. Many first and second century men, certainly most pagans and probably quite a few Christian men too, would have been uneasy about the injunction to love and treat their wives as their own bodies.

When I was growing up priests and teachers probably emphasized the prohibitions too much. But today the pendulum has swung and there is too much silence in pulpits and schools, too few attempts to explain the reasons for Christian teaching on sexuality, marriage and family.

Those energetically promoting the continuance of the sexual revolution, often for financial reasons, are not silent and often resent those who resist them by pointing out the long-term advantages of Christian living and the damage done by promiscuity, broken marriages, abortion. They like to run the line that the 'Church is hung-up about sex'; 'The Church should stay out of the bedroom'.

But whether people agree with the Church or not, we all intuitively know that sex is extremely important, more than entertainment. One important reason why people stop church-going is often Christian sexual teaching and one reason many come to Christ is the emptiness and pain of pagan alternatives.

For a start, none of us would exist without the sexual union of our parents. But the significance of our sexuality does not stop there.

Sex is not a comfortable topic for many people. In their discomfort with sexuality, people tend to go to one or other extreme; liberal abandon or conservative prudishness. There would still be some today a bit surprised by St Paul comparing the unity of Christ and the Church to Christian marriage.

Sexuality is God's gift to be treasured and celebrated. An asexual Church is as unholy and unredeemed as a sex-mad society. But there is a way through both distortions to wholeness, integration and truth.

Pope John Paul II has pondered this issue, and his bold conclusions have surprised many people. His *theology of the body* was explained in a series of 129 talks given between September 1979 and November 1984. They build on passages like this one from Ephesians and the theology of the body is very popular among Catholic university students. There are study groups at Sydney University on this very topic.

The essential point is this: by reflecting on sexual difference, male and female, and the desire for union with the opposite sex, we discover the deepest reality of human identity and we even enter some way into the mystery of the Trinitarian God.

The creation story in the Old Testament book of Genesis tells us that Adam and Eve were made for each other. At the core of their beings, man and woman experience a deep desire for unity. We are made to love and be loved.

Our masculinity and femininity draw us beyond ourselves to the other. This 'made for the other' is apparent in the differences between men's and women's bodies. Neither makes sense by itself, but only in union with the other.

The original harmony between men and women was ruptured when Adam and Eve chose to disobey God. They mistrusted God's love and plan for them, and asserted their own will over His. But far from making them free, the result was to trap them in selfishness.

They no longer looked on each other as a reflection of God's image, but with lust and the self-centred desire to manipulate the other.

It is from the trap of selfishness that Jesus – God-made-flesh – promises to free us, and this freedom involves our sexuality.

The Church views the sexual union of man and woman as sacred and sacramental. The Church does not say 'no' to practices such as pre-marital and extra-marital sex because it is against sex, but because it is radically for sex and the total, unreserved, mutual self-giving it expresses in marriage.

Society's efforts to dodge or avoid the challenge of the Christian sexual ethic have often reaped tragic results and deep personal hurts. The theology of the body offers a fresh insight into who we are and helps us embrace the truth about sexuality. This much criticized passage from Ephesians is a wonderful source for both study and prayer.

Sexuality is a highly sensitive topic. John Paul II recognizes the universality of the human struggle. No person has sexuality perfectly worked out! Redemption is a journey. It takes time.

'Be not afraid!' says the Pope echoing Jesus. Paul's teaching on marriage and the theology of the body though strong and confronting, are not meant as a condemnation but as an invitation to discover anew the gift and freedom of our sexuality. When so many people are frantically searching for happiness in the wrong direction, following the advertisers and being caught in emptiness and dissatisfaction, Christian teaching still provides genuine peace and freedom, but at some cost.

24 August 2003, St Mary's Cathedral, Sydney

Wisdom

Readings: *Wis 6:12-16 (The unknown author of the book of Wisdom, written around 100 years before the coming of Christ, describes wisdom as something 'resplendent and unfading', 'readily perceived by those who love her'.); 1 Thess 4:13-18.*
Gospel: *Matthew 25:1-13 (Christ tells a parable or story of ten bridesmaids who were waiting to meet the bridegroom and only five had sufficient oil to relight their lamps when they went out. Those without oil left to buy some, and when they returned the bridegroom had arrived and the doors to the wedding feast were closed and locked. Jesus warned his followers to 'stay awake, for you know neither the day nor the hour'.)*

Thirty-second Sunday in Ordinary Time – Year A

TO understand the Gospel of the wise and foolish bridesmaids we have to know a little bit about the marriage customs of the time, which I am told in that part of the world continued up until the end of the nineteenth century.

The climax of the wedding celebrations used to be when the groom went to the house of the bride.

He then collected the lucky lady and returned to his parents' house and it was only then that the actual marriage ceremony was performed and a new round of celebrations began.

Today it is the accepted thing for the bride to be a little bit late for the ceremony. The groom is in the church waiting hopefully and the bride often comes five or ten minutes late. But in the old style Jewish wedding it was not a fashionable five minutes, sometimes they would wait for hours for the groom to arrive and it is suggested that there were two reasons for that, neither of them particularly edifying. The first was that they would be haggling over the presents, which had to be given to the bride's relatives. Or, and this is a modern touch, they were arguing fiercely over the amount of money in the marriage contract that the bride would have to receive if she was divorced by her husband – and he could do that as easily as both husband and wife can divorce one another today – or over what money the bride would get if the husband died.

It is interesting to note that the foolish bridesmaids were blamed and punished not because they went to sleep, but because they had not brought enough oil with them to last during that long time. It is not a nice story particularly. It is not universally reassuring, which is the way we like our stories today, but it certainly tells us something about life. Good intentions are an indispensable start, but they are rarely enough. We are a bit lazy, a bit thoughtless and sometimes, perhaps often, we can pay severely.

So what do we mean by wisdom? Should all of us, young and old, even the youngsters here today, pray to become wise? Why is wisdom so important in the Old Testament? The first reading today is from the Book of Wisdom and, as all the youngsters who have been confirmed know, wisdom is one of the gifts of the Spirit.

Wisdom is not the same as cleverness because very intelligent people can sometimes be very foolish and you need a very clever person to think up reasons for the silliest of views. Wisdom is not always the same as being cunning because some evil people are very cunning, but we do not call them wise. With wisdom we can see beyond self-interest, beyond the short term and beneath the surfaces, beneath appearances. I am not sure that many, if any, people are born wise – they learn from experience and many, many people without much formal education can be very wise indeed. Some call this intuition and I am not sure whether it is the Asian religions or the Russians who sometimes talk about possessing a third eye, that is an eye that can see deeply into human problems.

To be wise you have to be driven by love. Haters are not wise, although they too can sometimes be very cunning. Not all the people who pray regularly are wise, but regular prayer is a great help to wisdom – it gives us time to be quiet, to settle down, to quieten our envy or anger or resentment at the way we have been treated. Sometimes our feelings can lead us badly astray, for example in the family.

The regulars will probably recall that I have often quoted Lady Longford and I am going to inflict her on you again. The Longfords were an interesting family – I think Lord and Lady Longford are both still alive, they are English obviously, and I think they are both converts; he certainly was. One Englishman said that when Longford was at university he went hunting. He fell off his horse and hit his head and he became a socialist and a Catholic. He is a great campaigner for many good things, a very interesting fellow. He wrote a short book on humility, which is very good, and then he wrote three volumes of autobiography. His wife, Lady Longford, was asked by a press reporter: 'You are a strong Catholic, you have been married well over thirty years, did you ever think of divorce?' She said: 'No. I have never thought of divorce, but I have often thought of murder.'

Now that's a good Catholic response and sometimes when our feelings are running in a different direction we decide to love and then our feelings catch up. Sometimes when we feel so deeply we can act as though we do not need to think clearly and in the last few weeks with the discussion about drugs we have had some examples of that. People who feel so deeply that something needs to be done about drugs, and I entirely agree with that, are inclined to agree with anything that is being suggested.

Wise people do not talk too much, certainly they think before they act and they think before they talk. And wise people are not afraid to seek advice, not afraid to talk about their problems, not with everyone but with a trusted few people whom they think are wise. Wise people do not ask one person after another the same question and then change their mind with every person they speak to. Wise persons do not live their lives as though they are immortal, as though the days of our youth are the only good years. They know that they cannot live forever. Not only that, they know that they will be judged by our merciful God for the type of life they have led. And wise people never despair, no matter how bad the situation.

Going back to the second reading today from St Paul, wise people do not live like people without hope. They know they are superior to the animals, that death is not the end and that God has a special reward for those who suffer disproportionately, for those who cop more than their share of suffering.

It is not easy to be wise, but if we were lucky enough

to grow up in a loving family, to know that God loves us, know the difference between right and wrong and know what it is to pray, then we are well on the way to wisdom. We pray for so many things. Please God we pray in thanks too and in worship and for forgiveness; but we pray for health and jobs and prosperity and peace in the family and exams and sometimes we even pray for sporting success. We should also pray for wisdom. Husbands and wives, so they will love one another wisely. Parents, so that they will bring the children up wisely, not spoil them, not be selfish or weak with them or too lazy to care for them effectively and discipline them. Children, even from a young age, should pray that they won't bring suffering and sadness to their parents or their brothers and their sisters. Finally, we should pray for wisdom in the leaders of our Church and our political leaders, judges and magistrates, all leaders. Wisdom is necessary for good people, for good families and for a good and just society.

Sunday 7 November 1999,
St Patrick's Cathedral, Melbourne

Parable of the Talents

***Readings:** Prov 3:1-6; Rom 12:3-13 (St Paul exhorts the Romans to exercise the gifts given to them by the grace of God and to serve the Lord, persevere in prayer and to be hospitable.)*
Gospel: Matthew 25:14-30 (Christ tells a story about a man going away who entrusted his money to three servants – giving one five talents, one two talents and the other one talent. On his return,

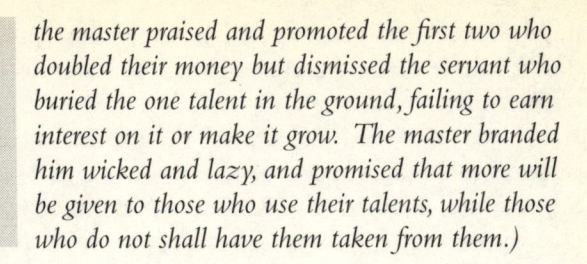

the master praised and promoted the first two who doubled their money but dismissed the servant who buried the one talent in the ground, failing to earn interest on it or make it grow. The master branded him wicked and lazy, and promised that more will be given to those who use their talents, while those who do not shall have them taken from them.)

MARY Tyrone, a mother in one of Eugene O'Neill's plays says at one time, 'Not one of us can help the things life has done to us. They're done before you realize it, and once they're done they make you do other things until at last everything comes between you and what you'd like to be, and you've lost your true self forever.'

This very modern viewpoint, which is quite un-Christian, provides a fascinating contrast and complement to Christ's parable of the talents, and today's passage from Romans.

Christ's story as recounted by St Matthew is a simple one, with strong parallels in Luke's gospel story of the nobleman who travelled abroad and left his money with his servants to be invested. A talent would now be worth two or three thousand dollars, and the servants (good capitalists) who doubled their money through trading were commended, while the third fellow who made no profit is censured. In a parallel passage in one of the apocryphal gospels, a third category of servant is introduced who in fact squanders his money on bad girls and flute players, but no such charge is laid against our servant. He was not a waster, he simply did not make a profit!

This is only one of the warning parables preached by Christ. Others were of the blind leading the blind and both falling into a ditch, the useless salt, of the house built on inadequate foundations to be swept away in the flood. These parables would have been interpreted by the people as being directed against the religious leaders of the time.

Had they used or abused their trust? Had they helped others or heaped burdens upon them? Had they opened the door to the Kingdom, or closed it? Had they reflected the light, or distorted, perhaps completely obscured it?

But Christ's stories do not tell us about bad Jews, they are about us, and help us to understand ourselves. The parable of the talents might have been used in the early Church to keep people on their toes, especially those disappointed by Christ's failure to return quickly, but it is directed to us today.

Are we, as individuals and as a group, doing our share? Are we struggling to understand, and then act out, our role in a much-changed world?

We sometimes underestimate the social and religious changes of recent decades. I believe there has been a radical change of sensibilities, which is not the same as a generation gap, between those who grew up before the Second Vatican Council, and those who grew up after it; a radical change of sensibilities which is roughly paralleled by the differences between the pre-television and television generations. These need not imply a communication gap, because people of different viewpoints can talk together, sometimes even happily, but the differences remain.

Catholic youngsters today are less open to discipline, have less instinctive respect for authority, are less guilt-ridden and puritanical in matters of sex, less sectarian, more inclined to say what they think, probably more likeable than my generation, and more likely to be either ignorant, or confused about the values they hold. Let no one think that only non-Catholics make up 'the disinherited defrauded rout', described by that fine Australian Catholic poet James McAuley,

> Who do not think or dream, deny or doubt,
> But simply don't know what it's all about.

More than ever the Church has a vital role to play in society to help and enlighten.

We could be the yeast in the loaf, the salt that savours. A contemporary historian has claimed that the story of Australian civilization is a story of struggle between three rival concepts of man, those of the Catholics, the Protestants, and the Enlightenment.

What a tragedy if our side of the discussion went by default! Just as in the Old Testament times, we dare not forget the teachings or principles we have learned. Not only kindliness, but loyalty to this tradition must be tied around our neck, and written on the tablets of our heart. We are not masters of the faith of our fathers, free to dispense that little we find acceptable and undemanding. We are the servants of this faith, bound in duty to preserve it intact, whether we like it or not.

We Australians are easy-going people, a nation of spectators, and not just at sport. This is one reason why we are attracted by Mary Tyrone's sentiments.

But fortunately or unfortunately, and this is a basic theme especially in St Matthew's gospel, Christ forces us to make a decision. Every person has to decide and especially, if he or she is a teacher or parent, is also obliged to help others to decide. Our tasks, each in our different way, are to help our pupils use their individual talents for good. Our task is to see that the themes of this Mass, fulfilment through service, peace through integrity, honour through devotion are written on the tablets of our hearts, and in the hearts of those we teach.

This is difficult. It requires competence, hard work, persistence, loyalty, hope (sometimes hoping against hope) and above all the love which St Paul spoke of. The word 'love' in English has a variety of meanings and covers a multitude of sins, but the word St Paul used has a more precise meaning which used to be translated as charity, and is better expressed now as kindliness and affection.

No adult is a successful person without it. No teacher can even make first base without it, and children know whether we possess it. It too can make up for a multitude of sins.

Adapted from the Aquinas College Institute of Catholic Education, Ballarat, graduation address, 3 December 1977

The Beatitudes

Readings: *Zeph 2:3, 3:12-13; 1 Cor 26-31.*
Gospel: *Matthew 5:1-12 (Jesus addressed the crowds, giving them nine Beatitudes, beginning 'Blessed are the poor in spirit, for theirs is the Kingdom of heaven …' He reassured His followers that their 'reward will be great in heaven'.)*

Fourth Sunday in Ordinary Time – Year A

IN today's gospel we have Our Lord's great sermon on the mount. In another gospel (Luke's) it is situated on the plain. In the translation of the word *makarios* the word 'happy' was rejected in favour of the word 'blessed'. It is difficult enough to make sense of what Our Lord is teaching by using the word 'blessed', but this is almost impossible if you substitute 'happy'.

Jesus was often provocative; what in Australia we might call (with no disrespect) a stirrer. He was able to catch people's attention so that they started to think and puzzle over what is taught.

The Beatitudes are a disconcerting mix of qualities, each bringing a different reward. We might divide them into three groups:

> a. personal qualities; such as poor in spirit, gentle, merciful, pure in heart;

> b. those who want justice (what is right) and those who are peace makers; and

> c. a third group of those who mourn, and those who are persecuted, abused or calumniated for doing or saying the right things, for speaking up for Christ.

The rewards are various, some belonging ultimately to the next life, although Our Lord believed the Kingdom of God began in the here and now.

One in particular deserves a passing reference; 'the pure of heart will see God'. In a world like ours when people are relentlessly pursued by pornography, told promiscuity is the norm and urged to buy, in order to be happy, it is not too surprising that the number of unbelievers has increased five or six times in forty years.

What was Our Lord trying to tell us? He was not talking just to his special followers, to the apostles, but has something for all of us. Many of the qualities belong to a person who is humble (the same sort of person praised in the Old Testament reading from Zephaniah). The humble person is not fishing for compliments. Humility was not a virtue for classical Greeks, being the opposite of pride which they valued. Humility is about being honest, especially honest with yourself. It is the work of a lifetime and means admitting our need for God and our own weakness, rather than believing that we owe nothing to anyone and are self-made!

Like much of the New Testament (and Matthew especially), the Beatitudes are quite clear about reward and punishment. Some feel uncomfortable with this. The German philosopher Immanuel Kant preferred to teach that 'Virtue is its own reward!' But Christ's teaching does have advantages for us in this life and certainly in the next, far beyond anything we deserve.

The attitude to suffering spelt out in the Beatitudes is very different from that of the secular world. Suffering need not be meaningless and can be turned to good. This is the central truth of Christianity, otherwise the crucifixion is meaningless. God loves sufferers in a special way!

The Beatitudes offer both ideals which are difficult and occasionally impossible for us to live up to, and values that are important in God's world. Different groups have different values. A small example is the way some people are bored to tears by talk about sport, whereas I love it. A more important example is that very rich people occasionally have no time for Christian values.

The Beatitudes are the values of heaven. They are clearly not the values of the secular world, or what we might consider to be common sense. Those whom today's world often consider losers are shown to be much closer to God's heart than those who consider themselves winners.

How does our personal list of priorities compare with Jesus' list? We should use the Beatitudes as a checklist for ourselves personally, not for others. Are we peacemakers or trouble makers? Does trouble follow us regularly? And do we always think it is someone else's fault?

Are we merciful or unforgiving? Are we gentle or hard and tough when we should be kind? Are we pure in heart or often trapped in lust? Are we humble in spirit, not much interested in possessions or are we hungry about money and possessions, even putting them before our family?

Do we want justice for all or do we refuse to think about the battlers because we are pretty comfortable? Do we look for God in our sorrow or are we too easily tempted to bitterness; to a chip on the shoulder? Do we believe the persecuted will have things made right for them? Or have we become cynical? (I remember speaking to a Cambodian official a little while after the fall of Pol Pot, who said 'This world is not for the weak' and laughed long and bitterly at Christian promises.)

I am sure that no one scores 100 per cent regularly, much less all the time, but to the extent that we can answer in the way Christ wants, we do achieve a real freedom. We often forget this. A greedy person, a promiscuous person, a liar, a vengeful person – none of these is free; they are imprisoned, they are slaves. They are not happy.

Christ's teaching will set us free. More people would continue to practise their religion, more people would become Catholics if we truly realized this. Christ is the liberator. The truth will set us free and the Beatitudes are a big part of the truth.

3 February 2002, St Mary's Cathedral, Sydney

The Acid Test
(Love Your Enemies)

> *Gospel:* Luke 6:27-38 (Christ tells the crowds to 'do good to those who hate you' and 'pray for those who mistreat you'. He urges us to stop judging and condemning so that we will not be judged and condemned ourselves.)

Seventh Sunday of Ordinary Time – Year C

WE are now concluding that short period of 'ordinary time' in the Church's liturgical year between the Christmas season and Lent, which begins this week with Ash Wednesday. I cannot resist telling you of the youngster last year from Grade 1 or 2 who told me that ordinary time was when nothing happened!

If the youngster had been older we could have explained that plenty should be happening in ordinary time, when we should be concentrating on doing everyday things well, family life, work, community building, worship and daily prayer.

Today we would also be able to explain that in the gospel we have proposed for us the stiffest test for Christians, Christ's Commandment that we love our enemies.

In Luke's Gospel this teaching immediately follows Jesus' preaching of the beatitudes, blessed are the poor, hungry, those weeping, those who are persecuted.

We have heard these teachings many times and we still hear them with a mixture of unease and partial disbelief or disapproval.

If we have been slapped once we should offer the other cheek for a slap. If our cloak has been stolen, we should offer our tunic also. We can imagine how those who heard this for the first time would have reacted.

There is no doubt that Our Lord was attention seeking, not for himself, but for His teaching. People in every age are tempted to hear what has been said, but refuse to engage with the content. We might feel that we know that already or that we do not agree or that we could not be bothered examining this too closely, because we have problems enough without more extreme religious burdens or requirements.

But there should be no mistake. In this passage we are at the heart of Jesus' revolutionary moral teaching that we should return good for evil, love our enemies, pray for those who hate and curse us.

I have recounted once or twice the story of the catechist chief in the Papua New Guinea highlands when they were being opened up by Catholic missionaries. He was translating the sermon when the priest explained the Christian teaching that we should not kill. The chief was amazed, interrupted the sermon to check with the priest that he had the message correctly and then returned to explain to his people this extraordinary teaching, 'Jesus says that you must not kill. Did you hear that? Do as he says. And if anyone of you should kill I will kill you!'

We often react in a similar way, although we are too sophisticated generally to be caught out so publicly.

Some people are more hot tempered than others, coming to the boil and going off the boil equally quickly. Some are very slow burners, but once ignited it can need a miracle, or perhaps many years before the fires of hate and revenge are doused.

It is often harder to forgive those who hurt our loved

ones than it is to forgive those who hurt us. Nonetheless even those who accept Jesus' teaching on forgiveness at the intellectual level, or the level of principle, have to wrestle with their feelings. Sometimes we do not feel one bit like forgiving. We can be full of genuine outrage at what has been perpetrated and very angry.

At this stage it is still useful to count to ten, at least in matters of lesser moment when we know we have a short fuse. More importantly we should pray, either for ourselves to master our feelings and do the right thing; or we can try to pray for the persons who have done the wrong thing, even when we feel that such a prayer would choke us.

A couple of clarifications, which can in fact make our situation more difficult at a practical level.

The obligation to forgive does not have to mean that the need for punishment is abolished. Children and adults sometimes need punishment, although this is to be meted out by the appropriate authority, e.g. parent, teacher or perhaps adults, police and judiciary.

Secondly it is important to remember that the obligation of compassion, the obligation to forgive, not to condemn and not to judge, must not mean that we abandon the public defence of Christian moral teaching, and decline to teach the Ten Commandments.

The answer lies in the old Christian maxim to hate the sin and love the sinner. This is absolutely at one with the Christian obligation to forgive.

Often we are tempted to hate both the sin and the sinner. Sometimes we might detest the sinner and not care too much how he is sinning.

But the need to forgive does not mean that anything goes; nor does it mean that Christian teachers should not be heard in the public forum.

It does mean that we shall be judged as we judged

and we shall receive, at the final judgment, what we have handed out.

22 February 2004, St Mary's Cathedral, Sydney

Suffering that Saves

WHILE I was preparing this article on Pope John Paul's latest apostolic letter *Salvifici Doloris* on the Christian meaning of human suffering a terrible tragedy struck one of the small country communities I serve. A young mother and two of her three beautiful young children were killed in a car accident. A few weeks ago a school-mate of the young mother had also died tragically on the road. These brute facts, which none of us can completely escape, added a new dimension to this small article. The families involved and all the local community were again confronted with one of life's great mysteries.

Pope John Paul II is extraordinarily well qualified to write about suffering. The Pope from his early adult years had no immediate family to sustain him. On top of this he lived through the immense suffering that was Poland's Nazi occupation and Communist rule. He claims that his years in the quarry as a forced labourer were worth more to him than his two doctorates. Who would we be to deny this!

The Pope's suffering might have destroyed him or wounded him terribly.

Few would have blamed him if this was the case. In fact, these terrible times have strengthened and ennobled him, and given him that immense compassion which is so appreciated by the sick and the suffering he visits.

Salvifici Doloris has six basic chapters with an introduction and conclusion. It is a meditation or reflection which draws heavily on the Pope's philosophical expertise and equally heavily on an exegesis of the Old Testament, especially the Book of Job, and the New Testament narrative and teaching on the meaning of Christ's suffering.

Suffering is a mystery which cannot be completely unravelled by our intelligence, but Christ's teaching gives us many pointers and the outlines of the correct approach. Our Lord is with us especially in difficult times. Sometimes it is difficult to see beyond the cause of our sorrow; sometimes even this suffering can be diminished and twisted simply into our personal reactions. This is a self-centred sorrow which places the sufferings of others on the periphery. It is natural in the first shock of suffering to see nothing at all but our loss.

It is human to protest and ask why, particularly when some suffering seems so pointless. At best we see only dimly. Christ Himself prayed in the garden at Gethsemane that His cup of suffering should pass Him by: He even asked from the cross why God His Father had abandoned Him.

Death and suffering are somehow deeply related to sinfulness. There is no doubt that suffering can sometimes be a recognizable punishment for sin, e.g. the suffering that an aggressor might undergo, or the health consequences of too much alcohol or indiscriminate sex; damage to the environment from human selfishness or ignorance. But Our Lord repeatedly ruled out any necessary connection between suffering and personal and family guilt. As the Book of Job pointed out in the Old Testament, the innocent often suffer and those close to God seem to suffer and do suffer more.

Our Lord never hid the reality of suffering from His

followers. He promised them no charmed life, no heaven on earth. The Christian does not ignore suffering, like the heroes in old-fashioned films – riding into the sunset to be happy for the rest of their lives. Christ rebuked St Peter who wanted Our Lord to avoid His trials and troubles. The Christian tries to see through the trouble and beyond it.

It must be a consolation to us that Christ, our leader and teacher, suffered also. Not only was He an innocent sufferer, unlike many of us, but He went to His suffering willingly. This teacher who taught by example was not only a man but was God. If God allowed His Son to suffer in such a fashion it becomes harder for us to complain about our sufferings, great or small.

Our Lord is not only united in a special way with those who suffer, but He told us that through His suffering He saved us. He is our redeemer as well as our creator. It is no fluke that for 1700 years the cross on which slaves died, with a young man in his death throes on it, has become the first symbol of Christianity.

Suffering can take us closer to God; our sufferings can be used to help others and even to make up what was lacking in Christ's own suffering. Everyone is called to complete the suffering of Christ. Or suffering can poison us, harden our hearts, confirm us in idolatry – worship of self.

So what does this mean in practical terms? It means, for example, offering up the pain of a serious illness in reparation for sins – one's own, or those of others – maybe for those souls in Purgatory for the longest time who have nobody to pray for them. Or maybe it can mean offering up a particular cross to God in the prayerful hope of receiving a worthwhile favour – a safe pregnancy and birth, for example, or the return to the faith of a family member, for wise leadership in the

Church and the world, or for justice for someone being persecuted unfairly.

This central conviction about Christ, our faith, gives new content and meaning to suffering, which becomes a coin with two sides. Glory, peace, happiness and ultimate justice are the other side of the coin. However, without faith and a loving God there is no coin, only meaningless suffering, which can be met with dignity and even heroism. But without faith there is no silver lining to the cloud, no light beyond the darkness.

Our Lord did not tell us to lie down before suffering, but to fight it and diminish it in every way we can. It was He who told us the story of the Good Samaritan. It was He who spent his life healing and helping as well as teaching. The Church has always, both communally and as individuals, preached and practised the necessity of helping those who suffer.

Salvifici Doloris is an apostolic letter of eighty-three small pages. It is not always easy reading. All of us would have to wrestle with some parts of the document, but suffering is no easy mystery and this letter is more than worth the effort it requires.

It is written from the heart and speaks to the heart.

From Light *magazine, October 1984*

A Republic for Australia

THE question of becoming a republic is not the most important challenge facing Australia. Nearly all of us would agree on this even as we disagree about what are the greater challenges. There has been no Boston tea party;

no complaints about taxation without representation. We are not rewriting the constitution after a long and violent struggle against apartheid. As we are already a sovereign and independent nation, we are not grasping for freedom because our imperial masters have been weakened by years of war.

None of this implies that the question is unimportant.

I speak as an Australian citizen who is a Catholic archbishop. There is no mandate to express a single political opinion for the Catholic Community which now comprises more than one-quarter of the Australian people, much less for the 70 per cent of Australians who are Christians. Opinions on these matters differ among us.

Catholics and Christians, like many others, recognize that in a democracy, the people, under God, are the source of authority. We want to strengthen and preserve parliamentary democracy, and our precious inheritance of freedom and tolerance. We all want what is best for the Australia of tomorrow, even as we might disagree about the means to achieve this.

Almost since European settlement began there was a lively tradition of political activity in the Catholic communities. There were Catholic prime ministers in Australia many years before there was a Catholic president in the United States.

In fact for a combination of religious and ethnic reasons, and almost unintentionally, Catholics here, then largely Irish, were among the first to think of themselves as Australians. It was Archbishop JB Polding, first Bishop of Sydney, who first spoke of 'Australia for the Australians'. Dr Mannix, in the conscription debates, was heavily criticized for putting Australian interests first. Naturally there were other traditions too, much more sympathetic to the British Empire.

For many years Catholics were a poor, self-conscious minority, denied educational justice, often prickly and hostile to Christians of other denominations. Most often the other churches returned these compliments!

Cardinal Moran, Archbishop of Sydney, frequently spoke in favour of Federation in the 1880s, but his candidature for the 1897 Sydney convention was rejected amid deep religious bitterness and he even felt unable to participate in the Federation celebrations in 1901.

Times have changed, generally for the better. Some Catholic schools have children who have come here from more than sixty nations. The Catholic community is an educated, and often prosperous, part of the mainstream. And most importantly the old antagonisms among Australian Christians have almost entirely disappeared.

Catholics have many reasons to thank God and their fellow Australians. We are proud of what we have built and are keen to work together for a better future.

Many Australian Catholics, here for some generations, through intermarriage now share a British heritage too. We acknowledge cheerfully the English prototypes of all our great civil institutions, parliament, the law, our universities and we share, of course, the precious heritage of our common language. Some of us have more personal debts. I completed my tertiary education in England in those bygone days when the British Government paid all the academic fees, not only of its own students, but of foreign students too. The histories of Britain and Australia have been inextricably linked, not least by the suffering of two World Wars. All this helps us understand the immense affection, usually unstated, that allows us to be such uninhibited opponents in sporting contests.

But the British Crown is no longer an appropriate

symbol of Australian nationhood, not because it is British, but because it is not Australian. Despite easier travel and communications between the ends of the earth, the Crown has lost much of its mystique and power to inspire, particularly among young Australians.

Even if Britain had not joined Europe, and it has, we need the republic, an Australian head of state, to remind ourselves that we are on our own in climes very distant from the homes of most of our forebears. Our neighbours need to see this, to see we are proud of our traditions but committed to the region, keen for friendship and co-operation, but proud, disciplined and emotionally self-sufficient.

There is no reason to imagine that our good sense will evaporate with the passing of the Crown, the passing of hereditary monarchy. Our freedoms will continue to be preserved by intelligent, committed democrats and ultimately by the Australian people at the ballot box.

The higher, more important dimensions of our quest were captured poignantly at this 1998 Constitutional Convention by Graham Edwards, Vietnam veteran and survivor of many years in politics. He pointed out that most Australians believe it acceptable for Australian men and women to fight for this country, to die for this country. How could we think, he asked, that it is not good enough, not acceptable 'for an Australian man or woman to be head of this country'. There is only one answer to this question.

The new head of state needs to be a symbol of national unity, defender of the constitution, and above the day to day adversarial politics of the parliament. While the Senate retains the power to block supply, the new president will need the capacity to act as an umpire.

Partial codification of the reserve powers, if it could be achieved, could help to prevent the repetition of the worst aspects of 1975. No future prime minister should be tempted to think he or she can remove the president with a phone call and no president should find it necessary to plan the dismissal of a prime minister in secrecy.

My own preference is for the direct election of the president by the people. With carefully defined and limited powers, such a position should not rival the prime minister's.

Despite the campaigning which would accompany these elections, this close popular involvement in the appointment of the head of state would strengthen the bonds between the people and the leadership, strengthen the sense of ownership and pride.

The people's choice would help to purify the deep nationalism of the Australian people into a patriotism of service, to unify us in times of peril and especially inspire our young people to altruism even to heroism, away from selfism, from preoccupation with personal difficulty.

A move to a republic, when it comes, will complete the gradual peaceful evolution of the Australian nation.

Adapted from Constitutional Convention speech, 11 February 1998

7

The Church, Yesterday, Today and Tomorrow

Matthew, the Fine Poet

> **Gospel:** *Matthew 6:24-33 (Jesus speaks of our dependence on God, stating we cannot serve both God and mammon. He urges us not to worry about clothes and material possessions but to learn from the wildflowers that do not work or spin. Seek the Kingdom of God, He urges, and everything else will be provided. And do not worry about tomorrow, which will take care of itself: 'Sufficient for a day is its own evil.' Or in other words, this Gospel passage would be a strategic planner's worst nightmare!)*
>
> *Eighth Sunday in Ordinary Time – Year A*

TODAY'S Gospel is undoubtedly one of the most elegant passages in the New Testament: a passage of lyrical simplicity, the work of a fine poet; but with a conclusion that could only have been spoken by a simpleton – or by the Son of God.

The sixth chapter of St Matthew – like the whole Gospel – has this peculiarity; little attempt is made to arrange events chronologically, and historically isolated statements are grouped together under some logical heading. We have at least two such headings in this passage. The first tells us of the impossibility of serving two masters; while the second tells us of the birds of the air, and the lilies of the field – and it is this second portion that enchants and disturbs us.

We instinctively realize that we cannot serve two masters – even if our entire life is devoted to the search for a compromise. Deep in our heart, we know that we have chosen and must continue to do so.

But the next verses are a different matter. 'Don't worry,' says Christ, 'about your life, about your food, clothes, etc.' – and at once twentieth-century man protests. Surely our whole history from the Stone Age to today has been prompted by man's concern for himself and by his fear of and concern for creation. Surely the wonders of philosophy and literature have been forged – not by a careless disregard for the nature of man – but by anxious enquiry into human experience.

Yet Christ continues: 'Seek ye first the Kingdom of Heaven and its justice – and all these things shall be added to you' – and once again, we rise to protest. How much of the beauties of life did Christ experience, as He was harried, misunderstood and then crucified? So much of history, especially our own, seems to have been dominated by wickedness, or brute stupidity. Did the Father help Czechoslovakia as she aspired to a primitive justice and was crushed after the Prague Spring earlier this year? Did the Father help Ghandi; the two Kennedys; Martin

Luther King and countless others who only wished to help their fellow man — and received no earthly reward?

And as further examples, perhaps blasphemies, tumble from our lips — the voice of the carpenter's son breaks in gently, but with terrible insistence (as it does here in this Gospel) 'You men of little faith'. Which of us would presume to deny the accusation?

In spite of our enormous achievements, perhaps because of them, and certainly because of the great evils that this progress brought, or the evils this progress has failed to conquer, our spirit of faith needs constant renewal. The wonders of our age require a wonderful faith; a faith and humility so we can commit ourselves to something which must and does lie beyond the evidence.

'Might is right'! Society no longer imposes God upon us in a world where man has done so much — where we are tempted to wonder if there is anything we cannot do. Rarely before have we needed to be reminded so insistently that Christ loves us and cares for us here in this life.

This Gospel passage is not a demand that we concentrate on heaven — and forget the earth; 'the Kingdom of heaven is among you' says Christ. Nor is it a demand that we concentrate on our soul and things spiritual and forget our bodies. The very examples Christ gives are the glories of his material creation — man himself, the lilies, the birds. But it is a demand that we get our priorities right within the scheme of human history, and that our first concern be for the omnipotent God, who is within and beyond this history. This cannot be done without faith — faith that was a stumbling block to the Jews; and sheer folly to the pagans.

And so we pray that as wars drag on in Biafra and Vietnam, with Russian troops in Czechoslovakia, and with the Church in the throes of her greatest upheaval since the Reformation – we pray that we may believe that God loves us – all of us, and that we may believe that if we did seek first the Kingdom of God, all these other things would be given to us.

8 September 1968, preached to the Oxford University Catholic Chaplaincy

The Picture Behind the Altar

LAST night after I had begun to prepare a few words of teaching for today's ordination sermon I was distracted by the magazine *Alma Mater* of the seminary where I studied in Rome, which usually has news of other ex-students.

In my time there were more than sixty nationalities at Propaganda Fide College, so the news is world-wide. There was an item from Romania, where things are still very difficult for the Church, telling of the death of two priests, each of whom spent ten years in jail. The writer said that all twelve bishops in Romania were jailed at some stage, but there was no Judas among them! All remained faithful. Another letter from China told of the death of Father Paul Siao, who had thirty-five years in Communist jails.

A little while ago on a visit to Rome I visited the Venerable English College, where at the height of the Protestant Reformation for year after year every student ordained for the English mission was captured by the authorities and died as a martyr. The picture still stands behind the altar in the chapel where the students gathered to sing the *Te Deum,* the hymn of praise and thanks, as the news of each martyrdom came through.

I am not suggesting for a moment that such a fate lies before our two deacons-to-be. Neither am I suggesting that any of us knows what the future holds; we have troubles enough today.

What I am trying to do is to remind you all that at this diaconate ordination we stand before a great mystery; two men are to be ordained into a sacred office which goes back to the apostles, back to New Testament times. They are called to a special, official and demanding life of service. The confessor and martyrs I mentioned suffered primarily because of their devotion to Christ and because of their refusal to break with the Pope, the successor of St Peter, the rock-man on whom Christ built the Church. They also suffered because of their office, because the opponents of the Church knew instinctively how important sacred office is for the everyday life of the Church.

The task of the Church is primarily supernatural, beyond nature. The great charism of the Salesians is to work with young people – and to prepare them for eternity, for heaven rather than hell. We love this world, we serve it, develop it, believing that in eternity in some strange way there will be a new earth as well as a new heaven. But deacons and priests are not just social workers or teachers or promoters of development (although we do all this and love doing it); priests and deacons are witnesses to a Kingdom which very much includes the world but goes far beyond it; a Kingdom whose values are radically different from what the newspapers and television consider important.

Deacons are entrusted to preach this Kingdom; to preach Christ and His values. They have no mandate to do otherwise. Such preaching is an essential part of their service.

They are called heralds of the Gospel as the Book of Gospels is given to them. They will be exhorted to believe what they read, to teach what they believe and practise what they teach. Like John the Baptist, they will have to call people to repentance as well as to faith. They will be moral teachers, a difficult task requiring courage and cunning and God's help.

Eleven days ago in Rome, the Holy Father Pope John Paul II spoke to a group of United States bishops about teaching young people. 'It is clear,' the Pope said 'that the controversies and dissent of past decades are of little interest to them. They are not inspired by a Gospel which is diluted, disguised or made to seem effortless. Every effort should be made to guarantee that catechetical and religious education programs, Catholic schools and institutions of higher learning and in particular, the preaching ministry of the Church, present serenely and convincingly but without embarrassment or compromise – the whole treasury of Church teaching.'

The new encyclical of the Holy Father, which will hit the press officially next Tuesday, *Veritatis Splendor* 'The Splendour of Truth' reaffirms the basics of our Gospel morality. It is already controversial and much needed.

'One of the key pastoral problems facing us,' declared the Pope in this same recent address to the US bishops, 'is the widespread misunderstanding of the role of conscience, whereby individual conscience and experience are exalted above or against Church teaching. All those who teach in the name of the Church … should proclaim, in opposition to all subjectivism, that conscience is not a tribunal which creates the good, but must be formed in the light of universal and objective norms of morality.'

So our new deacons will have to explain to

their congregations, pupils, youth groups that the virtues, the two great Commandments of love, the ten Commandments – that all this is still 'in', and it is still a Christian requirement. A difficult and challenging task.

They will also have to serve their people in a real and persistent manner. They will be leaders and healers – but servant leaders. Young deacons have not earned the status of chiefs; regular service, not the place of honour, will be their role. And if in fact they do become chiefs of a sort (parish priests or principals or something else) they will still have to be servants.

Another essential dimension of their service will be their daily prayer for themselves, for their work, for the People of God – their daily Mass, meditation, prayer of the Church. We cannot expect God to bless us if we pray only spasmodically; this is especially true for deacons and priests. That is why the office, the prayer of the Church is an official obligation for deacons and priests. It is at the core of their Salesian life, an essential element in their service – not something to be fitted in when all the other important work of the day allows.

With such a core of faith, service and self-discipline at the centre of their lives, they will be wonderful examples of Salesian joy, igniting the fire of enthusiasm in thousands of young hearts.

2 October 1993, Salesian Diaconate ordination, Melbourne

The Priesthood

THIS morning's packed Cathedral faithfully reflects the gratitude and rejoicing of the Catholic community of Melbourne at the ordination of three young men to the priesthood. Every bishop, and certainly this one who happens to be Archbishop of Melbourne, thanks God for such a blessing. We rejoice when a man enters the seminary to test his vocation. It is a much greater blessing when the long years of preparation, prayer, study and pastoral work are completed, when ordination is requested and a life's work of faith and service is about to commence.

Three ordinations a year is good. Which of us can claim with confidence that the archdiocese is spiritually healthy enough to deserve such a blessing? These things are hidden and that is God's business. But it is a sobering thought, which returns us to our prayers and the performance of our duty, to remember that we need more than this, at least four or five priests ordained each year, and for many years, to stabilize our situation.

God always calls enough young men to be parish priests, although 'enough' is defined differently in different ages and countries. But it is also certain that sometimes, too often, God's call is not heard, drowned out by worldly static. Our Lord used another metaphor of the seed which struck and then was choked by larger, more numerous weeds.

So the other side of the coin, after acknowledging our duty of gratitude to God, is a request from me to you all to pray for vocations to the priesthood. Priests and bishops are only a very small part of the Church. As priests we are ordained to worship God and serve the baptised and the outside world. This is the age of the laity because we have rediscovered the riches of baptism and because the secular pressures are so strong, coming into our lounges and offices every day through TV and the internet. More and more lay leadership will be needed just to stay where we are, to maintain our present strengths.

For Catholics, ministerial priests and the baptised are not in competition, much less conflict. They are complementary. Cardinal Newman said that the Church would look funny without the laity, but without the priests there would be no Church at all, only a gathering of Christians.

Every priest represents Christ, the head of the Church. Our Lord called priests to be shepherds of the flock, fishermen of souls. Paul said that priests are ambassadors of Christ. All this remains true, even in an age of public clerical scandals, such as our own, unequalled in Australian history. The treasure remains in the earthenware jar, even when the jar is cracked and filthy.

It was Our Lord Himself who chose the passage from Isaiah, which we heard, to describe to His own people what He was about. He got no thanks for His pains as the locals thought His claims pretentious, over the top. These claims also spell out the priest's duties to his people: to tell the truth to the poor, to remind them of God's justice, to console the sad, to visit the imprisoned, to comfort the mourners and inspire hope in the downcast.

All this is a tall order, but they are Christ's marching orders for us.

Our Lord is the greatest teacher in history, judged from the extent and longevity of His influence. His parables still haunt and disconcert us today. So too every priest must teach regularly what we have received from Christ and the apostles. Paul hammers this home to his unruly congregation in the port city of Corinth, without finesse and without too much imagination. The word of God is not to be watered down as the truth is announced without shame or subterfuge. Such truths reveal the glory on the face of God, Paul claims, and the priest is at his best when he is simply a conduit, a conductor for God's power, when his weakness and his strengths do not impede the free flow of God's grace.

Usually this does not mean heroic self-sacrifice; no melodrama, no abject humility, no dust and ashes, but regular service of those close to us, day in and day out. This is the true Christian alternative to pagan lordliness.

Naturally, our abilities as priests differ from area to area of Church life. Some are better community builders; others are instinctive consolers; some thrive on administration; others can teach and preach very easily. The list could go on.

However, there is another dimension to priestly life, which every priest can do well (because, we are told, God does most of the work) and that is to pray well and regularly for his people. It is probably the most important part of our work.

Western society is infecting our Church, sapping our vitality. We are tempted to place the search for Transcendence, the worship of Mystery, on the margins; for those few so inclined. Being interested in God can become like music or ballet lessons for the children. More radically, others reduce God to an extension of the human person, the ground of our being.

The Gospel tells us that the pure in heart will see God, so it is no surprise that so many today find it hard to believe. All this means that the priest must also pray for himself, as regularly as he prays for his people, that his faith remain strong and be a stimulus to hard work and initiative, not just an inert and receding backdrop. The priest needs to be regularly near God with his people in his heart. He will be able to help his people so much more, if his prayer regularly takes him beyond his daily concerns. Sometimes his prayer will be easy and beautiful, at other times it will be dry and distasteful, but prayer is founded in the daily round of small triumphs, routine and occasional disappointment. Prayer is not an extra, an embellishment; it is part of our work, part of our duty towards God and our people. As good seminarians, these ordinands know how to pray. We hope that during the priestly years that lie ahead their prayer life will deepen further, to become one essential part of their persona, their very selves.

And so I remind you, my brothers, that you must pray daily for your people as you pray for yourself. Daily Mass, daily prayer of the Church, daily meditation and devotion to Our Lady are essential parts of your priestly work and duty.

'We ask that you share with all mankind the word of God you have received with joy. Meditate on the law of God, believe what you read, teach what you believe, and put into practice what you teach.

'Let the doctrine you teach be true nourishment for the people of God. Let the example of your lives attract the followers of Christ, so that by word and action you may build up the house which is God's Church.

'In the same way you must carry out your mission of sanctifying in the power of Christ. Your ministry will perfect the spiritual sacrifice of the faithful by uniting it to Christ's sacrifice, the sacrifice which is offered sacramentally through your hands. Know what you are doing and imitate the mystery you will celebrate. In the memorial of the Lord's death and resurrection make every effort to die to sin and to walk in the new life of Christ.

'When you baptize, you will bring men and women into the people of God. In the Sacrament of penance, you will forgive sins in the name of Christ and the Church.' Only a priest can forgive sins in the Sacrament of Reconciliation. In Mother Teresa's words, only the priest can pour out the Blood of Christ into the wounds of sin to heal them. 'With holy oil you will relieve and console the sick. You will celebrate the liturgy and offer thanks and praise to God throughout the day, praying not only for the people of God but for the whole world. We ask you to remember that you are chosen from among God's people and appointed to act for them in relation to God. Do your part in the work of Christ the Priest with genuine joy and love, and attend to the concerns of Christ before your own.

'Finally, conscious of sharing in the work of Christ, the Head and Shepherd of the Church, and united with your bishop and subject to him, seek to bring the faithful together into a unified family and to lead them effectively, through Christ and in the Holy Spirit, to God the Father. Always remember the example of the Good Shepherd who came not to be served but to serve and to seek out and rescue those who were lost.'

May God and His love always be with you and may your family, friends and your people always support you through prayer and through loyal friendship.

From the ordination ceremony for Reverend Fathers David Cartwright, John Kennedy and Mark Withoos, 15 July 2000, St Patrick's Cathedral, Melbourne

Religious Life in the Third Millennium

THE Feast of Candlemas celebrates the Presentation of Christ in the temple forty days after the birth of Our Lord. The feast was celebrated in Jerusalem from about 350 AD and the Emperor, Justinian, ordered it to be celebrated in Constantinople in 542 AD, after which it spread through the East. It seems to have started in Rome with Pope Sergius (700), who was born in Antioch in Syria.

Today, throughout the world, there is a day of prayer for Consecrated Life. In St Peter's, the Holy Father blesses the candles surrounded by religious from all parts of the world. Thus we unite ourselves in prayer with the Universal Church and especially for the vitality of religious life.

The religious state is one way of experiencing a 'more intimate' consecration, rooted in baptism and dedicated totally to God. In the consecrated life, Christ's faithful moved by the Holy Spirit, propose to follow Christ more nearly, to give themselves to God who is loved above all and, pursuing the perfection of charity in the service of the Kingdom, to signify and proclaim in the Church the glory of the world to come.

The *Catechism of the Catholic Church* puts it well:

> The vocation of religious women and men, sisters, brothers, etc., takes a variety of forms. The commitment and consecration of the religious life play a major role in our Church. There is great witness value in 'pursuing the perfection of charity in the service of the Kingdom'. By their self-sacrifice (celibacy, poverty, obedience), by lives of prayer and service, religious men and women remind us of the 'glory of the world to come'.

The Catholic Church in Australia is gifted with the rich and diverse charisms of many Congregations. The Spirit, the author of these gifts, is still active today in the various Congregations endeavouring to live in the spirit of the Gospel and in the spirit of their founders. The diverse Congregations are called to continue the mission of Jesus in the context of the Church and society today.

Today is a recurring annual occasion for the wider Church to thank the religious for their continuing and historic contribution to Catholic life. We have reason to celebrate – to give thanks for the past, to appreciate the present and to ask God's blessing on the future.

On this Candlemas feast as we recall the example of Anna, the prophetess, living a life of fasting and prayer, never leaving the Temple and then telling all and sundry, who were looking forward to the deliverance of Israel – telling them of the Christ child; as we recall the example of Simeon too, who told Mary that a sword would pierce her heart as her Son would be a cause of division, provoking both the rise and fall of many in Israel, I am pleased to be able to recommend to your reading and meditation the Pope's letter on the start of the new, the third Christian millennium.

A beautiful piece of work; the best translation into English of a papal letter (according to Clifford Longley in the *English Tablet* – a magazine not noted for its orthodoxy or enthusiasm for Roman documents), since Cardinal Manning translated Pope Leo XIII's *Rerum Novarum* in 1891 – it is well worth your prayerful attention.

At one point the Holy Father asks what was the heart, what was at the core of our Jubilee celebrations. His reply is simple, 'the contemplation of the face of Christ'.

It is the Christ known in prayer, and confessed publicly, who urges us again at the dawn of a new millennium to put out into the deep, onto the ocean of a new century opening before us. It is not a time for looking back, much less for settling into laziness. Rather we should be inspired with a new energy, so that we be rooted in contemplation and prayer – resolved first of all to be worshippers and friends of Christ, to resist the itch for continual movement, and a disturbing restlessness.

The Holy Father notes that many people ask us to show them Jesus, rather than asking us to talk about Christ and he insists that only the experience of silence and prayer will give us a deeper, faithful knowledge of the Great Mystery.

He reminds us that we will not be saved by a formula, but by a person. It is not a matter of inventing a new programme; the programme already exists in the Gospels and the Church's living tradition. It is to live the life of the Trinity and so transform history until the fulfilment of the heavenly Jerusalem. The programme does not change, but it does have to be adapted to every age and local community. The call to holiness has to be at the heart of every pastoral plan.

Religious above all are called to a high standard of ordinary Christian living; to be distinguished genuinely in the art of prayer; more open to the experience of contemplation, to the great mystical tradition of both East and West.

The Holy Father wants those in consecrated life not to become mediocre Christians, lest they become Christians at risk; slip further, progressively undermined; become liable to succumb to the allure of substitutes, alternative religious proposals, even far-fetched superstitions.

While the Holy Door might have closed behind us, it was only to open more widely the door which is Christ, as we return to our ordinary everyday Christian living. We pray that Mary our Mother, the Star of the New Evangelization, will guide us wisely into the future.

The Church can only reflect the sun, which is Christ Our Lord. This is what the Fathers of the Early

Church called the mystery of the moon. Because of our sins and weakness, we are often full of shadows, unable to reflect the light of the sun. It is only by acknowledging the primacy of Christ and the primacy of the interior life, holiness and grace that we hope to struggle some distance towards also being lights in the darkness.

2 February 2001, St Patrick's Cathedral, Melbourne
Feast of Candlemas.

A New Parish

Readings: *Is 2:1-5, Rom 13:11-14.*
Gospel: *Matthew 24:37-44 (Jesus warns that just as it was in the times of Noah, we do not know when the Son of Man will come so we should be vigilant in how we lead our lives.)*

First Sunday of Advent – Year A

I remember an Irish-born Cistercian explaining that in his home village there was a practice of leaving a light in the front window of each home on Christmas Eve, so that if Mary and Joseph were to return, there would be a welcome there for them.

Many or most Catholic homes in his village had this light in their front window. A beautiful practice.

It is the start of Advent today; the start of the season of preparation for the feast of Christmas, the celebration of the birth of the Son of God, Mary's Son among us. The term *advent is* from the Latin 'advenire' to come.

We know that Christ came among us more than 2000 years ago. We would not be at Mass this morning if Christ were not welcome already in our hearts. We know of life's two certainties: death and taxes. So we will all meet Christ again at our death.

The readings are a contrasting mixture of joy and sadness, hope and fear, anticipation and dread. The psalm's refrain asks 'Let us go rejoicing to the house of the Lord'. It will be daylight soon and we are people of light, not those chained by habit to drunken orgies, promiscuity or jealousy. All people will go to the mountain of the Temple of the Lord, where the swords of traditional enemies will be turned into ploughshares, spears into sickles to collect the harvest.

But the gospel warns us of the careless, unthinking days before the great Old Testament flood, where Noah escaped in the Ark and most people carried on right up to the disaster and never knew what hit them. Christ tells us again that we do not know when the master will come, so we should be on our toes, be prepared.

Every adult knows both sides of this coin, of good personal times, happy and carefree, and of the times of personal crisis or tragedy. Nations too know times of peace and prosperity; of tragedies like September 11 and of uncertainties like our present period. The war continues against terrorism; we are not out of the woods yet.

I am sure you will all be preparing for Christmas here in this new parish. Christmas is a feast I love: extra people in the church, traditional hymns, happy family gatherings. But I know too that Christmas can be very hard for some who are alone; or caring for someone sick or dying; or caught up in some ongoing sadness or strife. Part of our preparation for Christmas should be to help someone like that … visit our old relatives; help a poor child to receive a decent present; take out those usually shut-in at home for a Christmas dinner. That would give a core, a substance, to our preparation for Christmas.

In this parish you have your own particular dimension to your Christian advent, because here you are the pioneers of a new Catholic Christian community in this developing area. Here you will build a community of faith and love to support one another in good times and bad times. Here you will build a church, a place of worship, for regular prayer and the Sacraments, where your children will be baptised and married, where some of you will be buried, where your sins will be forgiven. Through many years of prayer this will become more and more a sacred place. Your community should be like a powerhouse of faith and love for the local community, like yeast in a loaf, like a river of life watering the district.

You will build a school, to prepare your children for this life and for heaven. Please God it will prepare them well on both counts. Support your parish priest in his pioneer work; support him personally. I am sure he will serve you well.

I am sure you will take great pride in being the Catholic community's pioneers at Carnes Hill. On many jubilee occasions, silver and golden, people, some of them very old will tell me they helped to plan or build the school or hall or church. Sometimes it is their children or grandchildren who remember with pride their family's contributions. It is a privilege and an honour, as well as hard work and hassles.

Like the Irish homes with the candle in the window, may our Catholic parishes be places of welcome, childlike faith and love.

2 December 2001, Carnes Hill Parish, Sydney

Installation Sermon as Archbishop of Sydney

Readings: *1 Kings 17:10-16; Rev 22:1-5;*
Gospel: *John 8:2-11. (Christ forgives the woman caught in adultery.)*

TONIGHT we are in the birthplace of the church in Australia. The first bishop for any church in Australia was installed here. He was John Bede Polding, shortly afterwards the Archbishop of Sydney. The first bishop in a young church, in a new land, on an ancient continent. With Polding a fresh branch of the apostolic succession was created and tonight is renewed.

In Australia the 166 years since the coming of Polding seem a long time − our nation is only this year celebrating the Centenary of Federation. Our calendar which marks time from Our Lord's birth tells a different story − 2000 years is a long time even in the history of monotheism, which originates with our father in faith, Abraham, 1900 years before Christ Himself.

As we pray tonight for God's continued blessing on this archdiocese and on my office of worship, service and leadership as the eighth archbishop, the three historical reference points remind us of the brief period of time allotted to each one of us in the swift succession of the generations.

Tonight therefore, I ask you, the people of Sydney, not only for your support and friendship, but also for your constant prayers so that together we may discern and follow the Holy Spirit and seize our opportunities to consolidate and expand the Kingdom of God among us, building on what we have received from the past. At this point, may I thank my predecessor, Cardinal Edward Clancy, and commend him for his splendid contribution to building up the Body of Christ here in Sydney and in the wider Church.

Opportunities abound in many different areas. For as long as we have been on this continent, the Catholic Church has embraced these opportunities for service and helped construct the social capital, the fund of decency, at the core of Australian life. A central part of that core has been a multitude of lay faithful, married and single, who have lived out their baptismal promises in the love of Christ. A central challenge that still remains is reconciliation with the original inhabitants.

Most Australians do not enjoy the steady rainfall we receive in Sydney. Much of our continent is dry, so we Australians understand the imagery of water, its life-giving power. Like the early Christians we understand what is being claimed of the streams of crystal clear water issuing from the throne of the Lamb to nourish the tree of life.

For over 200 years the different Christian traditions have watered the heartlands of Australian life, served the battlers, built communities, brought compassion to the suffering. It matters little whether the Catholic community is best compared to the Murray or the Murrumbidgee or the Darling Rivers, but we are a river, a source of life, beside the other Christian rivers.

Our task is to ensure that these spiritual waters continue to run strong and deep; that the source is not blocked; that the flow does not fall away to a trickle; that the water does not turn sour and brackish; that not too much is lost into billabongs, closed backwaters without escape, where the water can only eddy in circles, as it evaporates or seeps into the sand.

Contrary to some claims, the Catholic Church is not about power and prestige, but about worship and service. We are more than a service club; certainly not a political party.

We are a community of individuals and families, united in worship around the one true God and the Lamb, the scriptural term used to describe the Son of God, who was born of Mary the Virgin, who died to redeem us and rose again as our personal Saviour.

Our source of grace, of the spiritual energy, which, for example, inspired more martyrs to give their lives for the faith last century than in any other century, is Jesus of Nazareth, incarnate Son of God, who was born in a stable in Bethlehem, refugee in Egypt, missing in the Temple as a teenager, hidden from history until He began his three-year ministry as a teacher and healer of sins and sickness; who wept over Jerusalem, condemned the hypocrites and exploiters, consoled the women on the way to Calvary and was helped by a stranger, Simon of Cyrene. He is our model. He is our Messiah. Loved by many, followed by some, hated by a few, He was crucified, buried and rose again. We call this man-God, Jesus Christ, our Lord and Saviour.

It is our sacred duty to hand on this torch of faith, this sustaining conviction of the centrality of Jesus Christ to all people young and old. This faith we offer to the wider community, where the collapse of denominational prejudice offers new opportunities as many seek for meaning and a sense of direction in their lives.

All cultures have struggled to approach and to reverence the Transcendent, which has moulded human development in a bewildering variety of ways. But for Christians the first Commandment will always be to love God, that eternal Mystery of Love, Beauty and Truth, ever ancient and ever new. The good God and His only Son must not be shunted from centre stage by any human good or activity; not by life issues, or family or social justice work or inter-religious dialogue.

It is here we have our central challenge. The most significant religious change in Australia over the last fifty years is the increase of people without religion, now about one-fifth of the population; more among young people.

All monotheists, Christians and Jews, Moslems and Sikhs, must labour to reverse this. We must not allow the situation to deteriorate as it had in Elijah's time, 850 years before Christ, where monotheism was nearly swamped by an aggressive paganism, by the followers of Baal.

Please God this challenge will be answered in many ways among our lay faithful and religious orders. We know the Holy Spirit will continue to flow where He wills, but one constant in all Catholic history is the need for priests, for vocations to the ministerial priesthood. Our Lord Himself appointed the twelve, called forth the shepherds, the fishers of men. St Paul underlined the importance of ambassadors for Christ. Without priests our parishes will wither and die.

These stark realities should not be hidden from young Catholics, from young parents. A priestless parish is a contradiction in terms, because there is no parish without the Sacraments, without baptism, eucharist, reconciliation. We should pray tonight that in the years ahead a sufficient number of young men will be on a wavelength that enables them to hear Christ's call to the priesthood, to join those gallant priests expending themselves in faithful service and prayer in the Archdiocese and elsewhere.

Let me turn now to our Gospel reading; not a passage chosen for the installation of every bishop! It illuminates a significant area of Christian moral struggle, personally and communally.

Christian teaching on sexuality is only one part of the Ten Commandments, of the virtues and vices, but it is essential for human wellbeing and especially for the proper flourishing of marriages and families, for the continuity of the human race.

In contrast with these scriptural perspectives, one or two local writers seem to suggest that sin is a recent Sydney invention; 'Sin City' or 'Tinsel Town' has a contemporary local resonance! However, human weakness also flourishes in other parts of Australia and the beautiful passage from St John's Gospel reminds us that human perfidy is as old as the Garden of Eden. To a greater or lesser extent we all bear the mark of Cain; we all need a Redeemer, and Christian compassion encompasses every group of persons, especially those trapped in prisons not of their choosing.

Any genuine religion has two important moral tasks; firstly, to present norms and ideals, goals for our striving; and secondly, to offer aids for our weakness, forgiveness and healing for every wrongdoer and sinner who repents and seeks forgiveness.

This Gospel passage demonstrates these criteria. It represents a supreme teaching moment, highlighting the delicate balance between Our Lord's justice in not condoning the sin and His mercy in forgiving the sinner.

Unresolved questions cloud the incident. Why did the mob bring the woman to Jesus? It was probably a trap, where they hoped to accuse Him of harshness and cruelty if He went one way, or of breaking the Mosaic Law if He was kind.

Had a vengeful husband set up the incident and the witnesses? What did Jesus write in the sand? The best known tradition is that Jesus wrote the sins of the would-be executioners; another that He exposed the husband's role in the incident.

Whatever of that, her accusers fled one by one and Jesus was left alone with this fearful, wretched woman. There was no one to condemn her; certainly Jesus did not. But He did not praise her nor endorse her way of life. Instead, He urged her quietly, 'Go and sin no more'.

Spiritual integrity can always be regained by repentance; God would always wipe the slate clean for genuine sorrow and amendment, even for the men determined to execute her.

The Church at her best has always struggled, however imperfectly, to diminish fear. Especially today it is fear, not doubt, which is the polar opposite of faith.

The widow in Elijah's story conquered her fear of dying and took that further step to give from the little she had for herself and her son. Her faith and generosity prefigure Mary, the mother of Jesus. This cathedral is under her patronage and only last week we Catholic bishops rededicated Australia to her protection. From Mary, Help of Christians, Patron of Australia, I ask for special help as I begin my work as Archbishop of Sydney.

God is good. We are destined for heaven. Suffering can be transformed and occasionally bested. Christ will come again in glory. All shall be well. All manner of things shall be well.

This is the Christian message to our world, as it has been for 2000 years.

As eighth Archbishop of Sydney I rededicate myself tonight to believe, live and teach these simple, beautiful truths. So help me God.

Installation sermon as the eighth Archbishop of Sydney, St Mary's Cathedral, Thursday, 10 May 2001 after five years' service as the seventh Archbishop of Melbourne

The Church and the World

Matthew 10:16-23 (Jesus urged His followers to be as 'shrewd as serpents and simple as doves' as they faced persecutions for their beliefs and teachings.)

GRACE usually works through nature. We know of the images of the body of Christ; of the vine and the fruitful branches and the dead branches. If we are to be regular channels of grace, icons of Christ Himself, we priests need to pray regularly.

In Chapter 10 of Matthew, the apostles had been named by our Lord and sent out on their missions to different towns and villages, and the verses are part of their riding instructions. Our Lord begins by mixing His metaphors; or perhaps by giving a fascinating variety of comparisons from the animal world. The apostles were sent out as sheep among wolves and urged to be as cunning as snakes and as simple or gentle as doves; a rare and unlikely combination of attributes.

Many years ago in the seminary I remember someone urging the point that we should be as cunning as serpents to another seminarian from the country, with a flat Aussie accent. 'Yeah,' he conceded, 'but in the right proportions.' He was suspicious of too much cunning!

Jesus then went on to outline to the apostles some of the opposition that they would encounter, explaining that the Spirit of the Father would be with them, helping them in these trials.

Thank God we in Australia at the moment avoid the worst of these troubles and persecution; unlike our Christian brothers and sisters in Indonesia, China and India. We should remember them in prayer and solidarity.

However it would be a bad sign if the Catholic community produced no negative reactions at all; a danger signal, that either we had retreated into a ghetto, pulling our heads in; or that we were so concerned with one another, with our internal issues, that we wanted the world to pass us by, undisturbed.

There should be some tension between the Church and the world. In one of Pope John Paul II's first publications as Pope he reminded us that the cross is a sign of contradiction. The basic tension should not be between different groups of Catholics or even between different communities of Christians; we need to be outward looking in our service and in our witness and engage the world around us. While we shouldn't be looking for trouble, and should emphasize what we have in common with all people of goodwill, we would not be preaching the whole of the gospel if we only received applause from the neo-pagans around us.

I don't think this is a lesson only for bishops, although it certainly applies to us, but it is also something for priests to ponder in their local communities. Once in a while at least, we shall be obliged to teach in a way some find objectionable; to reprove those who are conspicuously doing the wrong thing.

As Paul reminded us, our task is to preach Christ and His teachings. Some of us are tempted to say too much; sometimes to be too oppressive. At other times we can be cowed into silence, unwilling to speak up as we should. Charity in all things sometimes obliges us to call a spade a spade.

Let us ponder not only the teachings of Jesus our Master but how and when he taught.

13 July 2001, Sydney Priests' Retreat

From Roman Student to Cardinal ...

Light

'Rejection lies in this, that when the light came into the world men preferred darkness to light; preferred it, because their doings were evil.'

FROM the very first verses of Genesis where darkness hung over the face of the earth, until God created light; through all the Bible writings until the last chapter of the Apocalypse, where we read that 'there will be no more night, no more need of light from lamp or sun; the Lord God will shed His light upon them, and they will reign for ever and ever' (Apoc 22:5), the sacred authors have used the mystery of light to explain the mystery of salvation.

Salvation history is often described as a struggle between the children of light and the powers of darkness; a description which always differed radically from similar Chaldean myths. Nonetheless there was a real development of this theme in Old Testament times; e.g. it was not until the Wisdom literature that the symbolism of light was applied to God Himself, and a similar development and ambiguity is found in the discussions around the direct application of the Isaiahan prophecy, we read this afternoon. Was the light of the world for Isaiah a contemporary prince, a representative of the Davidic house, or was it Jesus Christ, the God-man? The question is of more than academic interest even in our day, for the fundamental ambiguity remains. Is Christ the light of the world, or is the Church?

For any Catholic, this ambiguity can only be resolved at the end of time when Christ shall be all in all, or as St Augustine said, there shall be only one Christ loving Himself. In the meantime, we as the Church have the awesome dignity of being the light of the world, and the equally awesome responsibility of being faithful to light. The Second Vatican Council Decree on the Church was beautifully entitled *Lumen Gentium*, quoting from Pope John XXIII, '*lumen Christi; lumen Ecclesiae; lumen gentium*' (the light of Christ; the light of the Church; the light of nations').

Trained as we are in the categories of Greek thought (a far cry from the refreshing un-metaphysical outlook of the Jews), we are often tempted to explain fidelity to the light in terms of a willingness to accept the new theology, or new pastoral methods, or the necessity for seminary reform. How often we are tempted to think that those who disagree with us must have sinned against the light, and despite our eloquence and our logic seem to prefer to remain in their unfortunate condition!

Unfortunately (or perhaps fortunately) for our purposes, St John and St Paul do not measure our fidelity by theological competence (or by the degree in which we subscribe to the new theology, or our enthusiasm for any faction), although they would certainly be the last to deny the importance these affairs, or their relevance to the ultimate things. Nonetheless this way we do not get to the heart of the matter. But fidelity to the light is not merely an intellectual condition, a product of faith, for the just man lives by faith, and by faith we move from the light into the life of the Trinity, and there is only one certain sign of our faithfulness in this regard – whether we love one another. As we read in the 1st Epistle of St John: 'the darkness has passed away now, and true light shines instead ... It is the man who loves his brother that lives in light.' This is the acid test; this is where we most often fail and this is why we have not yet brought all men to Christ. If we loved one another, every other necessary quality would follow; we should be faithfully receiving the light from Christ, and faithfully transmitting it in the Church.

At this point, gathered as we are not merely because of our common religion, but also because of the culture which we share, it is opportune for us to recall the epitaph Cardinal Newman chose for himself '*Ex umbris et imaginibus in veritatem*' – Out of the shadows and away from phantasms into the truth.

We too, as the first-born of the Council, must always realize that the intellectual contribution of Newman, and so many other great theologians has only borne fruit because these men continued to love God and all other men in the midst of the suffering and miscomprehension which was their lot. May we share to some degree in the message that Newman has left for us; but most of all may our whole life be like his a steady profession from the shadows and darkness of egoism and self-deceit so that when the light of the Lord shines upon us, we too may reign for ever.

Talk to the Newman Society Bible Vigil,
Propaganda Fide College, Rome, 23 April 1967

Santa Maria Domenica Mazzarello (2004)

Gospel: *Luke 15:1-3, 11-32*
(The Prodigal Son.)

IT is an honour to be a Cardinal of the Holy Roman Church and to take possession of this new parish church only opened in 1997. As an Australian it is interesting to see that also here in Europe, not only in Australia, the Church has to erect new parishes, construct new churches in the new suburbs. As a Cardinal of the Church of Rome I am happy to support this work.

Before preaching on the gospel I wish to say a few words about the miracle of the unity and universality of the Catholic Church. This unity is not a first class miracle like the resurrection, but it is a miracle of grace, a providential development, centred of course on Jesus Christ, and then on the college of bishops, successors of the apostles, around the Pope, the successor of Peter, the rock-man on whom the Church is built.

Over the centuries the Church has suffered much from schisms and heresies, especially in the first 1000 years through differences about the divine and human natures of Christ, the mystery of the Incarnation.

In 1054 there began the tragic separation of the East and the West, between Rome and Constantinople. Then in the sixteenth century we had the Protestant Reformation, whose effects continue today particularly in Australia.

Unity is neither built nor maintained easily. It needs

eternal vigilance, prayer and hard work.

As a cardinal and a bishop it is part of my duty to support the Holy Father in maintaining this unity, both locally, within parishes, dioceses, and nation, but also internationally, across the continents.

This is also a unity with the past which is open to the future. We are the children of many generations of witnesses. We rejoice in the Catholic tradition, because as GK Chesterton wrote, tradition is the democracy of the dead. Bishops and cardinals in particular are called to be defenders of this holy tradition, which is rich and diverse, not dead and uniform.

Extract from the homily preached in Italian on taking possession of the Church of Santa Maria Domenica Mazzarello, Rome, 20 March 2004

8

The Last Things

Because Non-Smokers Die Too

THE Feast of All Saints (November 1) and Commemoration of All Souls (November 2) are designed to focus the attention of Catholics on life after death. There are still good crowds at the Masses for both days, but for many Catholics the feasts are lost in the everyday rush. All of us should remember that we will die, and answer in love to our good God for our life.

A shadow has fallen over the afterlife in many ways. Obviously, funerals continue, as does family sadness at losing a loved one. A lot of attention is often focused on the tragedy of young people coming to unexpected deaths in car accidents and other mishaps. Death is still very much around us, but the danger for believers is that like the non-religious society in which we live, we too can prefer to work mightily not to think of death, or what life might be like after death.

We seem to be losing the awareness that life presents all adults with a series of choices in faith and morality. In a very real sense, we constitute ourselves, under God's grace, by the choices we make when faced with challenges in these areas of life. It makes sense to accept that in the light of these choices, in the light of our faith and good works, we will be judged by our all-loving God.

In my youth, some of us saw God as strict and even unreasonable. We would have denied this charge if it had been put to us so baldly, but we approached final judgment with a set of attitudes that seemed to be based on such a premise. There has been a reaction to this. Fear of hell, or any sort of punishment, seems to have evaporated for many. Hell is often not a deterrent, even when some people are interested in reincarnation and frightened of the possibility of returning to this world as a powerless animal or insect!

Among young people, occasionally even in Catholic schools, knowledge of the existence of purgatory has disappeared. I have put the question to them: 'If you die and you're not quite ready for heaven, where do you go?' Sometimes I prompt primary school children in their silence by explaining that the word begins with 'P'. 'Pentridge'[1] has been suggested, or 'presbytery'.

A temporary state of purification or punishment after death before the eternal joys of heaven seems very reasonable. While none of us is good enough for heaven, a time of drycleaning or getting ready after death seems a strong and logical requirement.

If there is no awareness of the reality of purgatory, of the need for 'the dead to be loosed from their sins' (*Catechism of the Catholic Church* paragraph 1032; and 2 Macc 12:46), then the main reason to pray for the dead disappears. Without purgatory, prayer for the dead takes on the mask of an empty devotional ritual, with no

---

1 Pentridge was then the main prison in Melbourne.

intrinsic purpose except to act out our grief and respect in a civilized way.

So too, if God is good, the scales of justice need to work out in eternity, just as they surely do not always work out in this life. If the belief flourishes that everything is forgiven – that everyone goes to heaven – even without repentance, this soon translates to being uncertain whether anyone gets to heaven, or whether there is any Godly forgiveness beyond the human forgiveness of the victims.

The dead are very silent. We can be sure about the existence of the afterlife only because this was a central theme and promise in Our Lord's teaching. For adults, such a conviction about God's eternal rewards for those who love Him needs to be nourished by regular prayer and it is not unusual for such a belief to be sometimes put to the test. It is a marvellous blessing to believe in Jesus' promises about heaven, and Christianity is radically depleted, false to itself and its Founder, if we do not teach these beliefs to our young people. We should teach them to remember their departed loved ones, and the Holy Souls in general, especially those with no one to pray for them, in their Masses and prayers. Example is often the best teacher, and if your children see you arranging with your Parish Priest to have Masses said for your deceased loved ones they will hopefully grow up with the same custom and do the same for you one day.

It is also important to help the children understand the extraordinary healing qualities – in this life and the next – of the Sacrament of Anointing, and why, if at all possible, the dying should enjoy the benefits of a plenary indulgence at the hour of death. Both the Sacrament and the plenary indulgence can only be administered, of course, by a priest. Lay pastoral workers, while performing valuable roles in caring for the sick, can never take the place of a priest in these matters and this needs to be understood clearly.

The life of Christ gives us strong grounds for optimism about eternal life. We realize that Our Lord was born as a poor and powerless little baby. We know He suffered grievously for our sins and that He rose, against all expectations, triumphant from the dead.

We sometimes fail to appreciate the fact that Jesus chose to die; a more convincing proof of His genuine humanity than even His birth. We should take heart from this, knowing that He has gone before us, not simply into heaven, but through His death.

As St Ambrose, the Bishop of Milan, at the end of the fourth century wrote so beautifully, 'Christ need not have died unless He had willed it, yet He did not think a shameful death a thing to be avoided, nor that there was any better way to save us than by dying. So His death is every man's life. We are signed and sealed by His death. It is His death we proclaim when we pray, that we preach when we offer sacrifice. His death is victory and sacrament and, year by year, it is the world's great feast.'

Adapted from Kairos *magazine,*
All Saints & All Souls 2000

Duty

THERE were two important funerals last week in distant parts of the world. Both the dead were worthy of admiration. They had done their duty.

Constable Glenn McEnallay, twenty-six years of age, was buried from St John's Anglican Church in Taree in a ceremony attended by 400 police officers from around Australia, USA, and New Zealand.

Most of us never knew of him until his sudden death, but the town of Taree stopped, crowds lined the streets as well as the thin blue line of grieving police, and blue ribbons were visible all over the state on buildings and individuals.

Glenn's fiancée Amanda paid him a beautiful tribute; someone she loved who was an 'ethical and courageous policeman'. They were soon to be married and had even chosen four names for their children. All that promise was destroyed.

The constable was shot three times, 'doing the right thing, trying to protect us' as he followed a suspected stolen car. The murder was so unexpected and disproportionate; the most he might have expected was a bit of a chase or perhaps a punch on the nose.

It showed once again the dangers that police regularly face in doing their duty. We should not take their work for granted; more so today where the after-effects of drugs have driven up the crime rate and distorted people's reactions and perceptions.

Good, brave and just police (as they are overwhelmingly) are an immense benefit to our communities. When a policeman proves to be bad, the public feels betrayed as they do with a bad priest or a bad schoolteacher.

The second funeral service was in Westminster Abbey, London, for Elizabeth the Queen Mother.

Her long life of 101 years had seen immense changes, the disappearance of the British Empire, two World Wars and the emergence of a united Australia from a collection of colonies.

She came from a Scottish background of wealth and privilege and lived a life of considerable comfort. Few begrudged her this, although the customary knockers and nasties worked hard to bring her down to their own level when the news of her death was announced.

There were predictions that few would turn out for her farewell.

I was not surprised that hundreds of thousands paid their respects at a magnificent funeral, and millions watched. The English people might be a bit undemonstrative, but they are loyal, have long memories and are grateful for a job well done.

More than that she had been Queen of England at the finest hour in British history, when the British Commonwealth had stood alone against the Nazis, and she was there as the Allies fought to victory in Europe and the Pacific. Hitler paid her the ultimate compliment as 'the most dangerous woman in Europe'. In farewelling her with such affection and pageantry the English were only doing their duty.

The Queen Mother was a woman of dignity and good humour. She lived an ordered private life. She knew much adversity and suffering. Most family failings remain private, but this is not a privilege allowed to the Royals. All this did not sour her.

We don't need a bill of rights. Perhaps we could do with a Bill of Duties, but we certainly need exemplars who do their duty like Glenn McEnallay and Elizabeth Windsor.

The Sunday Telegraph, 14 April 2002

Sir Bernard Callinan

WE are gathered here this morning in the cathedral he knew so well for the funeral of Bernard James Callinan, Companion of the Order of Australia, Knight Bachelor and Commander of the Most Excellent Order of the British Empire, who died on 20 July at St Joseph's Towers after several years of debilitating illness.

We come to acknowledge publicly his outstanding achievements, to thank God for his contributions to our city of Melbourne, to Australia and beyond, and to commend his Christian soul to our loving God.

Bernard was extraordinarily versatile with an unusual range of interests and achievements. Family man and engineer, soldier and educator, builder and committee man, his enthusiasms ranged from football to literature, from the Atomic Energy Commission to the Church. Central to his personality and his varied accomplishments were the facts that he was a patriot, a leader and a fine Catholic; a truly Christian gentleman.

He was born on 2 February 1913, in Moonee Ponds, and educated by the Sisters of Charity at St Columba's and then by the Christian Brothers.

He remembered the four Brothers at St Kevin's as excellent teachers, especially Br 'Jummy' Kenny the science master, who also alternated week-about with Br Rahill for religious education. Blessed by his birth into a family of faith, even as a young man Bernard was active in parish life.

It was the Brothers in senior school at the old St Kevin's who laid the intellectual foundations for the integrity we so admired. These Brothers gave him a knowledge of the essential doctrines of faith and morals, of the problems associated with religious belief. They taught with certainty that these problems could be solved and that, in their solution, lay the answers to the riddles of life.

By the time I first came to know Sir Bernard more than twenty years ago he was not just shrewd and experienced. He was a wise man, strong and uncomplicated because his values were certain and consistent. As a Christian he knew the relative merit of things; he was a clear thinker, not distracted by emotions, far-seeing, regularly able to assess all aspects of a situation. His many different friends knew what he stood for. The Brothers made a big contribution to all this.

Bernard's brother, Jack, pointed him towards engineering at Melbourne University, where he enrolled at the age of seventeen in 1929, and then suggested that he apply for a job with Mr A Gordon Gutteridge in 1935. It was the time of the Great Depression when unemployment reached 30 per cent (excluding wives and those under twenty-one). A couple of years earlier not one engineering graduate had found employment.

Bernard's application was successful and the rest of his life was shaped in an engineering direction. Before the decade was out the Great Depression was followed by the Second World War.

We find it hard to imagine today the mortal peril of Australia after the December 1941 attack on Pearl Harbor. The mighty British base at Singapore, which ordinary Australians had been led to believe was impregnable, fell quickly in February 1942. The conquering Japanese army advanced 5000 kilometres in a few months, confident and apparently invincible, with nearly all of South East Asia in their grasp. The enemy was at our very shores.

Volunteering at the start of the War, he quickly

transferred to the newly formed Independent Companies, the Commandos, who became part of the ill-fated Sparrow Force landed on Timor.

After the Japanese capture of the island the 300 Australian Commandos withdrew to the hills to fight on successfully against odds which saw them outnumbered eventually by 100 to one. For months no one in Australia knew they had survived.

We all know there was no Japanese invasion of Australia and one significant cause was the efforts, courage and fighting-skills of these two companies of Commandos who helped to immobilize 30,000 Japanese troops at Australia's darkest hour. As Nevil Shute wrote of them 'Few soldiers in history can claim to have done more than that'.

Originally second in command of the 2/2 Australian Independent Company, Bernard later commanded all our forces in Timor, before they withdrew safely. In that campaign he was awarded the Military Cross and mentioned in dispatches. He later received the Distinguished Service Order for his work as Commanding Officer of the 26th Australian Infantry Battalion in Bougainville and Rabaul and from 1973 to 1978 he was honorary Colonel of the 4/19 Prince of Wales Light Horse Regiment.

Bernard Callinan led a small band of heroes, whose exploits will pass into Australian legend as the only Allied troops in 1942 between India and Eastern Papua who had not surrendered to the Japanese. We should always remember this.

Bernard drew great strength from his wife and family. He and Lady Callinan were a distinguished couple, as she was always an unfailing source of support and advice. His book on the campaign in East Timor, *Independent Company*, was dedicated 'To my wife who knew and did not speak'.

He was proud that they had five sons; a result that he claimed was achieved with the planning and skill of an engineer! He was a model of the self-discipline he encouraged for his sons, unpretentious with them, a good sounding board in difficult times.

He delighted in their achievements and especially those of his grandchildren. He set high goals but did not prescribe directions for individuals. His family always knew that he loved them and he lived and died knowing that they loved him too.

Sir Bernard was undoubtedly one of the most outstanding Catholic laymen in Australia in the last fifty years. He was the only chairman in the seventeen-year history of the Institute of Catholic Education, a position offered to him by Cardinal Knox with the promise that it only involved a few meetings a year. He was chairman of the National Catholic Education Commission, a member of the Pontifical Council for Justice and Peace, one of the small group of planners who set up the Australian Catholic University.

While his Catholic faith helped shape his personality and guide his public life, there is no doubt that he brought the cast of mind of both engineer and soldier to his faith, to his patterns of believing. He studied life's problems, religious or otherwise, drew firm conclusions in his concise fashion and then worked resolutely to implement them.

He was a determined and resolute man and, I was told, a pugnacious soldier regularly looking to attack. But there was another side to him, more easily understood because of his religious convictions. His record demonstrated a commanding personality that was not immediately apparent behind a somewhat reserved, almost shy exterior; and his friends remarked on his genuine humility.

Sir Bernard recognized and accepted the clear lines of religious authority. He had no difficulty in bowing in worship before the one great God and would have had no problem in announcing that he was unworthy that Christ should enter his house. While he was under no illusions about the personal strengths of priests and bishops, he always treated us with scrupulous courtesy and respect and accepted, without hesitation, the proper religious authority of Pope and archbishop. He was devoted to the Mass, the Sacraments and the daily rosary. His Catholicism, among the best of its type and generation, was the informing principle of his life which so enriched this nation by its presence.

Sir Bernard served Australia with distinction in six years of war; he served it with equal distinction in peace for almost sixty years. Many aspects of his service have not been mentioned in this sermon; his work in the post-War reconstruction with Gutteridge, Haskins and Davey, his leadership roles in the construction of the new Parliament House and Latrobe University, his long-term involvement with the Institution of Engineers, his presidency of the Melbourne Club and the Melbourne Cricket Club.

He was a man for many seasons, who cared for the spiritual fabric of our country as much as he worked to extend and improve its physical infrastructure. He was loyal to a fault; to his principles, to his family and to his comrades-in-arms, his friends in every rank of society. We were privileged to know him.

In faith and with confidence we commend his valiant soul into the hands of the one true God whom he served so well.

Panegyric at Sir Bernard Callinan's Requiem Mass,
St Patrick's Cathedral, Melbourne, 26 July 1995

Elizabeth Anscombe

ELIZABETH Anscombe was an English philosopher, who died in England on 5 January 2001 aged eighty-one. She was one of the best known Catholic personalities when I was at Oxford University from 1967 to 1971.

Oxford has always had plenty of eccentrics, as well as those with remarkable intelligence. Elizabeth was both eccentric and recognized as a giant in the world of twentieth-century philosophy. The conjunction of these qualities is rare enough, but she was even more remarkable for her faith and her courage, qualities that are not universal anywhere, including among academics.

Gertrude Elizabeth Margaret Anscombe was born in 1919, the youngest child of Alan Wells Anscombe, a schoolmaster at Dulwich College, and his wife, Gertrude Elizabeth. She had two older twin brothers.

Educated at Sydenham School and St Hugh's College, Oxford she eventually became a university lecturer and Fellow at Somerville College, Oxford (in which her portrait now hangs). She became a Fellow of the British Academy in 1967.

He name will always be linked with the Austrian Ludwig Wittgenstein, arguably the greatest philosopher of the twentieth century. She was one of his literary executors and translators and in 1970 was appointed to the chair of philosophy at Cambridge, which he also had held.

Anscombe travelled widely and lectured in many countries including Australia. In 1941 she married Peter

Geach, who also achieved considerable philosophical renown. They had seven children, but she did not like to be called 'Mrs Geach' and, in academic circles, she continued to be known as 'Miss Anscombe'. It has been said that someone looking for Mrs Geach at the door of their Oxford residence was told by her that there was no such person there. There is no doubt that Elizabeth Anscombe and Peter Geach were a devoted couple, loving parents and deeply Catholic.

Anscombe became a convert to the Church in 1940, allegedly after reading GK Chesterton's Fr Brown detective stories. But she had problems making the leap. She was worried about the teaching of the sixteenth-century Jesuit, Luis de Molina, according to whom, in Anscombe's words, 'God knew what anybody would have done if, e.g., he hadn't died when he did'. She found that she could not believe this doctrine. Fr Kehoe, the Oxford Dominican instructing her, was amused by her reaction and rightly thought it compatible with Catholicism. So Anscombe converted.

Elizabeth always had the courage of her convictions, and was never frightened to oppose majority opinion. I have nowhere encountered a more formidable exponent. This was seen dramatically in 1968 as she defended Pope Paul VI's teaching against artificial contraception. Always dressed in slacks, often with a Kimono-type top, she wore a monocle and often carried a small brown paper bag for her cigars. She could be fierce, and if you entered the lists against her, no quarter was given. At the first large university meeting to protest the teaching, she and her husband arrived about an hour late as she had been walking and thinking in the Christ Church Meadow with her Denzinger, i.e. the collection of official Church teachings! Another memorable public occasion soon after that, marvellous for the courtesy and quality of the argumentation, was her debate on the pill with Fr Herbert McCabe, an English Dominican writer.

Some years earlier, although she was no pacifist, in 1956 she had strenuously opposed an honorary degree from Oxford University for America's former President Harry S Truman because of the atomic bombing of Hiroshima and Nagasaki. 'Choosing to kill the innocent as a means to your ends is always murder', as she later wrote when reflecting on the episode. As the ex-president entered the Sheldonian Theatre, Elizabeth knelt outside, arms outstretched, praying the rosary in reparation.

She wrote a pamphlet on transubstantiation, defending the Real Presence of Our Lord in the Eucharistic species. She recounts how after teaching her child about this, she returned to her pew after communion. The child asked 'Is He in you?' When Anscombe replied 'yes', her three-year-old child prostrated herself.

In a 1957 talk on the BBC she had argued that the moral philosophy then taught in Britain was corrupting the young and in 1958 in her paper 'Modern Moral Philosophy' returned to the attack, claiming that the concepts of obligation and duty were remnants of a type of moral thinking which no longer survived. It was a staggering claim, extreme and provocative, but one long-term effect was to make 'virtues ethics', the revival of interest in Aristotle's notion of human virtues, and of the good human life, one of the central areas of philosophical study today. This is a good thing, inside and outside the world of philosophy.

To a young priest just out of the seminary she was a wonderful exemplar, showing that prodigious intelligence was compatible with Catholic faith and that rarified learning could and should be used to defend simple people and great, if simple truths. Catholics who aspired to faith and orthodoxy walked a bit taller as a result of her efforts. She was a great woman. We can be sure she rests in peace.

From Kairos *magazine, 25 January 2001*

BA Santamaria

WE are told that one sure mark of the false prophet is that all people speak well of him. In death, as in life, Bob Santamaria has triumphantly escaped such a fate.

Bartholomew Augustine Santamaria was born in 1915, in the Melbourne suburb of Brunswick, the first of six children of Joe Santamaria and Maria Terzita, who had migrated here from the Aeolian island of Salina to escape poverty just before the First World War.

He was educated by the Christian Brothers, ultimately at St Kevin's College, where he was dux of the school, then winning his way to Melbourne University through a scholarship like three other members of his family. To me, he always retained something of the self-confidence, directness and instinct for struggle and competition that then characterized the Brothers' schools.

His personal story is a wonderful example of the openness of Australian society, of the interplay of two different Catholic cultures; of the capacity of the Irish-Australian Catholic education system, then without government funds, to promote social mobility and build on the strengths of Italian faith and family. He himself wrote, 'I have never had any doubts about my identity. I was born in Australia. It is my country and I owe my primary loyalty to it. About this there is no room for confusion. The rest of me is Aeolian, my blood, my background, my earliest memories.'

When he visited Salina as an adult he marvelled that those tiny islands could have bred so sturdy a people with their 'instinct for stability' which he so prized.

It was his Aeolian background, he claimed, which gave him his values; the sense of family, the necessity of religious belief, the importance of accumulating some modest property for a degree of independence and the love of Italy and the Italian way of life.

The Italian-Australian community has made many wonderful contributions to Australian society. We are especially in their debt for BA Santamaria.

Bob grew to manhood in the Brunswick of the Depression. He saw unemployment and poverty. The brothers at St Kevin's gave him reasons for believing and in the Campion Society as he was introduced to the Catholic intellectual tradition he came to realize that ideas are powerful, that ideas provoke consequences.

Dr Daniel Mannix was then Archbishop of Melbourne and Pius XI was the Pope, a great champion of lay Catholic involvement in the world (Catholic Action), a strong opponent of capitalism, Communism and Fascism and a regular advocate of the application of Catholic principles to public life. He was a strong, perhaps even a tough Pope.

However, these were important background factors rather than the defining issue of Bob's long career, which was the Spanish Civil War between Franco and the Communists.

The great English historian AJP Taylor wrote that 'The Spanish question far transcended politics in the ordinary sense. The controversy provided for the generation of the thirties the emotional experience of their lifetime.'

In Australia, Bob himself wrote that the Spanish Civil War reshaped his own priorities and that his primary concern was the freedom of religion from persecution by the State. Here the fire was lit.

The debate in March 1937 in the Public Lecture Theatre at Melbourne University on the topic 'That the Spanish Government is the ruin of Spain' has entered into Catholic legend. Manning Clark wrote about it a number of times. It was held before a packed, rowdy audience of at least 1000 people, two-thirds Catholic, many of them working class militants from the Catholic Young Men's Society.

Bob Santamaria was part of the three-man affirmative team and he provoked uproar as he declaimed, 'When the bullets of the atheists struck the statue of Christ outside the cathedral in Madrid, for some that was just lead striking brass, but for me those bullets were piercing the heart of Christ my King.'

The good Catholic turn-out ensured that when the motion was put, it was carried amid 'unparalleled scenes of enthusiasm' as one report described it. Santamaria's cry of 'Long live Christ the King', a phrase coined first in the Mexican persecution of the Christians, drew thunderous applause.

It therefore comes as no surprise to us now that soon afterwards Archbishop Mannix offered young Bobby Santamaria, a new graduate in law and arts, a position in the recently formed National Secretariat of Catholic Action.

Bob Santamaria (few called him Bobby except his parents and Manning Clark) struggled, indeed flourished, in the hard world of Australian politics for sixty years. The verdicts of his friends and enemies are various and conflicting not only on his strengths and weaknesses, but even on his successes and failures. More than ever then, commentators today find it difficult to accept that the engine of his life, the central unifying motivation was his Catholic faith; but Spain is a help in understanding this.

He had decided, like St Paul in the letter to the Romans, to be on God's side and he worked tirelessly to ensure that nothing – no power, height or depth – came between him and the love of God made visible in Christ Jesus. In faith, and of necessity and from long experience, he came to realize that if he was to triumph at all it was through the trials which beset him.

He went to daily Mass and his religious devotion was deep, reserved and conventional. He had huge and hidden reservoirs of compassion for individuals, which never obscured his clarity of mind about principles and issues. It was Thomas Carlyle who wrote last century that 'a man who does not know rigour cannot pity either'.

He well knew the hazards of working with the leadership of the Church as he had in fact lost his first pay packet playing cards with an Irish-Australian priest friend! And many times he experienced the wrath of Church opponents as he espoused unpopular doctrines and practices.

Nor do I believe that his well known pessimism can be completely understood without a background of Christian hope. It is true that he did recently tell his grandson who was organising a seminar on 'Signs of Hope' that there were no such signs. He did believe strongly in the consequences of original sin, that flaw or fault-line that runs through every community and every human heart and that makes all improvement costly and difficult. But he also believed that our good and just God would implement in the next life the promises outlined in the beatitudes by His Son; and balance things up, even things out for the poor, oppressed and suffering.

Then the Lord of hosts will prepare a rich banquet

for all peoples, wipe away every tear, remove our shame, put aside the burial shroud.

These deep convictions of his were not retained without struggle. He knew the enticements to agnosticism, to set the great issue of God to one side as too difficult. He spoke of the silken thread which sustained personal faith, but for him it was a thread which never broke and which strengthened him magnificently in his last illness. He died a beautiful Christian death.

The Catholic community in Australia owes BA Santamaria a great debt for his leadership in the fight against Communism in the unions; for his indispensable contribution in obtaining financial justice for all Christian schools from state and federal governments; for his authorship of fifteen of the Bishops' statements on social justice; for his brilliant alliance with Archbishop Mannix, where he progressed from the status of a young disciple to being suspected, inaccurately, of exercising an excessive influence over an ailing and declining archbishop.

However, some would believe that his greatest religious contribution has been during the last ten or fifteen years as different forces contended for the soul of Catholicism. Here BA stood squarely with the Holy Father.

No other person had the intellectual skills or organizational ability nation-wide to inform Australian Catholics of the nature of the challenge they faced. It was his last great struggle and the issue is far from settled.

There are minority forces in Australian Catholicism who want to subordinate gospel morality to individual conscience. Some want to use this to expand beyond recognition the limits of proper sexual activity. Some reject not only particular Papal teachings, but would like to sideline Papal authority itself. Others see the ministerial priesthood as one relic of a vanished clerical age.

Even more seriously some do not see Christianity as a revealed religion. So the divinity of Christ is impugned, the Trinity redefined and the worship of the one true God relativized and minimized. It is increasingly hard work to convince our youngsters of the evils of abortion and euthanasia, let alone contraception.

Thanks to Bob Santamaria much more of this struggle is now in the open, with the issues available to public scrutiny. This represents progress. He could not remove or much deflect the mighty forces damaging faith and morals in the Western world, but he has managed to alert an increasing number of us to the folly of embracing the forces seeking our destruction.

Once again, Bob was an effective agent of God's provident concern for our community. He changed the course of Australian religious debate on both faith and family. He inspired many of us to join him in the long twilight struggle between good and evil, between faith and unbelief. We thank God for this.

Bob Santamaria would be annoyed if we did not pray during this Mass that he be loosed from his sins. And I do this willingly, but without deep conviction about the need.

He did know the attractive force of the principle that the end justifies the means. But he resisted this. He loved greatly his Church, his family, his nation and because of that he knew God's love and forgiveness.

He has left us, but his legacy remains. As we await the resurrection of the body we also have to keep up the struggle with hope and strength. His close friend, the distinguished Australian poet, James McAuley, has pointed our way.

> It is not said we shall succeed,
> Save as his Cross prevails:

The good we choose and mean to do
Prospers if he wills it to,
And if not, then it fails.

Nor is failure our disgrace:
By ways we cannot know
He keeps the merit in his hand,
And suddenly as no one planned,
Behold the Kingdom grow!

    3 March 1998, St Patrick's Cathedral, Melbourne

Sr Clare Forbes

Readings: Wis 3:1-3 (The souls of the righteous are in the hand of God and while their going from us may seem like a disaster, they are at peace.)
Rom 14:7-12 (St Paul tells the Romans that we live and die for the Lord and not ourselves. He warns them not to pass judgment on others, and that each one of us will be accountable to God.)
Gospel: *Luke 24:1-11 (St Luke tells of how Mary Magdalene, Joanna and Mary the mother of James and others went to Christ's tomb at dawn with spices they had prepared but found He had risen from the dead. His eleven remaining apostles, however, did not believe them.)*

RECENTLY at the funeral of the Melbourne priest Fr John Keaney, his twin brother Matt, a Jesuit who preached the sermon, quoted a crusty old Irish priest who left instructions that at his funeral he didn't want his corpse lying in the church and some priest lying in the pulpit!

Sr Clare would probably have thought this instruction equally appropriate, perhaps even more necessary, when a bishop was preaching the panegyric. At any rate we certainly need no more than the truth as we commend, in faith and confidence, the soul of Sr Clare Forbes into the hands of our loving God, as we thank God for her life and achievements and ask God to release her from the effects of her sins, if that might still be necessary.

Sr Clare chose the readings for today's funeral Mass, even nominating the translations which she wanted to be used. They are short, to the point. They explain what was central to her faith and the second reading in particular sets out how she lived her life and prepared for her death.

It is to God that all must give an account of themselves, when they stand before the judgment seat of God, because Jesus the Christ is the Lord, not only of the living but also of the dead. Whether we are living, or dying, we can and should do it for the Lord.

Clare was grounded in the faith in a wonderful family and in the parish of Bungaree, which is well known for the strength of its faith community and its family life. One of the small mysteries is why this parish has produced so few priests (and there is still plenty of time to change this!), but Bungaree has produced nuns aplenty and Clare was one of them. She never lost the treasures of faith which her family passed on to her. She nourished them regularly, year in and year out, with daily prayer, Mass, meditation and prayer of the Church, so that when she came to speak of the spiritual life she spoke with authority.

It was this nourished faith which enabled her to grace so many situations and gave her the strength to die with such courage and dignity. Some leave us quickly and apparently without pain. Some leave us tragically, out of time. Others are called to God with full knowledge of their approaching death, with the prospect of considerable suffering. Sr Clare was in this last group and she handled this final period, not without struggle, in an exemplary way. As a religious she had made a radical commitment to Christ and His gospel and she stuck to that vision right to the end.

Clare was born the eldest daughter of Stan Forbes and Anne Hanna. Her sisters Joan and Dorothy, who married and brought up good large Catholic families, survive her as do Helen and Anne, who also joined the Mercies at Ballarat East. Her only brother Stan died as a boy of ten years in 1943, the year she entered the convent.

She attended St Michael's School in Bungaree, then run by the Presentation Sisters, before coming to Sacred Heart College. She always had a robust common sense and a down to earth approach to life. Apparently when she was three, a cyclone hit Bungaree causing considerable damage and distress. Clare was given a sip of brandy to settle her down afterwards. When the parish priest Fr Mulcahy called on his rounds and enquired how she was, she replied that she wasn't the best but was sure she would be better if she could have a bit more brandy and soda!

It is also claimed by the family that her first words were spoken on a visit to an aunt and uncle's place in Melbourne (it is difficult to imagine there ever was a time when Clare could not speak). Apparently she wandered into a bedroom, which contained three mirrors. Seeing herself in turn in all three of them, she broke her silence by exclaiming, 'Oh my God!'

Sr Clare spent twenty-five years in the Convent in

Victoria Street, Ballarat, completing her formation and working in the College. In those days she was known as Sr Ignatius, 'gracious Ignatius' to many of her students, whom she influenced deeply. Those were days of unparalleled expansion, a proliferation of vocations to the religious life.

While Clare had no regrets whatsoever about belonging to the Church of today, and struggled vigorously inside and outside the congregation to implement the reforms which followed the Second Vatican Council, she once remarked to me that she was saddened by the fact that so many of the strengths of that period had gone from us.

She was religious superior in Charlton from 1969 to 1972, acting director of Sacred Heart Teachers College in 1973, Deputy Director of Aquinas College from 1974 to 1982. In 1977–78 she completed a Masters of Education at the Jesuit University, Boston College, where she was recognized as an outstanding student, and inducted as a member of the Alpha Sigma Nu Society, a Jesuit honour society reserved to those who made an outstanding contribution to their universities.

Her most important work was as Congregational Superior between 1981 and 1989. It was just before she stepped down that she suspected she was ill. Typically, and with full knowledge of what she might be doing, she did not go to the doctor until the chapter was concluded.

She was interested and involved in many other areas of society and the Church, the Soroptimists, the Australian College of Education, the Victorian Council of Churches. She was especially devoted to ecumenical work and dialogue with the Anglican and Uniting Churches.

By any human standards, Sr Clare's life was a full and happy one, a life of distinguished and varied service.

The eighties were still a difficult time for religious congregations, even if the worst of the turbulence had passed. Such were the differences then, as they are now, that it was quite impossible for any one person of any persuasion to please everyone. Sr Clare provoked keen disagreement at times.

The Anglo-Irish poet WB Yeats, in lamenting our times, spoke of the ceremony of innocence being drowned, of things falling apart, 'the centre cannot hold'. 'The best,' he wrote, 'lack all conviction, while the worst are full of passionate intensity.'

Clare was the perfect response to Yeats' lament. She was energetic, vigorous in argument, passionate about her causes, as only those with Celtic blood can be. I remember reading once that the colleagues of Gladstone, the nineteenth-century British Prime Minister, used to live in fear and trembling of Gladstone's latest cause, which he invariably argued with an almost frightening energy and enthusiasm. Clare was like that. She felt things deeply, her struggles cost her a lot. As congregation leader she was universally respected, much loved and she cared deeply, very deeply, for the welfare of every nun in her congregation.

She was a great supporter of the priesthood and of priests. This never stopped her from disagreeing with priests, or bishops, but there was never any doubt we were working for the same one great God, the same one, holy, Catholic and Apostolic Church; we were on the same side.

The gospel she chose to be read today, where the women reported correctly that Christ was risen, that the tomb was empty and the apostles thought they were talking nonsense and would not believe them, is entirely typical of her relationship with the men of the Church, whom she liked so much, with whom she worked so well and who so often reduced her to a good natured but despairing exasperation.

Speaking personally, words cannot express how much I owed her as friend and supporter, tactical adviser and spiritual mentor. She reinforced, as no one else did except my mother, my own devotion to Our Lady. She was born on the feast of Our Lady of Perpetual Succour and believed it significant that she received the news the cancer had spread to her brain on the feast of Our Lady of Guadalupe, to whom she had a special devotion.

We pray for her today; it would be presumptuous to do otherwise. But we also pray in thanks for her life of hard work, faith and service.

Sr Clare had come to realize, in her heart as well as her head, that God did not simply love everyone, or more easily everyone else. She realized that God loved her, with her weaknesses as well as her strengths. That was why she chose the first reading. The souls of the just are in the hand of God, and no torment shall touch them ... They are in peace. May this be our prayer, conviction and consolation.

18 February 1992, St Alipius Church, Ballarat East

Memories of Mum and Dad

Mum

> **Reading:** *Eccl 3:1-11 (There is an appointed time for everything, and a time for every affair under the heavens – a time to be born and a time to die ...)*

THE first reading, which is from the Old Testament Wisdom literature, written about 200 or 300 years before the time of Our Lord, reminds us that we cannot fully understand what God is doing in our lives and the lives of our family and friends, let alone larger communities and nations.

But we can become sure of some things; this is part of growing up and growing old, and certainly part of becoming a convinced Christian. We can slowly (or quickly) become convinced that there is a God who loves us and is interested in us, who demands much of us, who promises eternal life to us, and has a task for each one of us.

One consequence of a fairly long illness is that it enables the family of the sick and dying to come to terms with what is happening. In fits and starts, slowly at first but inevitably they come to realize that the time for birth, for planting and healing, has passed, that now we are at the time for parting and for death.

For Christians this cannot be just an occasion of sadness, or grief, without hope. Just last night one of our parishioners from the East told me that it was hard to give condolences to a priest; the clear implication that priests above all must take seriously the promise of eternal life. Wouldn't we be delighted, he added, if our mother was to meet the Queen or the Pope – and of course the dead have gone to meet someone much more important.

This is true of course because we are sons and daughters of God, not slaves dominated by fear, but it is only one side of the coin. We are still waiting for the final revelation; we are still limited as we wait for our bodies to be set free.

But we believe in Christ that the dead such as my mother have been set free and have come to the glory of the children of God. So our Mass this morning as well as being a consolation is also a celebration of thanksgiving and of hope.

My mother was born in the Ballarat East parish and married at St Alipius. It is appropriate that she be farewelled from here. She was a woman of great strength and faith: a faith I suspect that was very Irish, and probably in particular a faith typical of the west of Ireland in its certainties and in its impatience with theological subtleties.

She knew as well as St Paul and any of the gospel writers that any human achievement meant hard work, struggle and sometimes sorrow. She and Dad worked enormously hard that their children would have opportunities not open to themselves. Mum was very proud that her children, through the grace of God, and luck and strong management direction from her and Dad availed themselves to some extent of their opportunities.

I ask you then to pray in this Mass a prayer of thanksgiving for the good she accomplished; to pray in the hope of the resurrection that she may be loosed from her sins and to pray for all of us in the family.

Requiem Mass for Margaret Lillian (Lil) Pell, 23 April 1980

Dad

> **Readings:** 2 Macc 12:43-46; Apoc 21:1-7 *(The author, believed by most of the early Church fathers to be St John, envisages a new heaven and a new earth where God wipes every tear from our eyes and there shall be no more death, mourning or pain. He envisages a new Jerusalem, the holy city and says the thirsty shall be given a gift from the spring of life-giving water.)*
> **Gospel:** John 14:1-6 *(St John recalls some of Christ's reassurances to His Apostles at the Last Supper. He told them that in His Father's house there are many dwelling places, and that He was going to prepare a place for them so that where He is, they (and we) also may be.)*

WE come together on this beautiful autumn morning in Ballarat to celebrate the Eucharist for my father and to commend his soul to the care of our loving God. We do this here in St Alipius Church where he was married and from where Mum was also buried.

He would certainly agree with some of the sentiments in this morning's gospel. He would not want us to be too much troubled, too disturbed at this time. Recently he repeated many times that he had had a good innings, had enjoyed a good life. On a lighter note, during the last few months in hospital he often urged us, his family, to be on our way, not to be wasting too much of our time with him as 'he was all right'! To the extent that he understood and accepted our teaching on life after death, he would have agreed that either there were many mansions in the Father's house or there were none at all.

Dad's grandfather Frank was one of the first British colonists in Dunedin, New Zealand. His son and Dad's father, also George, came to Melbourne and then moved on to Western Australia, with tens of thousands of others, after the bank crash here in Victoria in the 1890s. His mother's people – the Connollys – lived at Scotsburn before also moving to the West, where Dad was born and lived for thirty years. He came to Melbourne for the Melbourne Cup in 1936, saw the light and never went back!

He was a good athlete, being captain of Perth City surf lifesaving club, and at one stage was leading contender for the heavyweight boxing championship of the British Empire. He fought under the name of Bell because his mother did not approve. She knew eventually but went along with the strategy, probably because she realized there was no way she could have stopped him.

He worked on the mines in Kalgoorlie, came to this district as manager of the Gordon goldmine where he first met my mother and later managed mines in Bendigo, Tasmania, the Northern Territory and New Guinea. For twenty-five years we had the Royal Oak Hotel here in Ballarat, where he dispensed hospitality, administered justice, kept the peace and incidentally built and maintained a sense of community which was as good as that in many of our parishes. I see some of these old friends here today. All who met him agreed that he was a great character, who regularly expressed himself colourfully and eloquently, sometimes with a pungent humour. I think he was a remarkable man.

Dad was not noted for the depth or extent of his religious enthusiasm. When I was about to leave school, with the typically biased eye of a parent, he rather fancied my prospects in life and was dismayed when I told him I was going to train for the priesthood. He lamented then to Sr Anne Forbes, a good friend of the family, that as I was now joining the Church I might just as well have been a 'bloody dill'... 'But,' he added, 'you probably don't want dills, do you?'

Over the years this first reaction changed dramatically as he became increasingly sympathetic and openly supportive of Catholic views and activities, especially, but not only, when they touched the lives of his children and grandchildren.

Dad was devoted to his family. Like most Australian men of his generation, he did not wear his heart on his sleeve (and was none the worse for this), but his devotion to his family was complete. I only realized fully how lucky I was in my parents as I grew older and saw a bit more of the world.

Often in talks or sermons on the family I have told people that as a child and an adult it never once crossed my mind that my parents did not love me; I never doubted for a moment that they would do anything they could to help us. If every adult could say this honestly about his or her parents our world would be a much better place. It is this quality of love which enables us to be sure that good people in their dying pass from death to life.

I know that Dad would have approved the second reading where Christ, in the Holy City, the new Jerusalem, is giving 'water from the well of life free to anybody who is thirsty'.

He would have been pleased for another reason. Like most of us, he too affected to being anti-British, at least in unimportant matters like cricket matches; when it was a matter of importance, e.g. war, things were different. In fact, he was very proud of his origins, of the people and tradition to which he belonged. It is this Scriptural passage of course which Blake used as one starting point for his marvellous poem on the new Jerusalem, which English people now sing just as we sing 'Waltzing Matilda'. Dad would have been pleased with this reading and thought it only right and proper.

As Catholics, all traditional Christians are called to believe in life after death and the resurrection of the body. It is a belief which pre-dates Christianity, being a strong conviction of the major strain of later Judaism. It was 'an altogether fine and noble action' to offer sacrifice for those who died; it was a 'holy and devout thought' to pray that 'they might be released from their sin'. This was a belief of the Jews and it is our belief too that God rewards with eternal life all those who love and serve others.

My father was a strong man, physically and personally. He was sometimes gruff and always honest. He told it as he saw it. A private man in many ways he had high principles and kept to them.

As he was devoted to Mum in her last sickness, so too he was blessed in the love and care our sister Margaret lavished on him. He suffered with dignity and died peacefully, consoled by Catholic prayers. It is a privilege as his son and as a priest, with faith and full confidence to commend his soul to the care of our loving God.

From the Requiem Mass for George Arthur Pell,
27 April 1985

9

Conscience: 'The aboriginal Vicar of Christ'

Conscience: 'the aboriginal Vicar of Christ'

ANY discussion of right and wrong, including discussion of the role of individual conscience, receives a jolt when we consider the example of Christian martyrdom. St John Fisher is such an example.

We know of the pivotal role Cambridge men played in the diffusion of Reformation teachings in England, especially through the meetings of young theologians at the White Horse Tavern (known to the undergraduates then as 'little Germany'). Cambridge University also provided one of the few heroes of the Catholic resistance, the only bishop sufficiently clear headed and courageous enough to understand the importance of the underlying issues. This was of course the Bishop of Rochester.

It was fascinating during the Jubilee Year to visit the Tower of London and learn that Churchill ordered, towards the end of the Second World War, that the room Fisher occupied should be refurbished. This was no example of a belated religious enthusiasm, but a prerequisite for Churchill's determination to imprison Hitler in the Tower if he survived the War. The room Fisher used happened to be the one chosen.

St John Fisher is one of my heroes. I have a copy of the Holbein drawing of his portrait on the wall of my office.

My enthusiasm is partly due to clerical solidarity with a brother priest, as an alternative to the wide popularity of the layman Thomas More.

Much more importantly, any person in public life who has spoken or taken a decision which provokes opposition understands the ultimate penalty Fisher suffered, and the importance of friends and public support in any controversy. One of the most admirable characteristics of the martyrdom of Fisher (and More) is his fortitude in isolation, in the total absence of peer support.

Neither do I believe that St John Fisher died for conscience's sake. He died for truth, because he would not subscribe to untruths.

In his encyclical *Veritatis Splendor* ('The Splendour of Truth') in 1993 Pope John Paul II claimed that the Church was facing a genuine crisis which touched the very foundations of moral theology.[1] He explained that this crisis was no longer a matter of limited and occasional dissent but of an overall and systematic calling

---

1 *Veritatis Splendor* §5.

into question of traditional moral doctrine.[2]

Today in England and Australia it is a moot point whether the crisis has lessened or deepened, or indeed whether the situation remains basically as it was. Rome has spoken, but in the English-speaking world there is no evidence that the matter has been successfully concluded.

The Pontificate of John Paul II

Pope John Paul II is an historical anomaly. We risk categorizing his outstanding achievements as being normative for the papacy. This is particularly a danger for young Catholics who have known no other Pope. In fact no Pope in history, even Pope John XXIII, has exercised such an influence in so many fields. This is partly a consequence of the mass media today, but more particularly it is a consequence of his unique contribution. *Veritatis Splendor* was discussed everywhere throughout the Western world. The major papers in just about every Western capital city editorialised on this encyclical. His defence of human rights against Communism and totalitarianism was pivotal. These are but one part of his extraordinary achievements. An important task for the future will be to assimilate his teachings and put them into practice.

This encyclical had been announced on the Feast of St Alphonsus in 1987, but did not appear until six years later, after the publication of the *Catechism of the Catholic Church*. It was eagerly awaited by admirers of the Pope and also by his opponents inside and outside the Church. The traditional loose alliance of dissidents were well organized to orchestrate a chorus of dissent in the media, as they had done so successfully in 1968

---

2 VS §4.

against Pope Paul VI's encyclical *Humanae Vitae*.

However the world had changed since 1968 in a number of significant ways. First of all the scope for dissent had enlarged immeasurably. In 1968 the arguments for individual judgment or private conscience were advanced on the topic of the new means of contraception, which it was alleged, with some justification, was disputed even within the Catholic tradition. Today, what remains in dispute are the grounds for moral argumentation itself within the Catholic and indeed Christian tradition, and the controverted areas now include every area of sexual practice, and many issues which touch human life. Consequently there are also significant debates on marriage and family life. There has been no period in Church history where such a range of moral teachings has been rejected and the rejectors have continued to insist on remaining within the Church and aspiring to change Church teaching. Also there has probably been no period in Church history where so many have been able to do this without effective retribution. To my knowledge no bishop has taken up the recommendation of the Holy Father in *Veritatis Splendor*[3] to take away the title 'Catholic' from Catholic institutions which are deviating significantly from sound moral doctrine.

In 1968 many in the Church were optimistic that the progressive reforms of the Second Vatican Council would soon bring wonderful fruits, and that dialogue with the world would be one of the means for this. *Humanae Vitae* was a valuable corrective to this inflated optimism. The collapse of the Church, for example, in Holland and French-speaking Canada then lay in the future, as did the exodus of many priests and religious

---

3 VS §116.

and the radical decline in vocations to the priesthood and religious life in many parts of the Church. Today we are much better aware of the consequences of the acid rain of modernity on our Catholic communities, of our minority status as serious Christians everywhere in the English-speaking world, and of the damaging power of the neo-pagan world of communications. Probably too we are better aware of the fruits of internal dissent.

However Pope John Paul II has been an immensely more powerful influence than Pope Paul VI. Pope Paul was fated to lead the Church at an intensely difficult time but he will not rank with Leo the Great or Gregory the Great. John Paul II will, and one major reason for this will be his moral teaching, especially as outlined in *Veritatis Splendor* and *Evangelium Vitae* ('The Gospel of Life' – 1995).

No Primacy of Conscience

Sections 54–64 of *Veritatis Splendor* are the best short piece written on conscience since Cardinal Newman's *Letter to the Duke of Norfolk* in 1875. It is a sophisticated and accessible piece of work, quoting section 16 of the Second Vatican Council's Constitution on 'The Church in the Modern World' (*Gaudium et Spes*) about the voice of conscience always summoning us to love good and avoid evil. 'For man has in his heart a law written by God. To obey it is the very dignity of man; according to it he will be judged (cf. Romans 2:14-16).' Naturally, though this law is written in our hearts, it is not our heart's law: it is God's law. There is an explicit reference to the development in the Church's moral doctrine similar to the development in the doctrines of faith, provided the original meaning is preserved intact.[4]

---

4 VS §53 & n.100.

The encyclical is not fundamentalist.

Naturally I accept the teaching of the Second Vatican Council and *Veritatis Splendor* on the crucial role of conscience for us all. However for some years I have spoken and written against the so-called 'doctrine of the primacy of conscience', arguing that this is incompatible with traditional Catholic teaching. Not surprisingly this has in turn provoked a number of hostile public criticisms and quite a number of letters from friends and acquaintances attempting to persuade me of the error of my ways.

My object is twofold: firstly to explain that increasingly, even in Catholic circles, the appeal to the primacy of conscience is being used to justify what we would like to do rather than what God wants us to do. Even within Catholic discourse two different notions of conscience are at work: a) neo-pagan or secular, which feels free to override official Catholic moral teaching, even when it is confirming New Testament teaching, and b) a Christian understanding of conscience which recognizes explicitly the authority of New Testament moral teaching and the official Catholic affirmation or development of that teaching. My second claim is that conscience does not, even in the second and Catholic sense, enjoy primacy, because conscience always involves a human act of judgment which could be mistaken, innocently or otherwise, and the consequences of all decisions have to be played out in some ordered human community. Every human community has to limit the rights of its members to 'err', however error is defined.

One should say that the word of God has primacy or that truth has primacy, and that a person uses his conscience to discern the truth in particular cases. Individual conscience cannot confer the right to reject or distort New Testament morality as affirmed or developed by the Church. To use the language of *Veritatis Splendor*, conscience is 'the proximate norm of personal morality' whose authority in its voice and judgment 'derives from the truth about moral good and evil'.[5] That is so for everyone, but in a special sense for Catholics, for whom the Church's moral teaching cannot be just 'another view', along with dissenting theologians, academics or the media.

Whatever the pressures for conformity produced by public opinion and the mass media today, there is a healthy rhetoric about respect for the rights of the individual, including the right to private judgment, in the English-speaking democracies. Today we value our freedom of speech, however much political correctness and prevailing taboos in the media limit public discussion with invisible parameters, like the proverbial glass ceilings. We take it for granted that all citizens have a freedom to choose their career, their home and all adults presume unreflectingly the right to choose a spouse – or now, increasingly in Australia, a temporary partner. Just as people have the right in a democracy to choose their religion so too some Catholics feel they should be able to choose the type of morality they follow and remain 'good' Catholics. The title 'smorgasbord Catholics' is not rejected as an insult, but as a proper right and title. Of course, no one actually 'chooses' a morality: conscience is not the ability to make morality out of nothing. Too often, though, it is presented as moral source, not moral knowledge.

Unless all kinds of implicit Christian assumptions are made explicit, the claim to the primacy of individual conscience easily becomes in our cultural context the

---

5 VS §60.

same as a claim to personal moral autonomy. Fine though autonomy is, in Christian hands this has tended to become code for 'rationalization of personal wishes' and there is no dignity in that, unless our wishes are for the genuine good. A wish isn't dignifying just because it's mine. Most Western moral philosophers since the eighteenth century, with the exceptions of the Marxists and the Christians, have followed Kant in advocating some form of moral self-legislation and government (autonomy), as distinct from heteronomy or rule by others. Kant would be appalled by contemporary autonomy liberalism. He believed in objective morality ('practical reason') which autonomy gives us the means and opportunity to follow, never a self-made morality of private preference.

We should ask what is the extent of the agent's freedom to follow his own will? In response one can usefully give two versions of moral autonomy. The first emphasizes the person's right to choose in the areas of life generally open to moral evaluation, leaving the limits outside which the agent might curtail his right generally unspecified. The second version of autonomy, the more practical version, always spells out in some way the constraints necessary for social life.

Those Catholics who appeal to the primacy of conscience cite a number of classical references. The first comes from the Second Vatican Council's 'Declaration on Religious Freedom' (*Dignitatis Humanae*), which states that religious freedom 'has to do with immunity from coercion in civil society'; 'the truth cannot impose itself except by virtue of its own truth'. However these advocates often leave unsaid the conciliar teaching from the same paragraph that religious freedom 'leaves untouched traditional Catholic doctrine on the moral duty of men and societies towards the true religion and towards the one Church of Christ'.[6] So while the Declaration explains that in matters religious 'no man is to be forced to act in a manner contrary to his own beliefs ... within due limits', it also goes on to say that all men are 'bound by a moral obligation to seek the truth, especially religious truth'.[7]

The American Fr John Courtney Murray, SJ, who had such a profound influence in the production of the Declaration wrote in his introduction to the English translation: 'The conciliar affirmation of the principle of freedom was narrowly limited – in the text. But the text itself was flung into a pool whose shores are wide as the Universal Church. The ripples will run far. Inevitably, a great second argument will be set afoot – now on the theological meaning of Christian freedom.'[8] In other words *Dignitatis Humanae* speaks of relationships between State and Church, and between the State and individual. It does not deal with the relationship between the magisterium and the baptised.

A second reference frequently quoted, and indeed cited by the Holy Father himself in *Crossing the Threshold of Hope* comes from St Thomas Aquinas, who explains that if a man is admonished by his conscience, even when it is erroneous he must always listen to it and follow it.[9] The supporters of primacy of conscience do not go on to explain, as Aquinas does and John Paul II has done over a lifetime of writing, that the binding force of conscience, even mistaken conscience, comes from the person's belief

---

6 *Dignitatis Humanae* §1.
7 DH §2.
8 John Courtney Murray SJ, *The Documents of Vatican II*, gen. ed. Walter M Abbot SJ (Chapman, London & Dublin: 1966), p. 674.
9 Pope John Paul II, *Crossing the Threshold of Hope* (Jonathan Cape, London: 1994), p. 191.

that the conscientious decision is in accord with the law of God.[10] I also believe that a person following Aquinas' advice might not only err in an objective sense, but could be guilty for his mistaken views.

'The aboriginal Vicar of Christ'
A final passage, also frequently cited, is Cardinal Newman's famous declaration at the end of his *Letter to the Duke of Norfolk*: 'Certainly, if I am obliged to bring religion into after-dinner toasts (which indeed does not seem quite the thing) I shall drink – to the Pope, if you please – still, to Conscience first, and to the Pope afterwards.'[11] Newman was concerned about the Ultramontane claims of extreme infallibilists, facetiously explaining that if the Pope told the English bishops to order their priests to work for teetotalism or to hold a lottery in each mission, they would not be obliged to do so.[12] Here he is addressing a situation in which Popes issue orders – not moral teaching – that exceed their authority. Newman would of course believe that confronted with Church teaching, we all have the obligation to form and inform our consciences by that. But there is no doubt also that his understanding of conscience is very specifically Christocentric and God-centred, within the Catholic tradition.

> Conscience is not a long-sighted selfishness, nor a desire to be consistent with oneself; but it is a

---

10 Thomas Aquinas, *Summa Theologica* 1-2, 19.5. See also the Commentary *In Epistolam ad Romanos*, c.14 lect. 2 (ad v.5).
11 John Henry Newman, *Letter to the Duke of Norfolk* (1875): in *The Genius of John Henry Newman: Selections from his Writings* (Clarendon Press, Oxford: 1989), p. 267.
12 Ibid.

> messenger from Him, who, both in nature and
> in grace, speaks to us behind a veil, and teaches
> and rules us by His representatives. Conscience
> is the aboriginal Vicar of Christ, a prophet in its
> informations, a monarch in its peremptoriness,
> a priest in its blessings and anathemas, and even
> though the eternal priesthood throughout the
> Church could cease to be, in it the sacerdotal
> principle would remain and would have a sway.[13]

Newman carefully distinguishes this proper understanding of Christian conscience from its secular alternative, which is 'in one way or another a creation of man'. 'Conscience is a stern monitor, but in this century it has been superseded by a counterfeit, which the eighteen centuries prior to it never heard of, and could not have mistaken for it, if they had. It is the right of self will.'[14]

He also points out in a clarification which is more useful today than it was in 1875 that when Pope Gregory XVI and Pope Pius IX condemned freedom of conscience (a '*deliramentum*' or madness according to Gregory) they were not condemning what the Church now proposes, not condemning the notion of conscience Newman proposed, i.e. conscience in 'a high sense' as 'dutiful obedience to what claims to be a divine voice, speaking within us'.[15] They condemned a conscience which rejected God and natural law.

Newman also explains elegantly why conscience is 'the highest of all teachers, yet the least luminous'. It is because 'the sense of right and wrong, which is the first element in religion is ... so easily, puzzled, obscured,

---

13 Ibid., pp. 263-64. Cf. *Catechism of the Catholic Church* (1994) §1778.
14 Newman, *Letter to the Duke of Norfolk*, p. 247.
15 Ibid., pp. 251-52; 255.

perverted ... so biased by pride and passion, so unsteady in its course'.[16] He was completely correct.

Neither would Newman have hesitated to reject the notion that any secular notion of conscience has primacy. Might he claim that a proper notion of Christian conscience does have primacy? Would this be a primacy of honour or a primacy of jurisdiction or no primacy at all?

He is typically precise and limited in his claims, pointing out that conscience is 'not a judgment about any speculative truth', but 'bears immediately on conduct, something to be done or not done'.[17] He outlined a number of incidents from St Peter to Pope Urban VIII, who persecuted Galileo, when popes erred (and therefore were not infallible on those occasions), and acknowledges that 'conscience truly so called' does have 'the right of opposing the supreme, though not infallible Authority of the Pope'.[18]

He does not spell out the possible alternative consequences of refusing to follow an infallible papal teaching, but he differs from the Second Vatican Council in talking about the relationship between the magisterium and believers and follows Cardinal Jacobatius in acknowledging that if a person cannot 'conform himself to the judgment of the Pope, in that case it is his duty to follow his own private conscience, and patiently to bear it, if the Pope punishes him'.[19]

It is beside my purposes to debate whether it was wise for a pope to excommunicate Queen Elizabeth I or imprison Galileo, although in most cases popes and

---

16 Ibid., pp. 253-54.
17 Ibid., p. 256.
18 Ibid., p. 257.
19 Ibid., p. 261.

bishops who governed unwisely (or unjustly) were probably following their consciences. My concern is with moral teaching. Nor am I arguing that a person should act contrary to her personal conscientious judgment. However such a judgment is not the last word in a number of ways. First, is this conscience, or a wish? It is interesting that few argue that if your conscience instructs you to be racist or weak on social justice issues, it is acceptable to be so. Primacy of conscience only appears with the sexual, or like, issues.

Any moral ruling and the obedience or disobedience of the subject must be evaluated in the light of revealed Christian teaching and the various grades of authority of official Catholic teaching. Rulers and subjects might act correctly or erroneously, innocently or with malice, ignorantly or after deep study, but all will answer to God for their decisions. Also the Catholic authorities, primarily the pope and bishops as guardians of the apostolic tradition, have an obligation in truth to preserve and defend core Catholic teachings in morality as well as faith and to preserve prudently and charitably rudimentary Church order. Therefore it is possible that not only individual actions might exclude us from the body of believers, e.g. abortion, apostasy, attacking the Pope, but that explicit rejection of solemnly taught Catholic moral teachings (e.g. as defined in *Evangelium Vitae* on killing the innocent, abortion, euthanasia) might call into question our membership of the Church.

For these reasons no individual moral decision of conscience, nor any general conscientious moral teaching, has the primacy, i.e. is the ultimate judgment or decision. All actions and decisions are judged by conformity to the truth, or even to the Word of God. Truth and truth specified as the Word of God have primacy. It is interesting that when St Thomas deals with these matters, in his disputed question on truth, it is to a part of our minds called *synderesis* that he grants infallible knowledge of the human good. *Conscientia* or conscience is the act of applying that knowledge and this is fallible.[20] Without a good moral education, a sustained attempt to understand Church teaching, and a humble disposition, we will be vulnerable to erroneous conscientious judgments. There is many a slip between cup and lip – or between *synderesis* and *conscientia*.

Therefore in Catholic theological language the claim to primacy of secular conscience is a cliché, which only requires preliminary examination for us to conclude that it needs to be refined and developed to have any plausible meaning at all. I do not even favour the substitution of the primacy of *informed* Christian conscience, because it is also possible that with goodwill and conscientious study a devout Catholic could fail to recognize some moral truth, act upon this failure and have to face the consequences.

While occasionally at the theological level I feel that all I am doing is forcing my way through an open door, it is at the pastoral level that this espousal of the primacy of conscience has disastrous effect. Let me give you a crass but actual example, recounted to me by a friend who witnessed this encounter. A man asked this question: suppose I have been regularly 'sleeping with my girlfriend'. Would it be wrong for me to be receiving Holy Communion? Without hesitation the theologian replied, 'Vatican II has taught that in answering any moral question, you must obey your conscience. Just do that.' Such a teaching is insufficient and misleading. Does it mean there are no moral absolutes or authorities? Is it sufficient to follow one's feelings? Or was Charlie

---

20 Thomas Aquinas, *De Veritate*, q. 17, a. 2.

Brown correct forty years ago to claim that 'it doesn't matter what you believe as long as you are sincere'? That enquirer truly wanted to know, and the theologian gave him nothing, just left him where he was.

In many places, even in the Catholic world, the category of mortal or death-bearing sin is now an endangered species, because the unthinking presumption is that everyone is honestly doing his or her 'own thing', following conscience. Obviously public opinion places limits to this world of easy options, often coterminous with the limits of political correctness, but many areas of sexual conduct and activities such as contraception, abortion, euthanasia, the number of children are 'free go' areas, where one opinion is held to be as good as another.

This reflects the fact that there has been a dramatic shift in the tectonic plates of public moral discourse within the Catholic Church, and certainly within the ranks of the other Christian churches. The public disarray in the Anglican churches on the suitability of ordaining homosexually active men and women to the Anglican ministry is one spectacular example of this.

Conclusion
Once upon a time it was pastorally useful, sometimes necessary to explain the possibility of invincible ignorance among those who differed from us, because of the temptation to presume bad faith in opponents. Nowadays, it can mean 'invincibly wilful'. Now for many, tolerance is the first and most important Commandment. Therefore it is necessary and important for us to argue for the possibility of culpable ignorance that usually has been built up through years of sin and is psychologically invincible, short of a miracle. The idea of culpable moral blindness is discussed as infrequently as the pains of hell.

Jesus knew human nature very well and *Veritatis Splendor* quotes that marvellous saying of Our Lord from St Matthew's gospel: 'the eye is the lamp of the body. So if your eye is sound, your whole body will be full of light; but if your eye is not sound, your whole body will be full of darkness. If then the light in you is darkness, how great is the darkness!'[21]

Christian writers at different times have expounded wonderfully on the concept of culpable moral blindness. St Thomas More wrote his *Dialogue of Comfort Against Tribulation* in the final year of his imprisonment in the Tower of London, speaking there of conscience's susceptibility to corruption.

Even earlier, in 1377–78, St Catherine of Siena in her *Dialogue* spoke of the consequences of pride, sensuality, impatience and the consequent lack of discernment. These four chief vices constitute a tree of death. 'Within these trees a worm of conscience nibbles. But as long as a person lives in deadly sin the worm is blinded and is so little felt.'

Sin darkens the intellect. Old spiritual books used to say that as a commonplace, but today it has been largely forgotten. Those who live conscientiously by the Commandments are better judges of morality than clever people who live in sin. That can sound arrogant, but it is simply the truth. As Newman put it, it is a better ethical disposition that enables some to discover the truth. Newman also spoke of an 'ethical incredulity' that blocked some from accepting genuine evident miracles.[22] *Courage* to face the truth, *a desire to know* the truth, and *humility* in accepting it from others or from a higher

---

21 VS §63.
22 John Henry Newman, *Two Essays on Biblical and Ecclesiastical Miracles*. (2nd ed. 1907), pp. 183-84.

authority such as the New Testament and official Church teaching, play a greater part in having right moral and religious beliefs than native intelligence or cleverness.

My thesis, about the centrality, power and limitations of personal conscience in no way implies that the directives or teachings of individual bishops must always be obeyed or accepted automatically. As you know these are sometimes, perhaps often, contradictory. Wider considerations must be invoked.

My concerns are to maintain the purity of Christian conscience as it is used to identify moral truths. In other words to work so that a secular understanding of conscience does not replace the role of conscience as 'the aboriginal Vicar of Christ'.

3 March 2004, the 2004 Fisher Lecture,
Catholic Chaplaincy, University of Cambridge

Four Catholic Foundations

1. We believe in one God, Father, Son and Holy Spirit, who loves us.

2. We believe in one Redeemer, Jesus Christ, the only Son of God, born of the Virgin Mary, who died and rose from the dead to save us.

3. We believe in the Catholic Church, the Body of Christ, where we are led in service and worship by the Pope and Bishops.

4. We believe that Jesus, Our Lord, calls us to repent and believe; that is, to choose faith not doubt, love not hate, good not evil, and eternal life in heaven not hell.

This is our faith.
We are proud to profess it in
Christ Jesus, Our Lord.

Picture Acknowledgments

1. *Battesimo* (fresco) by Francisco Argüello in the church of The Most Holy Trinity in Piacenza, Italy
2. Advanced Telescope Supplies image, courtesy Peter J Ward 2004
3. Our Lady of Perpetual Help painted by Andrew Molczyk in Corpus Christi Seminary Chapel, Carlton, Victoria. Photograph by John Casamento Photography
4. *Return of the Prodigal Son*, c.1668–69 (oil on canvas) by Rembrandt Harmensz van Rijn (1606–69). Hermitage, St Petersburg, Russia / Bridgeman Art Library
5. *Ingresso a Gerusalemme* (fresco) by Francisco Argüello in the church of The Most Holy Trinity in Piacenza, Italy
6. Paintings by Mary Anne Coutts in the chapel of Aquinas Campus, Australian Catholic University, Ballarat
7. Paintings by Mary Anne Coutts in the chapel of Aquinas Campus, Australian Catholic University, Ballarat
8. *Noli me Tangere* or *The Apparition of Christ to Mary Magdalene*, 1303–05 (fresco) by Giotto di Bondone (c.1266–1337). Scrovegni (Arena) Chapel, Padua, Italy. Alinari / Bridgeman Art Library
9. Photograph by Brett Faulkner
10. Photograph by WinkiPoP Media
11. Servizio Fotografico de "L'OR", 00120 Città del Vaticano
12. Photograph by John Casamento Photography
13. Photograph by Max Herford
14. The chair of St Peter, 1665 (bronze) by Giovanni Lorenzo Bernini (1598–1680). St Peter's, Vatican, Rome, Italy. Joseph Martin / Bridgeman Art Library
15. Photograph by Kate Collins
16. Newspix / Bill Leak

Gospel Index

Saint Matthew
5:1-12	204
5:17-19	30
6:24-33	219
10:16-23	243
14:13-31	26
16:13-20	10, 89, 95
17:1-9	44
24:37-44	234
25:1-13	196
25:14-30	200
25:31-46	18
28:1-10	59

Saint Mark
14:12-16, 22-26	6
16:15-20	63

Saint Luke
1:26-38	75, 84
1:39-56	80
2:1-14	39
6:27-38	208
15:1-3, 11-32	154, 248
17:12-18	158
24:1-11	271

Saint John
1:1-14	42
1:6-8, 19-28	35
4:1-38	143
6:41-51	14
7:1-2, 10, 25-30	163
8:2-11	237
9:1-41	48
14:1-6	279
14:15-16, 23-26	67
15:9-17	1
18:1-19, 42	54
19:25-27	71
20:19-31	130